MARTIAL

# MARTIAL

## THE·WORLD·OF·THE·EPIGRAM

William Fitzgerald

UNIVERSITY OF CHICAGO PRESS · *Chicago and London*

WILLIAM FITZGERALD is university lecturer
in classics and fellow of Gonville and Caius College,
Cambridge.

The University of Chicago Press, Chicago 60637
The University of Chicago Press, Ltd., London
© 2007 by The University of Chicago
All rights reserved. Published 2007
Printed in the United States of America
16 15 14 13 12 11 10 09 08 07     1 2 3 4 5
ISBN-13: 978-0-226-25253-7 (cloth)
ISBN-10: 0-226-25253-1 (cloth)

Library of Congress Cataloging-in-Publication Data
Fitzgerald, William, 1952–
    Martial : the world of the epigram / William Fitzgerald.
        p. cm.
    Includes bibliographical references and index.
    ISBN-13: 978-0-226-25253-7 (cloth : alk. paper)
    ISBN-10: 0-226-25253-1 (cloth : alk. paper)
1. Martial. Epigrammata.  2. Epigrams, Latin—History
and criticism.  3. Books and reading—Rome.    I. Title.
    PA6507.F58 2007
    878′.0102—dc22

                                2006028344

To Red and Brian

# CONTENTS

# ACKNOWLEDGMENTS

My thanks are due first to the members of my Martial seminar in Berkeley in 2000 where the main lines of my approach were developed, and particularly to Pat Larash, who went on to write a fine dissertation on Martial and with whom I had many stimulating conversations. My colleagues in Berkeley made the three years I spent there among the happiest in my professional life. Kathy McCarthy and Ellen Oliensis were always inspiring interlocutors and examples in matters of Latin poetry. The three anonymous readers for the University of Chicago Press provided valuable criticisms and suggestions. Susan Bielstein's encouragement and kindness are much appreciated, as is the painstaking editing of Carol Fisher Saller. The book's dedicatees were the most generous hosts during the writing of much of this book and for that, and much else, I am deeply grateful.

# CHAPTER ONE

# MARTIAL·AND·THE·WORLD OF·THE·EPIGRAM

Martial is a major poet, but the fact that he has had to wait so long for the critical reassessment that is beginning to come his way is not surprising. He writes in a genre that it is not easy to take seriously, and Martial himself is at pains to tell us not to. Though we have become accustomed to discounting protestations of worthlessness by ancient poets, in this case we might think that the author has a point. In fact, points are all he seems to have, as one epigram after another reveals the sting in its tail, nudging us in the ribs, giving us the wink, inviting us to groan or soliciting our reaction in some way or other. Reading Martial is like eating a whole box of bonbons at one sitting, as one critic put it, and a colleague of mine marveled that I could teach a seminar on a poet who wrote the same poem over and over again. I could see her point. How does one *read* an epigrammatist?

We should be well placed to answer this question in the age of bytes and sound bites, of items, articles, snapshots, highlights, headlines, slogans, and the like; one would expect the epigram form to be congenial to our distracted culture, whose metaphors of attention include browsing, grazing, surfing, and cruising. These aspects of our own world go some of the way to explaining why Martial is a poet for our time, and they also encourage us to look at Martial's chosen form, the book of epigrams, as a particular vision or representation of the world. "World" is a versatile, not to say vague, word, but it serves to orient us toward what it is that makes Martial a unique and important poet. If "world" is the most general term for the form in which an environment makes sense, for the way in which its components relate, then the world of the epigram book is quite distinct from that of other genres. If "world" is what you confront and have to deal with, then the epigrammatist masters his world in a way that is uniquely his own. Again, if the world of a given entity is what surrounds it—that in which it is embedded—then the epigram book creates a very particular relation between inside and outside, between work of art and circulating book. Martial's epigram book is both an object that goes out into the world and a focal point about which a heterogeneous collection of readers and readings assembles itself as a virtual society, its consumption very much part of what it is. Finally, we may speak of the world of the book as the attitude it takes, the focus, selection or frame that disposes us to see things from a certain angle, and here too, Martial's books have something unique to offer.

One way to broach the distinctive world of the epigram book is through the paradoxes that the form implies. Since the epigram is the most closed of forms, the notion of a *book* of epigrams is paradoxical, as Martial himself acknowledges. Why write a book of epigrams, he asks, if brevity is the chief virtue of the form (8.29); it's easy to write epigrams nicely, but difficult to write a book (7.58); there's good, bad, and indifferent here—a book (of epigrams) can't be made otherwise (1.16). Since you can no more read a book of epigrams than you can eat a whole box of chocolates, Martial suggests that the reader pick and choose, or, as we might postmodernly put it, browse and graze. Whenever the end of a poem coincides with the end of a page, he tells us, you can make a *liber* into a *libellus* (10.1); more radically, "We have arrived at the bosses (*umbilicos*), but you, reader, want to go further . . . as though you had not finished what was already finished on page one" (4.89). Why would the book already be finished on page one? Not, as Shackleton Bailey would have it (1993, ad loc.), because the book might just as well not have been written, but because "you can finish the book wherever you want: each work (*opus*) is unrolled (*explicitum*) in two lines" (14.2).[1] The epigram being the most closed of forms, almost closure *as* form, you cannot continue an epigram; you can only start again, which is surely one of the reasons why Martial finds dicing an appropriate figure for writing or reading epigrams.[2]

Another paradox that attends the notion of the book of epigrams has to do with the occasional nature of the epigram. If the epigram is embedded in the day-to-day life of the Roman elite, improvised, perhaps, to lend a veneer of sophistication to a birthday, a wedding, a boat trip or a dinner, or, more broadly, to shed the glow of culture over relations between patron and client, then what happens when epigrams are assembled in a book? Have they been uprooted from the soil from which they draw their life, or have they rather been universalized, raised to a higher power for a different kind of audience, the anonymous *lector* who is our forbear? One of Martial's most significant puns is on the word *libellus,* both "petition" and "little book of poems." The pun points to two kinds of reading that his epigrams might elicit, depending on whether the reader is a (potential) patron or an unknown reader. Trailing a context which stubbornly clings to it, the transplanted epigram prevents the book from closing over its contents.

When we consider the associations of the epigram as a genre, we come up against more contradictions. The lapidary compression and closure of the epigram point to inscriptional uses—epitaph, dedication, monumental inscription. In this context, the epigram implies permanence, and Martial has his own unconventional figures for this: an ant preserved in amber, a brand or a tattoo.[3] But, seen from a different angle, the one-dimensional brevity and compressing wit of the epigram give it quite different associations, with the ephemeral, the improvised, and the spoken. The epigram may be a means of commemorating and preserving, but it may equally be an elegant waste of time not intended to outlast its occasion. Again, the very pointedness that lends the epigram its definitive and unmodifiable rightness, its inscriptional permanence, could also be seen as the trick that loses its potency after a single reading, rendering the epigram an object to be consumed and thrown away.[4] Food, like gaming, is an appropriate figure for the perishable aspect of Martial's epigrams, and it features frequently.[5]

A similar dialectic relates the two most common categories of epigram in Martial's books, the sceptic and the panegyric. Mockery and celebration are equally characteristic of the form, for, as Lawrence Manley puts it, "The impulse to immortalize by inscription could just as well become the satiric impulse to fix a neat, indelible image in a last, unanswerable word."[6] The attitude of the epigram to its world is as conflicted as its status is contradictory and these paradoxes of the form serve to complicate the "world" of the book of epigrams. I will return to questions of status and attitude later in this chapter, but first we need to look more closely at the paradox of a book that is at the same time a random collection of self-contained units.

## JUXTAPOSITION:
## THE EPIGRAMMATIC ENVIRONMENT

Martial may suggest that we browse his books (10.1), but it is clear that in some respects they are as constructed as any other books of Latin poetry. Opening sequences with programmatic and dedicatory material are the most obvious evidence of this, but there are also closural poems or sequences; some poems explicitly comment on the preceding, and parts of books may be distinguished from other parts as more or less suitable for, say, female readers.[7] When we focus in more closely, it is the heterogeneity of the material which is most apparent and *variatio* seems to be the main principle of arrangement. A typical sequence (6.12–18), which I will examine in chapter 4, interweaves three invective squibs (6.12, 6.14, 6.17); two panegyrical epigrams, of which one is high imperial panegyric (6.13), the other a touching consolation (6.18); an epideictic epigram on an extraordinary occurrence (6.15); and a Priapic poem (6.16). However, as we shall see, there is plenty to suggest that Martial is interested in making witty connections between consecutive poems, different though they may be in subject matter, tone, or genre. His penchant for playing on names in consecutive poems is but one piece of evidence for this.[8] It should not be surprising, given that individual epigrams manipulate puns, zeugma, antithesis, and double entendre to put things wittily together, that consecutive epigrams should be related by the same principles. In the course of this book I will produce many examples of this kind of relation and I hope to show that these juxtapositions allow Martial to apply an analytic wit to the structures of his society. For the moment, though, I want to focus more broadly on the environment of Martial's books, where heterogeneous poems confront each other without being explicitly related.

The most useful term we can enlist for the formal principle of a sequence of short but highly closed poems is *juxtaposition*, a term that suggests both closeness and separation. The combination of closeness and separation is not only characteristic of the epigrammatic sequence, it is also a feature of urban environments, and one that decisively affects the urbanite's experience. In Martial's Rome, orienting oneself was a matter of knowing what was next to what, as the frequency of the word *vicinus*, particularly in the urban itineraries, attests.[9] But a single neighborhood might bring together a very varied collection of people. When "the whole neighborhood" greets the addressee of 12.59 it includes a weaver, a fuller, a cobbler, an unshaven man, a man with a limp, another with a bleary eye, a fellator, and a cunnilinctor, all of them bearing down on the unfortunate man with a kiss. I will take up this poem, in connection with Martial's Catullus, in chapter 6, where I will argue that Martial urbanizes his urbane predecessor. Martial's city is not the locus of wit and sophistication that it was for Catullus, but rather a place of jostling variety. The city compresses what is heterogeneous into a close proximity, but it can also isolate from each other elements that are spatially close. Martial complains that, though his neighbor Novius lives so close that they can touch each other from their windows, he might be as far away as Terentianus, posted in Egypt, for all that the poet sees or hears of him (1.86). "There is nobody in the whole city so near and yet so far," he remarks (*nec urbe tota / quisquam est tam prope tam proculque nobis*, 1.86.9–10) In the city, people rub up against each other and at the same time are insulated from each other; they want to see each other more or wish they could avoid each other better; they penetrate each others' secrets or they try to disguise what proximity reveals. These paradoxes and tensions of urban experience, as chronicled by Martial, are the worldly counterpart to the juxtository environment of his books.

Juxtaposition is what we might call the zero degree of authorship; maintaining an attitude of deadpan, it is always deniable. For a reader to say that *x* and *y* are juxtaposed is not necessarily to imply an intention, either about the juxtaposition itself or about what is to be made of it. While we may be sure that Martial sometimes wants consecutive poems to communicate, we often cannot tell whether in a given case we are seeing things; perhaps we are exercising our own wit rather than discovering Martial's, or perhaps the random juggling of a finite number of themes and types of jokes will inevitably produce particular juxtapositions. The poem that follows Martial's complaint about Novius (1.87), for instance, mocks Fescennia for attempting, in vain, to disguise the smell of booze with perfumed pastilles. For Fescennia, there is nothing paradoxical about proximity and no disguising what it reveals.[10] The juxtaposition of these two poems, if we choose to let them confront each other, invites us to link the phenomenon of urban proximity with the proximities thrown up by the work itself.[11] But, more broadly, we might say that the theme "city business prevents friends from being together" and the theme "x tries to keep his/her dirty little secret but in vain" were destined to meet eventually, and here a random throw of the dice brings it about. Interpretive uncertainty of this kind is intrinsic to the world of Martial's books and part of the experience of finding our way around them; it is, in other words, intrinsic to a juxtository environment. So the aspect of the individual epigram that catalogues, defines, and fixes, making the epigram a self-interpreting form, contrasts with the deadpan of the epigram book's juxtapositions, in which the reader's decision to relate is not authorized, and the nature of the connection may be an optical illusion or an operation of chance.

The interpretive uncertainty of Martial's juxtapositions is particularly interesting for us, given that it is a large part of contemporary urban experience that we must choose whether to notice (or accustom ourselves *not* to notice) the juxtapositions that the urban environment casts in our face. Extremes of wealth and poverty, durability and disposability, meaning and meaninglessness, continually confront us with the question of what, if anything, we are going to make of their juxtaposition.[12] We may fail to notice; we may notice but choose to ignore; we may smile wryly; or we may seek an underlying structural rationale. This is very much the range of options with which we are presented in Martial's books. Juxtaposition is a significant urban feature of Martial's urban poetry, presenting the reader with an environment whose very interpretability is open to question and to choice.

In a more literary form, juxtaposition features in our own daily lives through the newspaper, that exemplary modern aesthetic form. One of its most astute historians speaks of the paradoxical effect of the newspaper's random juxtaposition of miscellaneous items, which "simultaneously confronted and studiously ignored each other."[13] This might be an apt description of the impression given by Martial's books. If newspapers, as Richard Terdiman argues, are "the first culturally influential anti-organicist mode of discursive construction," then Martial's books of epigrams are part of the prehistory of this antiorganicist mode.[14] Terdiman might have added that in the spirit of this antiorganicist form we celebrate the piquant juxtaposition as an *objet trouvé* of modern life: newspapers and magazines publish examples found by their readers, and there is a whole genre of photography that consists in recording ironic, poignant, or comic juxtapositions (billboards and the life that surrounds them are one of its most common forms); we pride ourselves on the wit that notices. I will be arguing that juxtaposition plays a central role in Martial's aesthetic, and that here we find in Martial a kindred spirit. But this is not the only aspect of Martial's "world" that has relevance for our own, and I will be pointing to such connections from time to time throughout this book.

## PERSONA, WIT, AND WORLD

Terdiman's observations on the newspaper refer to nineteenth-century Paris, which gave us that distinctive type of modern urbanity, the *flâneur* (stroller).[15] *Flânerie* is an activity closely related to the newspaper, which has been described by Vanessa Schwartz as "a printed digest of the *flâneur*'s roving eye."[16] She observes that "the *flâneur* is not so much a person as *flânerie* is a positionality of power—one through which the spectator assumes the position of being able to be part of the spectacle and yet command it at the same time." If the modern newspaper reflects a certain kind of urban persona (the *flâneur*) then we might by analogy ask what is the persona of Martial's epigram book, for the juxtapository epigrammatic sequence has a subjective and an objective side: it is both an environment in which the reader must orient himself and at the same time the characteristic form in which the book's persona engages with his world. To speak of an epigrammatic persona might seem paradoxical since, on the face of it, the epigram would appear to be a poetic genre that can dispense with persona; the concision, closure, and definitiveness of the form give it an impersonal air, and the tendency of the humorous epigram toward the quip lends it the anonymity of the joke.[17] So, what kind of person writes a book of epigrams? Martial himself appeals to Catullus as his model, and in doing so places himself in the tradition of Latin first-person trivial poetry, in which persona plays an important role. Writing books of first-person epigrams, Martial inevitably plays with persona.[18] Of course, this persona is far removed from that of the urbane, aristocratic Catullus, standing at the center of his circle of literary sophisticates. Martial's is a much bigger world, and his position in it is more precarious: as a professional epigrammatist his persona must be tinged with the character of the client Greekling. At the broadest level of the persona of the form, we might say that if world is what confronts you, what you must deal with and master, then the epigrammatist grasps and manages his world as a series of encounters or opportunities (dicing again). In the epigrammatic sequence the world has been broken down to be rendered manageable, and this is the attitude projected by the form itself, the equivalent of the *flâneur*'s roving eye for the newspaper.

In terms of content, Martial's persona has affinities with that of the satirist. As the poet of the city who observes its scandals with relish and complains of the difficulties of the client's life, Martial has inevitably invited comparison with his younger contemporary, Juvenal, and not always in his favor.[19] In 1970 W. S. Anderson drew an instructive contrast between Juvenal's anger and Martial's "naughty, basically tolerant *lascivia*" (18).[20] Ten years later Bramble's article on these two poets in the *Cambridge History of Classical Literature* directed a truly Juvenalian scorn at Martial, the "court-jester" who never gives offence, never pricks our conscience, and never makes us think (Bramble 1982). Though both poets cast themselves as social inferiors, there is an important difference between the ways they elaborate that persona. Juvenal is mad as hell and he won't take it any more; he pours out a torrent of abuse and resentment that readers can both enjoy as cathartic and reject as neurotic. Martial, by contrast, adopts the persona of the struggling dependant not to give voice to the resentment of the unrewarded but to explore the art of survival; hence Bramble's contempt. Martial casts himself as a *scurra*, defined by Ruurd Nauta as "a particular type of hanger-on, one who earned his dinner by entertaining his guests with his mockery."[21] Where Juvenal claims to be driven by an irrepressible anger, Martial seeks the license of institutions. As Nauta demonstrates, the fictional contexts of Martial's poetry are the banquet and the Saturnalia.[22] This association with the Saturnalia accounts for one of the most important themes of his work, namely the relations between rich and poor. Nauta puts it as follows: "The Saturnalia were characterized by playing out the relationship between the rich and the poor, in so far as these were bound together by gift-exchange and by sympotic hospitality. . . . On the one hand [Martial] had the licence to criticize, even if this licence was strictly controlled, so that he had to confine his attacks to fictional persons. On the other hand criticisms of deviations from the norm strengthen the norm itself, so that Martial's carnivalistic mockery of fictional patrons adds point and credibility to his serious panegyric of real patrons."[23]

This characterization of Martial's satirical strain, broad though it is, does not go far enough, for behind the criticism of breaches of hospitality and patronal obligation lies something more anarchic, opportunistic, and random. We can focus in on this from Art Spisak's attempt to identify Martial as a moralist concerned with the proper conduct of friendship, and thereby to rescue him from charges of mercenary begging.[24] One of Spisak's exhibits is 5.18, in which Martial excuses the fact that his Saturnalian gift to Quintianus is only "home-born books" (*libellos vernulas*, 4).[25] But gifts are like hooks (*imitantur hamos dona*, 7), whose deceitful ways Martial professes to hate. "Whenever he gives nothing to a rich friend, Quintianus, a poor man is being generous" (*quotiens amico diviti nihil donat, / O Quintiane, liberalis est pauper,* 9–10). Spisak seizes on the familiar point that gifts are hooks, a point often applied to *captatores* (legacy hunters), and claims that the poem is directed against a particular kind of giver.[26] But the wit of the final point resides in the paradox that the poor man is *generous* if he gives *nothing.*[27] It is the contradiction embedded in the concept of gift-exchange that is the target of this poem, not the wiles of the *captator.* If the receiver of a gift is expected, or rather obligated, to reciprocate, and to reciprocate in proportion to his status, then the poor man is making a profit when he gives to a rich man. Naturally, when all is functioning as it should, the will to give and the expectation of reciprocity travel on separate tracks. Martial not only prevents us from making the mental disjunction, but facetiously articulates a new etiquette based on the practical realities rather than the official story.[28]

It is a regular practice of Martial to strip the veneer of spontaneity from the social "rules," articulating what usually goes unspoken, and particularly the expectation of reciprocity that is central to relations between the elite. This expectation, which needs to be recognized and enforced in some informal way, loses its point if it becomes the object of calculation: naturally, you shouldn't feel that, when I ask you what *you* are working on, I do so in order to be given the opportunity to tell you about *my* current project (cf. 5.73). The arbitrariness of whether, on any given occasion, Martial will buy into the official version or expose the unspoken assumption is a function of the epigrammatist's opportunistic persona, but it is made possible by the cohabitation of these two conflicting models in the minds of his audience.[29] Here, Martial's contemporary Pliny provides a striking contrast. In Pliny's letters, the language of merit, desert, and friendship is constantly masking the elite's construction of networks of favors and influence. Hoffer (1999) has argued convincingly that Pliny's carefully constructed appearance of a "virtuous circle" of favors masks an underlying anxiety. Martial, who makes arbitrary and opportunistic decisions about whether he will support the fiction of spontaneity or expose and exploit it, seems to inhabit a very different mental world from Pliny, one that is virtually devoid of anxiety.

We can reapproach Martial's attitude to his social world through the epigrammatic form itself, and here it is useful to return to Terdiman, who notes the connection between the atomistic form of the newspaper's juxtaposed articles and developments in the social and economic environment. Relating the newspapers to the emerging department stores in Haussmann's Paris of the mid-nineteenth century, Terdiman argues that there is a relation between the anti-organicist mode of the newspaper's construction and the creation of a citizenry of consumers. In the end, as Terdiman argues, it is the logic of the market which requires readers trained in "the apprehension of detached, reified, decontextualized 'articles'—and the ambiguity of the term is itself significant. . . . It will prove impossible to detach the two elements of the newspaper's functionality—imparting information and selling goods—from each other."[30] Clearly the world of Domitian's Rome and the world of Haussmann's Paris are far removed from each other. The Roman capital boasted no department store, arcade, or newspaper; no capitalism, in fact. But I think we can make a connection between Martial's atomized, nonorganic books and social or economic aspects of his world. The epigram, by Martial's time, was embedded in the Roman patronage system, but the peculiar nature of its form tended to convert the elusive reciprocities of patronage into more sharply defined, atomistic transactions. Much of Martial's wit consists in subjecting *amicitia* to economic calculation, atomizing what should ideally be long-term relationships, based on *fides*, into a series of transactions. The circulation of Martial's books of epigrams also reflects the impinging of economistic understandings of social relationships on more deeply entrenched habits of gift exchange and reciprocity. Martial makes much of the fact that "he" is available at the bookstore, that those who want to read his works need form no relationship with the author himself, but can simply buy the book. He both celebrates and deplores this fact.

Though he may characterize himself as the humiliated dependant, Martial's chosen form can hardly avoid projecting mastery.[31] The succession of short, pointed, and various epigrams, so different from Juvenal's continuous and overwhelming rant, creates the fiction of a man who can successfully negotiate the adversarial and competitive world of the city, striking the difficult balance between *scurrilitas* and courtliness. He comes off on top in every encounter, and a large part of his mastery is the ability to cast experience as a series of discrete encounters. The epigram becomes the art of survival as Martial dishes the dirt, takes revenge, enlists allies, and solicits friends; he is a man to be reckoned with. Writing on Renaissance English epigram, Manley cites Georg Simmel to the effect that "an increased emphasis on intellectual precociousness, rather than emotional attachment, is the individual's principal defense against the anonymity of urban life."[32] Perhaps we cannot call urban life in ancient Rome anonymous in the sense that Simmel meant it, but Barbara Kellum (1999) makes a convincing case for the adversarial and confrontational quality of the urban environment. The epigram empowers the reader in the art of pricking and unmasking, the art of survival.[33]

The arbitrariness with which Martial supports or undermines a social illusion is at least partially a function of the fact that his is a world where honorary titles and status symbols proliferate and are often usurped; what people agree to notice or not is negotiable.[34] Martial himself was granted the *ius trium liberorum*, an honor which dates back to the time of Augustus, and he takes great pleasure in playing with the absurdity that someone could be *made* a father of three, both in his own case and that of others.[35] Again, the title *eques* had long since ceased to mean "cavalryman," but Martial likes to play with the lost meaning of the title, and with the insignia of equestrian status. The emperor could award equestrian status at will and, since a knight had to be freeborn, when he bestowed equestrian status on a freedman the emperor put time into reverse.[36] Even the title *Caesar*, no longer even an attenuated name, becomes a source of wit.[37] Characteristic of Martial's opportunistic attitude to honorifics is his play with the term *dominus*. During Martial's time it had become common to greet people as *dominus/domina*, a word that continued to have powerful associations with slavery in some contexts, while being more or less equivalent to "sir" in others. It was also common to address or refer to patrons as *dominus* and *rex*.[38] But, side by side with this honorific use, which inevitably carried with it slavish associations, were more neutral uses, starting with the habit of addressing a father as *dominus*.[39] Of course, it is characteristic of poets to resuscitate meanings that have been eroded by use, but these wordplays take advantage of the cognitive disconnection required in using certain honorific words. In 1.81 Martial facetiously makes the fact that Sosibianus greets his father as *dominus* prove that he is the son of a slave of his "father" (and thus, by law, his father's slave). But in Book 5.57 Martial tells Cinna, who has taken Martial's greeting to have a particular significance, that it means nothing, adding that sometimes he returns the greeting of Cinna's slave with the same word (*domine*). For the slave's greeting the word means something, but for Martial's return, nothing. Successful manipulation of this world lies in knowing when to take advantage of a meaning and when to let it go unnoticed.

## THE EPIGRAMMATIST ON HIS WORLD—OR OF IT

The persona of Martial the opportunistic epigrammatist sits uneasily with that of Martial the scourge of the upwardly mobile, and in some respects he exemplifies the very qualities he mocks. We could take as figures for the poet in this latter capacity the bouncers Leitus and Oceanus, whose job it is to ensure that nobody usurps a seat he does not deserve at the theater.[40] In Martial's Rome people are on the make, and the epigrammatist both polices and mirrors their mobility. The energy of the hustler who turns everything into an opportunity is reflected in the poet's ability to make language work for him, to make it pay off. This is perfectly exemplified in the extended play on the versatile verb *ago* in 1.79, which introduces a very busy man:

> Semper agis causas et res agis, Attale, semper;
> est, non est quod agas, Attale, semper agis.
> si res et causas desunt, agis, Attale, mulas.
> Attale, ne quod agas desit, agas animam. (1.79)

You are always arguing (*agis*) cases and, Attalus, you always have (*agis*) business. Whether there is or isn't something doing, you are always doing. If cases and business fail you, you

> drive (*agis*) mules. If you're running out of things to do, At-
> talus, why don't you do yourself in (*agas animam*).

Martial's zeugma (*res/causas/mulas/animam agere*), mirroring the
relentless busy-ness of Attalus, makes activities at opposite ends of
the social spectrum interchangeable. Attalus is probably a freedman, and just as his humanity has metamorphosed so his raw energy undergoes various incarnations as the verb *ago* searches for
objects.[41] In the process, what we may presume to have been the
biographical trajectory of Attalus, from slave to free, is reversed;
the slavish activity of driving mules emerges by a process of elimi-
nation as Attalus burns through the world, indifferently seeking
material with which to be busy. He is unmasked by his own activity,
as though his servile background were not a secret to be uncovered
but the destiny of his very success. The primitive meaning of *ago*
("drive": *agis . . . mulas*, 3) and the original servility of Attalus are
arrived at simultaneously, as the drive which underlies Attalus's
ascent is isolated from its objects. Attalus is finally consumed by
his own energy turning on him as it seizes on the last remaining
object, his own life. The epigrammatist steers this restless energy
into the trajectory of a life. Epigram is epitaph.

Where Attalus is betrayed by his own activity in the form of a
verb, Cerdo (3.16) is dogged by his origins in the form of a noun.

> Das gladiatores, sutorum regule, Cerdo,
>     quodque tibi tribuit subula, sica rapit.
> ebrius es: neque enim faceres hoc sobrius umquam,
>     ut velles corio ludere, Cerdo, tuo.
> lusisti corio: sed te, mihi crede, memento
>     nunc in pellicula, Cerdo, tenere tua.

> You're giving a gladiatorial show, Cerdo, little king of cob-
> blers. So what the awl afforded you, the dagger takes away.
> You must be drunk: sober you'd never have wanted to play
> with your own hide. You've played (given a gladiatorial
> show) with hide, then. But, trust me, now you must remem-
> ber, Cerdo, to keep yourself in your own skin.

The Attalus poem worked with the energy of its object, mimicking its adaptability and guiding its metamorphoses, but on a downward path which took Attalus through his servile origins toward death; this poem refuses the metamorphosis the social climber would effect, tying all the verbs to the same noun. Cerdo, "king of the cobblers," has given a gladiatorial combat (*ludus*), usurping an honor (*munus*) that should be reserved for those who came by their money in more dignified ways. If Cerdo's Greek name ("profit") suggests the antecedent of the relative *quod* (*quodque tibi tribuit subula*, 2), the complementarity of awl and dagger, stitching and cutting, brings to mind another noun, the *corium* (hide, skin) that is to feature in the rest of the poem. Martial's reduction of this honorable *munus* to a transaction between *sica* and *subula*, in which the cobbler exchanges animal hide for gladiator's flesh, prevents the translation of real into symbolic capital that Cerdo seeks to effect: money has not worked its usual metamorphosis. The expressions that play on skin/hide in the following two couplets reduce Cerdo himself to the level of the material with which he is "playing" in order to convert himself from cobbler to man of standing. The point is made most clearly in the fourth line, which is both literal and metaphorical: Cerdo is "doing this at his own expense" and "giving a gladiatorial combat (*ludere*) with his own hide," the shoe leather which has become gladiatorial flesh via money. By virtue of the fact that he is "playing" with his own profits Cerdo is also "risking his own skin," like the gladiators themselves, who stick to him as does the trade that has brought him fortune. The same combination of literal and metaphorical might be true also of the final couplet in which Cerdo is told to "keep himself in his own skin," that is, both to stay in his proper social position and to stick to the flesh that is his own (animal hide, not gladiatorial flesh).

Martial returns to Cerdo in the penultimate poem of the book, where the poet himself pulls off the very transformation that he had denied to Cerdo. In its prominent closural position the poem becomes an apologia, recalling other occasions on which Martial distinguishes between his life and his poetry, or asks his readers to grant him the license to play without giving offense. But in this poem it is Cerdo's life and art that are to be distinguished, not Martial's:

> Irasci nostro non debes, Cerdo, libello.
>     ars tua, non vita est carmine laesa meo.
> innocuos permitte sales. cur ludere nobis
>     non liceat, licuit si iugulare tibi? (3.99)

> You mustn't be angry with my little book, Cerdo. It was your craft, not your life that was injured by my poem. Permit me this harmless wit. Why should I not be allowed to play if you were allowed to slaughter?

As Martial alludes to one prong of his own apologia for his work, to attack vices, not people (*parcere personis, dicere de vitiis*, 10.33.10), he echoes another, namely that though the *book* is *lascivus*, his life is not.[42] But Martial's protestation is disingenuous, for the whole aim of the poem was to identify Cerdo with his profession (Cerdo-*corium*), to prevent him from transcending it. This poem simply adds insult to injury, since the punch line once again refuses Cerdo the honor of performing a *munus* by reducing it to the physical act of slaughter (*iugulare*), which brings us back to Cerdo's profession. Meanwhile it is Martial who has managed to transcend the brute reality of what he is inflicting on Cerdo. If the verb *ludere* in the earlier poem alluded to Cerdo's aspirations to give a *ludus*, only to mock them with a colloquial usage that brought us back to his profession (*corio ludere*), here it is appropriated by Martial to allude to the license that renders his mockery poetry rather than defamation, a "little book of poetry" (*libellus, OLD* 1a) as opposed to a "defamatory pamphlet" (*libellus, OLD* 1b). With the opposition *ludere-iugulare* Martial becomes the *editor* and Cerdo the gladiator. Of course, it is Cerdo who is "finished off" with that penultimate word, which manages both to perform an act of brutality and assign it to the victim (cf. *agas animam*, 1.79.4).

I have dealt with these poems at some length in order to demonstrate how Martial's opportunistic use of language mirrors, at the same time as it polices, the social mobility he observes in his world. Cerdo's attempt to transform real into symbolic capital is blocked by the same Martial who would parlay insult into art through his poetry. Is Martial, then, a poet as Attalus is a "doer" and Cerdo a cobbler? As profession, commercial item, gift, homage, decoration, weapon, entertainment, bore, social duty, and so on, Martial's poetry seems to rub shoulders with all the other professions, commercial items, and gifts that feature in the books. One more way to make a living; one more way to cultivate a patron; one more thing to send as a gift or buy at a store; one more thing to own or have stolen; one more way to impress or pretend; one more way to waste time or money. It has the privilege, also, of being the medium in which all these things, including poetry, appear.[43] To publish occasional poems in a book is to imply that they have an interest which transcends their immediate use; that they have not been used up. Perhaps, then, Martial claims that his poetry transcends those aspects of itself which it shares with other actions, relations, and objects. This tension has been well explored by Luke Roman, who formulates one aspect of it as follows: "The way in which Martial stages the fragmentation of his book into various social situations . . . suggests that the book is always disintegrating into multiple use-functions. The insistent quality of this fiction, however, is matched by discrete, but none the less important, expressions of Martial's concern with the book's existence as an integral entity."[44] Roman astutely attributes this duality to the dispersal of patronage in Martial's time: "If the poet were afforded the shelter of a grand patron [such as Maecenas] . . . he would be able to focus on an ambitious, integral work, rather than continuously pursuing many smaller gifts" (141). So the tension between the occasional and the transcendent (or "autonomous," in Roman's terminology) may itself have a persuasive (occasional) role to play, a loop which is typical of Martial.

Related to this tension is the paradox that Martial, the client-poet, complains that the demands of client service prevent him from writing poetry, but nevertheless creates a poetry whose dominant subject is that very service. Complaints about the paucity of patrons, the demeaning conditions of client service, and the meager returns of the profession of poetry are common. If Martial writes only epigrams and his output is small, that is because of all the extraneous claims on his time, or so he claims.[45] But in the meantime poetry is not so much wrested from this distracted life as produced by it: "While I accompany you and escort you home, / while I lend my ear to your natterings, / and while I praise whatever you say and do / how many verses, Labullus, could have been (*poterant*) born?" (11.24.1–4). The answer is "four." But the poem does not acknowledge its own existence; instead, the incommensurability of poetry and client service is driven home when Martial asks if it is fair that Labullus should swell his crowd of attendants at the expense of the poet's books (11.24.10–12). So poetry *does* transcend its world, but not *this* poetry, which is provisional for what could have been produced under more conducive circumstances.

## THE BOOK AND ITS READERS

A similar tension persists between the book as a second-order entity that floats free of the world it describes, detaching itself from the materiality it insists upon, and the book as a material object that has been bought, and is now being read, by someone who has thereby made a choice about how to use her time. The tension between the material/occasional and transcendent aspects of the book is not peculiar to Martial, and it is instructive to compare Catullus's version to Martial's. In c. 1 Catullus decides to give Nepos his book (*Cui dono . . . ? habe tibi*, 1, 8), but prays that the Muse keep it fresh for more than one generation (*quod, o patrona virgo, / plus uno maneat perenne saeclo*, 9–10). Martial transforms Catullus's dedication in order to refuse the same compliment to Quintus:

> Exigis ut donem nostros tibi, Quinte, libellos.
>   non habeo, sed habet bibliopola Tryphon.
> "aes dabo pro nugis et emam tua carmina sanus?
>   non" inquis "faciam tam fatue." nec ego. (4.72)

You demand that I give you [or dedicate to you] my books,
Quintus. I don't have any, but the bookseller Tryphon does.
"Will I give out cash for trivialities and buy your poems in
my right mind? I will not be such a fool," you say. Nor will I.

Everything has been reversed. Catullus generously announced his decision, but the put-upon Martial is reacting to an importunate request. Far from thinking, like Catullus's Nepos, that the poet's trifles *are* something (*namque tu solebas / meas esse aliquid putare nugas*, c. 1.3–4), Martial's Quintus refuses to shell out good money for them. Catullus plays on the senses in which Nepos can and can't have the book, and on the ambiguous status of the book itself.[46] So does Martial, but in a very different way. His *non habeo sed habet bibliopola* echoes Catullus's *habe tibi . . . quod . . . maneat.* Nepos can't quite *have* the book because it belongs to posterity, whereas Quintus can't have the book because Martial doesn't have it himself. When Quintus demands that Martial give him his books he is asking for a dedication, but Martial (mis)takes him to be requesting the physical objects themselves.[47] The book is a commercial item as well as a symbolic object, and the question of its value is partially a material issue; even the author has access to it only at a price, for he must pay to have it copied.[48] Of course, all this is disingenuous, an elaborate means of fobbing Quintus off. The allusion to Catullus tells Quintus that if he doesn't think Martial's trifles *are* something (compare Catullus's *namque tu solebas / meas esse aliquid putare nugas*, c. 1.3–4), then the author has no reason to grant him a dedication. It is characteristic of Martial that the best measure of what Quintus thinks of his *nugae* is whether he would be prepared to buy them. The Catullan allusion works to remind us that *nugae* might be something after all, but Martial substitutes for Catullus's Muse (*patrona virgo*, 9) the bookseller Tryphon, and erases the distinction between the author's and the buyer's relation to the book. Martial's play with the two dimensions of the book, dedicated and given, literary work and object, anchors the book more firmly in the material circumstances of circulation than does Catullus's similar play, and in the process it alludes to the heterogeneous character of Martial's readership.

Quintus, a potential patron, is one kind of reader addressed in Martial's books, but here he is mockingly assimilated to a quite different kind of reader whom Martial makes peculiarly his own, the anonymous *lector.* This character will have an enormously important afterlife in the history of the notion of a readership. Here again, we may use the newspaper as a handy reference point. One nineteenth-century Parisian editorial enthused on the newspaper's circulation as follows: "To read one's newspaper is to live the universal life, the life of the whole capital, of the entire city, of all France, of all nations. . . . It is thus that in a great country like France, the same thought, at one and the same time, animates the whole population. . . . It is the newspaper which establishes this sublime communication of souls across distances."[49] At the beginning of his *Liber spectaculorum*, Martial lists some of the nations represented by visitors to the games, and he concludes the poem with his own version of a "sublime communication of souls" as the resultant babel of tongues becomes one when the emperor is greeted as *pater patriae* (*Spec.* 3). There is more than a hint of self-praise in this effusion, for Martial will open his first book with the claim that he is *toto notus in orbe* (1.1.2), known and in demand across a wide and heterogeneous readership, addressed in the singular as *lector studiose* (dedicated reader, 1.1.4). The emperor, also known through copies, the statues scattered across the Roman world, is implicitly posed as a figure against which to measure the popular author. Complaining to a patron that his attendance at the former's *levées* is costing him valuable writing time, Martial laments the loss of "what Rome reads, the visitor demands, the knight does not despise, the senator has by heart, the lawyer praises, the poet criticizes" (11.24.6–8). Not exactly a "sublime communication of souls," perhaps, but a whistle-stop tour of the city as readership. Martial's strategy in books 1–12 is not so much to assimilate this heterogeneity to unity (or "universal life"), as to create a shifting set of relations between different elements of this readership. Some of these relations will manifest the tension between the occasional and the transcendent that I have been describing, for the appeal of Martial's books to an anonymous, abstract *lector*, standing for a diffused and numerous readership, suggests that the books have an aesthetic dimension beyond their use, and that the *lector* is their ultimate destination. But this is not the only way to understand the situation. Perhaps the *lector* is just a voyeur, who has missed, or is excluded from the real thing, shared between the poet and the addressees of the individual poems. Possibly, frustration will prompt the *lector* to abandon his, or her, anonymity and to become an honored addressee, a promotion rather than a loss of the transcendent position. Equally, the appeal to the *lector* serves the purposes of the occasional by providing a wider audience for the praise of the patron. If the poet wants to attract patrons, then he needs to show that he has a wide circulation. So the transcendent is folded back into the occasional. This oscillation between occasional and transcendent prevents the book from either congealing or disintegrating.

THE "SOCIETY OF THE BOOK" that I have just described will be the topic of chapter 5, and at this point it will be useful to take an overview of the succession of chapters. After a brief survey of epigram at Rome (Excursus), I will begin with two chapters focusing on a single book each, the *Liber spectaculorum* and Book 1 respectively. These are the first two books to confront the reader in modern editions of Martial and between them they make a neat contrast: the *Liber spectaculorum* atomizes and epigrammatizes a single event, breaking it down into a series of discrete moments, while Book 1 is the first of Martial's twelve books of miscellaneous epigrams, but one that will reveal an unexpected coherence, if not unity. The *Liber spectaculorum* is an appropriate place to start for several reasons, and not least because it celebrates the beginning of the new Flavian dynasty, with which Martial will be closely associated, and whose demise will be followed swiftly by the poet's departure from Rome for his native Spain. This chapter concerns the world of Martial in a more historically specific sense than the ones that follow. Titus's games, as Martial represents them, are the locus of a presence that obliterates the independent and potentially exemplary status of the past. Here the ideological requirements of the new dynasty, which cannot lay claim to an illustrious or divine ancestry, coincide with the claim of the epigram to be concerned with the here and now, so that this book introduces us to a characteristic epigrammatic attitude from the perspective of imperial ideology. If the *Liber spectaculorum* introduces us to an imperial author, the first book of Martial's "Dodecalogue" is programmatic for this author in a different way, since one of its prominent themes is the issue of what a book of epigrams might be, a question that is raised explicitly and implicitly during the course of the book. Book 1 carries over from the *Liber spectaculorum* not only the theme of the arena, which has a significant presence in the book, but also the question of the relation between exemplary past, preserved in lapidary epigrams, and the present, on which the epigram as an occasional form depends. The relation between past and present, then, plays on the tense coexistence of (occasional) ephemerality and lapidary permanence in the character of the genre itself. In Book 1, it is also associated with the process of entering the book. It is typical of Martial to cast the reading process in material terms, and here the various layers of prefatory material put into question where the book, or our reading of it, actually begins, which is one dimension of this book's interrogation of its own status. Can the book secure its own boundaries and maintain its integrity? What kind of coherence might it have? How does its concatenation of overlapping themes reflect on Martial's world? In these two chapters I will attempt to *read* two epigrammatic books.

Each of the two chapters on individual books also introduces one of the running subthemes of this book. I will be suggesting throughout, as I have already, that Martial is not only a poet of his times, but also a poet for ours. In the case of the *Liber spectaculorum*, I will be applying some concepts developed to describe the modern "society of the spectacle" to the ancient spectacle as Martial conceives it, and this will be the most focused attempt to read Martial through the modern. Another strain that runs through this book is the theme of slavery, a ubiquitous and extremely rich theme in Martial's work. In Book 1 it seems to have a structural function, but it features throughout his work to such an extent that it sometimes appears as an emblem of the form itself.[50] The commodification of the epigram form; the relations between client and patron; the celebration of the culture and lifestyles of the rich and famous; the unmasking of hypocrites; the uncovering of secrets and the expression of private sentiment—all of these concerns of the genre are, at one point or another, filtered through the subject of slavery. In the case of Book 1, slavery will play an important role in Martial's exploration of the varieties and complexities of possession, a subject that is a source of wit throughout his work.

Chapter 4 will take both a broader and a narrower look at the epigram book. It will be concerned with local effects of a kind that recur throughout the oeuvre and will tackle the central topic of juxtaposition. One way to characterize the juxtapository world of Martial's books is to ask if there are particular kinds of juxtaposition that recur. I will start with a polarity that is not only central to Martial's oeuvre but endemic to the genre itself, for the epigram's claim to fix its subject once and for all has the potential for both praise and ridicule. What is the effect of juxtaposing scoptic with panegyric? In this case I will try to characterize the experience of the reader who is required both to exercise suspicion and to suspend it as he moves between unmasking and flattery from one poem to the next. The rest of this chapter will be concerned with juxtapositions of status, and here again we will be confronted with opposites. Slaves will feature prominently in this chapter and particularly in connection with their polar opposite, the emperor. Is there an analytic wit behind these juxtapositions, and if so, what do Martial's juxtapositions of status tell us about the structure of his social world? We will see that some surprising analogies emerge from Martial's juxtapositions; among other things, it is clear that Martial understands the anomalous figure of the emperor by reference to a number of counterparts with whom he is juxtaposed, anomalous figures themselves, such as the slave, the author, and the *lector*.

Chapter 5 will deal with the society of the book. Martial's appeal to an anonymous "reader" (*lector*) is the beginning of a long history of the writer's relation to an unknown public, but the *lector* is only one component of Martial's imagined readership, which is variegated and layered rather than homogeneous. Martial's readers are made aware of the others with whom they share the book, and this virtual society produces shifting relations between different interests, statuses, and reading practices. Contrasting with the enthusiastic *lector* are the patrons who have no time to read frivolities, or who write poetry rather than read it; along with the predominantly male readership, there are matrons who read the dirty bits in secret or are warned, in vain, that the next bit is not for them; there are readers for whom the book is too long or too short; readers who are proud to find their name in the book, and others, less proud, who think they recognize themselves under a pseudonym; still other readers will never find their name in the book no matter how much they want to. Although all are reading the same book in one sense, in another they are not, since they will have acquired the book in different ways. Some are reading a presentation copy and others have been to the bookstore; others still will have been present at occasions where a particular epigram was improvised or presented. This is not mere variety but a network of relations that is constantly finding new configurations, new hierarchies. Sometimes we are to think of the unknown *lector* as the true imagined reader of a book in which occasional epigrams have been removed from their specific context and raised to the status of the universal; at other times, the *lector* is just a voyeur who wasn't there for the real thing. To read Martial, then, is to enter the society of the book. It is to be aware of the different readers with whom you are sharing the book and of the different ways in which you partake of it.

The final chapter will look at the dual capacity of the epigram to diminish and to exalt, but in the context of intertextual relations. This chapter will take us from Martial's Republican precursor, Catullus, to his Renaissance parodist, Johannes Burmeister. On the way we will visit a very important model, though not one whom Martial explicitly acknowledges as such, namely Ovid, and particularly the Ovid of the exile poetry. This chapter is concerned with the relation between different poetic worlds as the later poet reads the precursor through his own very different context. Catullus's urbanities will be subjected to a banalizing urbanization, while Ovid the exile will be recalled as Martial adapts Ovidian motifs to the more fortunate circumstances of the client poet. Finally, Burmeister will take us out of the ancient world with his Christian version, in parallel text, of the entire oeuvre of Martial, raising the question of whether there is such a thing as a parody upward rather than downward.

# EXCURSUS
## EPIGRAM·AT·ROME

When we use the term "epigram" today what comes to mind is more or less what Martial made of the form: closure, pointedness, wit, concision, and satire.[1] Martial chose the term "epigram" from a range of expressions used by Roman poets more or less interchangeably for collections of short, light, and personal verse—besides *epigrammata*, the list includes *nugae, lusus* and *ioci*.[2] Though he uses all of these words for his poetry, it is as a poet famous for "books of witty epigrams" (*argutis epigrammaton libellis*, 1.1.3) that he chooses to introduce himself in the first poem of Book 1, and it remains his favored term.[3] Probably, as Mario Puelma suggests, Martial intended to give a name, and with it a new canonical text, to the genreless *nugae, ludi, ioci*, and so forth of Catullus and others.[4] By Martial's time the Greek epigrammatists too were using this term and discussing the genre; like Martial, they assigned it a place at the bottom of the generic ladder.[5] But if Martial is alluding to Greek tradition in his use of this term, he is strikingly silent about that tradition when it comes to declaring his models, for all of the names he adduces are Roman, and at the head of the list stands Catullus. With the exception of Callimachus, the Greek poets we call epigrammatists are nowhere named by Martial, though their influence is everywhere apparent.[6] By Martial's time Greek epigram was a vital component of literary life at Rome, and we must now briefly trace its history.

## GREEK EPIGRAM

The word *epigramma* means "inscription," and examples of verse inscriptions on objects and monuments informing us who dedicated this votive offering or who is buried here survive from as early as the archaic period.[7] When epigrams migrate to books in the Hellenistic period, epitaphs, along with dedications and other "anathematic" epigrams, remain a significant component of the new literary form.[8] Martial features both types, and not only does he play with common epitaphic formulas but he also alludes to the inscriptional associations of the form through a number of characteristic figures that not only banalize the original but also situate it more specifically in its world: the stigma on a slave's face, or graffiti, for instance.[9]

The epigram was a form "destined by its very nature to be anthologized" (Cameron 1993.4), and we know Greek epigram almost exclusively through a succession of anthologies, subsumed into what we call the *Greek*, or *Palatine Anthology*, which was put together by Cephalas in the early tenth century. It contains earlier anthologies, most importantly the Garlands (*stephanoi*, literally "crowns") of Meleager and Philip. Around 100 BC Meleager composed an anthology of Hellenistic epigram, probably subsuming earlier collections by the authors themselves, parts of which may survive intact in their new home.[10] Meleager arranged poems in his anthology according to the four categories of erotic, epitaphic, anathematic (dedicatory), and epideictic (descriptive or narrative), all of which types feature in Martial. Meleager's organization emphasized the art of variation, juxtaposing different versions of the same theme, so that the reader might be treated, for instance, to thirty successive poems on the subject of the sculptor Myron's famous cow (*AP* 713–42).[11] This kind of arrangement survives in Martial's *Apophoreta* and *Xenia*, but nothing could be further from the arrangement of his twelve numbered books, which juxtapose poems that diverge sharply, often aggressively, in type, subject matter, and tone.

New evidence that Hellenistic poets published books of epigrams before the anthology of Meleager has surfaced in the form of the Milan papyrus, a third-century manuscript containing one hundred epigrams of Posidippus.[12] The arrangement of these epigrams is according to theme, as in the anthology of Meleager. Kathryn

Gutzwiller (1998) argues that poets as early as Anyte, Nossis (fl. 300 BC), and Leonidas (second quarter of the third century) composed their own collections, with programmatic poems and a range of content unified by particular focuses such as gender, age, class, philosophical ideology, or, in the case of the erotic epigrammatists, distinctive emotional perspectives. The most famous book of epigrams for the Hellenistic age was Callimachus's *Epigrammata*, a very varied collection held together, as Gutzwiller puts it, by Callimachus's self-reflexive position.[13] We would give much to know about the epigram books of Martial's most important Greek predecessor, Lucillius, and in particular whether he arranged his books by theme, as did his Hellenistic predecessors, or anticipated Martial's principle of *variatio*.[14] What we do know is that the opening of his second book, preserved in book 9 of the *Palatine Anthology*, is both programmatic and dedicatory.[15]

The *Garland* of Philippus of Thessalonica was presented to the consul Camillus during the reign of Nero. Between the anthology of Meleager and that of Philip, the thematic center of gravity had shifted from the erotic and symposiastic to the ecphrastic and epideictic. The Neronian epigrammatist Lucillius, much imitated by Martial, would add invective and scoptic to the epigram's thematic repertoire. This was an important development for Martial, but equally so was the fact that by the time of Philip's *Garland* Greek epigram and epigrammatists were firmly embedded in the world of client and patron at Rome, with important mutual effects.[16] When Lucillius dedicated his second book of epigrams to Nero he struck a pose familiar to readers of Martial:

> "From the Heliconian Muses let us begin our song," wrote Hesiod, while shepherding, as the story goes. "Sing, goddess, of the wrath," and "Tell me of a man, O Muse," said Calliope through Homer's mouth. And I too must write something as a proem. But what shall I write, as I begin to release my second book? "Olympian Muses, daughters of Zeus, I would not have got by if Nero Caesar hadn't given me some bronze." (*AP* 9.572)[17]

Lucillius teases Nero as Martial occasionally teases Domitian (1.5, 5.15), and in other poems we find him sharing quips and complaints with the emperor.[18] Greek epigram was now an essential element of social and court life, lending a veneer of elegance to the relations between patron and client, and consecrating the rituals and exchanges of Roman social life. Invitations, gifts, requests, and celebrations of significant events (birthdays, weddings, promotions, deaths) might all be accompanied by epigrams written by Greek poets for their Roman patrons. The association goes back to the end of the second century BC, when Antipater of Sidon and A. Licinius Archias came to Rome at about the time that Meleager published his anthology.[19] Archias celebrated the victories of C. Marius and L. Licinius Lucullus, and when Cicero defended Archias's citizenship in 62 he hoped, in vain, that Archias would write a poem in his honor (*Att.* 1.16.1). Philodemus's relation to L. Calpurnius Piso Caesonius is documented by several epigrams, including the ancestor of the Roman invitation poem, which ends with a hint that Piso might be more generous with his protégé (*AP* 11.44; compare the end of Lucillius' poem to Nero). According to Cicero (*In Pisonem*, 28–29), Philodemus celebrated all aspects of Piso's disreputable life (adulteries, lusts, dinners . . . ) in the most exquisite of verses. Epigrams served to "celebrate the moments," and not only the glorious moments, of aristocratic life, bathing them in the glow of instant culture: both Archias and Antipater were known as skilled improvisers.[20]

A generation later, under the first *princeps*, the relation has become more courtly.[21] Piso's son, L. Calpurnius Piso (the *pontifex*), was a patron of Antipater of Thessalonica, who celebrated the *translatio imperii* with an epigram in which Piso receives a sword of Alexander's.[22] The Hellenistic anathematic epigram, accompanying a dedication to a deity, was retooled to serve as accompaniment to a gift for a patron, with some of the conventions of address carried over to the new context.[23] This gift might be the poet's new book ("let Piso receive it gratefully, like Zeus who is won over by a little incense," *AP* 6.227) or the humble Saturnalian gift of a candle (*AP* 6.249). Prayers that had been addressed to deities were now directed at patrons and, particularly, emperors.[24] Finally, the wonders of epideictic epigram became the miracles of the emperor's arena, as we shall see in the next chapter.

From the time of Augustus, Greek epigrammatists had a significant presence at court, as witnessed, for instance, by the career of Crinagoras, a client of Octavia who wrote epigrams celebrating Germanicus, Tiberius, Marcellus, and Augustus himself.[25] Leonidas of Alexandria found favor at the court of Nero and survived the change of regime to flourish under Vespasian, a feat which Martial hoped (in vain) to perform after the assassination of Domitian. Indirect evidence of the activity of Greek epigrammatists at the court of Domitian is provided by Martial 9.11.14–17, which suggests that his poems celebrating the hair-offering of Domitian's *delicatus*, the eunuch Earinus, may have met with competition from Greek epigrammatists. Martial complains that the Greeks (*quibus est nihil negatum*, 14) allow themselves the metrical license to render the name Earinus more tractable in verse. Roman poets, whose Muses are more severe, cannot be that eloquent (*disertis*, 16).[26] But Martial beat the Greeks at their own game, and it may have been part of Domitian's policy to encourage Latin poets to make inroads into genres that had hitherto been dominated by Greeks.[27]

Roman patron and Greek epigrammatist often professed to share a dedication to the Muses, and from the time of the publication of Meleager's *Garland* we find Roman aristocrats getting in on the act. The consul of 102, Q. Lutatius Catulus, who knew Antipater, wrote two of the earliest preserved Latin epigrams, both homoerotic, and one of them inspired by Callimachus.[28] There is even a surviving Greek epigram by Germanicus Caesar (*AP* 7.31). From the beginning, the fiction of shared literary pursuits was a crucial element of the *amicitia* between Roman patrons and Greek poets.[29] The epigrammatists celebrate their patrons' literary endeavors and occasionally, so as not to devalue the coinage, they complain. Lucillius, for instance, grumbles about a patron who serves him lousy food and then washes it down with epigrams (*AP* 11.136), and Martial puts into close juxtaposition contrasting attitudes to patrons who write (7.42 and 7.46): in 7.42, it is carrying coals to Newcastle to send poems to Castricus, while in 7.46 Martial complains that Priscus wants to accompany his gifts with poems, and Martial must wait for the Muse to descend before receiving Priscus's gift.

One of the most interesting examples of a Roman grandee writing Greek epigram is Augustus himself. Macrobius (*Saturnalia* 2.4.31) recounts a fascinating anecdote about a certain "Greekling" (*graeculus*) who made several vain attempts to waylay the *princeps* and present him with an honorific epigram. When Augustus saw that the Greek was preparing to make another attempt he wrote out a little epigram of his own, in Greek, and had it delivered to the poet, who read it with visible admiration. The poet then dipped into his purse and brought out a few denarii, which he gave to Augustus, saying that he wished it could have been more. Augustus was amused, and had 100,000 sesterces paid out to the Greek.[30] The anecdote establishes that Augustus could write a Greek epigram with the best of them, and on the spot.[31] But it is most interesting for what it says about the epigram as a form. Short, formally closed, and evoking, ideally, a smile of pleasure, delight, or admiration, the epigram was a form waiting to be commodified. The Greek reads Augustus's epigram on the spot and then dips into his purse for a few coins as return for the moment of pleasure it has given. Of course, in doing this he is flattering Augustus as a poet of equal accomplishment, but clearly he also implies that the appropriate way to respond to such a "gift" is to pay for it. From their earliest inscriptional manifestations, epigrams were associated metonymically with things. In the late Republic and early Empire epigrams often accompanied gifts from poets to patrons, and sometimes vice versa; price tags, manufacturers' labels, and gift cards all at once, they both enhanced the value of the gift and assimilated some of the objecthood of the gift itself. The Greek's gesture is not only flattering but also witty in an epigrammatic way: his reversal neatly includes the hint of a request in his flattery—he would have given more if he could. Particularly relevant to Martial is the bald acknowledgment of what the epigrammatist might expect from the honoree. In this case, the transaction is atomistic and the exchange immediate, a far cry from the process by which Horace came to be included in the Augustan circle (*Serm.* 1.6.45–62). But the very monstrosity of the sum that Augustus pays out suggests that the value of this fiction of reciprocity, reversibility, and shared literary pursuits is inestimable. The anecdote succinctly encapsulates the tension between mystification and demystification that is endemic to the form.

Unfortunately, we do not have Augustus's Greek epigram, but what we do have, thanks to Martial, is a Latin epigram from the time of the siege of Perugia, in which Octavian insults Antonia in sexual terms similar to those we find inscribed on the infamous sling bullets used at the siege of Perugia.[32] As a form of propaganda or publicity, the epigram had the advantage that it could be easily memorized, repeated, and circulated:

> Quod futuit Glaphyran Antonius, hanc mihi poenam
>     Fulvia constituit, se quoque uti futuam.
> Fulvia ego ut futuam? quid si me Manius oret
>     pedicem? faciam? non puto, si sapiam.
> "aut futue; aut pugnemus" ait. quid quod mihi vita
>     carior est ipsa mentula? signa canant! (11.20.3–8)

Because Antony is fucking Glaphyra, Fulvia has resolved on this penalty for *me*, that I fuck her in turn. I, fuck Fulvia? What if Manius asked me to bugger him? Would I do it? I don't think so, not if I have any sense. "Either fuck me or let us fight," she says. What about the fact that my prick is more dear to me than my life? Let them sound the trumpet!

By reducing politics to sexual relations, and by casting the run-up to war as a brilliantly economical epigrammatic exchange, Octavian puts himself in charge of the situation. Judith Hallett is right to stress that Octavian is here establishing himself (against the background of accusations of passive homosexuality) as the phallic aggressor, but the propaganda value of this poem is as much a matter of its aesthetics, its commanding display of *sprezzatura*, as of its sexual politics. We do not have any evidence that Domitian composed epigrams, but early in his first book, Martial lets the emperor speak back with a couplet that recalls the exchange between Augustus and the *graeculus* and also bears an interesting relation to Octavian's Perugian epigram:

> Do tibi naumachiam, tu das epigrammata nobis:
>     vis, puto, cum libro, Marce, natare tuo. (1.5)

I give you a sea battle and you give me epigrams. Marcus, I think you want to swim with your book.

The prominence given to the two balancing Greek words in the first line brings to mind the Greek court epigrammatists, still a presence in Martial's day. Like Augustus in Macrobius's anecdote, Martial's Domitian forestalls the epigrammatist's request and reverses the transaction: the epigrams are the poet's return for the emperor's gift of a *naumachia*, not a performance that needs to be rewarded. Like the *graeculus*, "Domitian" makes a joke of the fiction of reciprocity, and the huge differential in power, confirmed by the rather sinister reference to the punishments meted out in the arena's fatal charades, is modulated into an exchange of wit between poet and emperor. Martial is addressed by his *praenomen*, a bold assumption of intimacy on the part of the author ventriloquizing the "emperor," but one that marks the latter as a *civilis princeps*. The poem's strained humor shows the difficulty of containing the relation between an increasingly distant emperor and his humble subject within the fiction of *amicitia* that had served earlier poets and patrons.

But the relation between epigram and court was not always benign. Like a joke, the scoptic epigram tends toward the anonymous, which allows it to stand for the voice of the people, or the subject's version of the ruler's edicts. The epigram's concision and memorability ensure that it is passed around, and that it sticks to its target. Suetonius (*Nero* 39) tells us that in the last years of Nero's reign "many poems in Greek or Latin were posted up (*proscripta*) or passed around." Three Latin couplets are quoted, one of which is particularly interesting for us, since Martial may allude to it in the *Liber spectaculorum*:

> Roma domus fiet: Veios migrate, Quirites,
> si non et Veios occupat ista domus.

> Rome will become a single house [i.e. Nero's palace, the Golden House]: move to Veii, citizens. If that house doesn't occupy Veii too.[33]

Suetonius tells us that Nero did not seek out the authors of this couplet, and that when they were reported to him he prevented them from being punished severely. Domitian was different, and

Suetonius describes him as inordinately suspicious. But perhaps it was not as paranoiac as Suetonius implies (*Dom.* 14.2) that Domitian suspected the worst when he discovered that an epigram of Euenus of Ascalon was being passed around at the time of his legislation curtailing the cultivation of vines. In the epigram (*AP* 9.75) a vine reminds the goat that is eating it that it will provide wine for the libation when the goat is sacrificed.

Suetonius's *Lives of the Caesars* is rife with references to anonymous epigrams directed at the emperors.[34] Centuries later, Martial's poetry would be plundered by the anonymous authors of Renaissance Rome who posted scurrilous epigrams on the torso of an ancient sculpture known as Pasquino. These "pasquinades" recycled phrases and epigrams of Martial to lambaste the popes, descendents of the emperors Martial had celebrated.[35] Martial's *Liber spectaculorum*, which will be the focus of the next chapter, reflects the existence of these anonymous squibs not only because it echoes the epigram on Nero's Golden House quoted above, but also because the end of the manuscript has attracted an epigram on the last emperor of the Flavian dynasty, which cannot have originally stood in its present position:

> Flavia gens, quantum tibi tertius abstulit heres.
> paene fuit tanti, non habuisse duos.

> Flavian clan, how much did the third of your dynasty diminish you. It would almost have been worth it not to have had the other two.

As he himself complained, Martial's celebrity made him a convenient Pasquino.[36]

# CHAPTER TWO

# STRATEGIES·OF·THE·SPECTACLE

The book that opens Martial's oeuvre, both in modern editions and in the chronological sequence of his surviving work, is unlike any of the following books, and yet it makes a fitting introduction to his work. Unlike the numbered books, it deals with a single theme, indeed a single event, the games given by Titus for the inauguration of the Flavian amphitheater in 80 BC. Furthermore, aspects of Martial's persona that will be important for his later work are lacking. Indeed Martial offers us very little in the way of a persona in this book; he speaks as a member of the audience, worshiping his emperor at the same time that he wonders at the spectacle the emperor has provided. Here Martial realizes the poetry of presence anticipated, as Mario Labate has shown, in Ovid's *Tristia*: the poet, present himself at the imperial event he celebrates, provides his audience with models of reception or response.[1] The *Liber spectaculorum* casts Titus's celebration as a succession of momentary, sometimes unscripted, events, as though to reflect the moment-to-moment elations of the crowd. The epigram's brevity, wit, and pointedness here serve to isolate slices from the continuous flow of attractions and render its highlights portable, like the favors distributed to the crowd by the emperor.[2] If we are not yet introduced to Martial the client-poet, this book nevertheless brings before us some of the characteristic attitudes of the epigram as a "modern" form, for here the epigram meets a kind of event that is peculiarly of its (early imperial) times. Above all, the spectacle as the epitome of presence, presided over by the divine presence of the emperor himself, provides Martial with the opportunity to explore one of the genre's proudest boasts, namely that it concerns the here and now.[3] Simultaneously exalting and deflating, the epigram pits a wondrous and ephemeral present against a past drained of its substance, and Martial is able to make an implicit claim for the epigram as the appropriate form for this content. It could be said that in this book epigram and spectacle mutually interpret one another, with the result that Martial's *Liber spectaculorum* provides a unique perspective on the strategies of the imperial spectacle.[4]

## SPECTACLES AND "THE SPECTACLE"

Standing at the head of Martial's oeuvre, the *Liber spectaculorum* threatens to turn away the modern reader at the very threshold of his work. Even a sensibility dulled by contemporary screen violence may find some of it hard to take. For sheer physical repulsiveness, *Spec.* 9, in which a criminal is mauled to death by a bear, is difficult to match.[5] The cruel gloating at human suffering and the mockery of the tormented which pervade the book remind us of what has made the Roman arena a source of such ambivalent fascination to Hollywood. Throughout the twentieth century the Roman arena played a key role in discussions of contemporary mass culture: Juvenal's "bread and circuses" model exerted, and in some respects continues to exert, a considerable influence on the study of modern mass culture in the form of what Patrick Brantlinger (1983) has called "negative classicism."[6] But sensational violence is not the only aspect of the arena that has struck the modern imagination with a mixture of fascination and disgust. The enormous amount of attention that has recently been paid to the spectacular aspects of Roman culture, and to the spectacles themselves, must be attributed in no small part to the fact that early imperial Rome and the West in its late capitalist phase are both, in their different ways, societies of the spectacle.[7] Recent work on the Roman spectacle shows the fruitful influence of contemporary concerns with the "society of the spectacle," as Guy Debord has dubbed it, declaring that "in societies where modern conditions of production prevail, all of life presents itself as an immense accumulation of spectacles. Everything that was directly lived has moved away into a representation."[8] Shadi Bartsch, in her study of theatrical doublespeak during the early Empire, compares the dominance of simulation in postmodern culture, and Matthew Leigh's book on Lucan takes as its theme the degradation of engagement into spectatorship, a common complaint of critics of contemporary culture.[9] Are the spectacles of ancient Rome part of the prehistory of "*the* spectacle"?

The origins of the (post)modern spectacle have been traced, in the work of Walter Benjamin, Jean Baudrillard, and T. J. Clark, to nineteenth-century Paris, where the citizen was being transformed into the consumer through the marketing and commoditization of areas of social practice once referred to as everyday life; there the industries of tourism, recreation, fashion, and display were on the rise, along with mechanical reproduction, advertising, and, in general, the precedence of sign value over use value, of copy over original. The relation between copy and original will be a significant theme of this chapter, but I will also address another aspect of the spectacle that was crucial to Debord, namely, "the spectacle as a new kind of power of recuperation and absorption, a capacity to neutralize and assimilate acts of resistance by converting them into objects or images of consumption."[10] In reaching back to the world of ancient Rome to find earlier traces of this, and other, spectacular strategies, I am going to stretch the notion of genealogy beyond its breaking point. In fact, it is not my intention to argue that Rome was a precursor of our "society of the spectacle"; insofar as one can apply the phrase to ancient Rome it has to mean something quite different from what was meant by Debord. For one thing, ancient spectacles did not produce "lonely crowds" isolated from each other in their submission to the spectacle: the ancient "society of the spectacle" involved both a wide range of political and social practices and a more active role for the spectator. Factors such as euergetism, honor, Roman identity, and monarchical politics situate the Roman arena in a very different context from the patterns of modern production and consumption which, according to Debord, are objectified in the spectacle. What I do intend to claim is that there is a certain logic to the workings of spectacle that postmodern "spectacologists" were not the first to articulate and, conversely, that some of the concepts developed to understand the modern spectacle may help us to understand what Martial is doing in this distinctively epigrammatic take on the spectacles and, with them, the glorification of Rome's second dynasty.

Debord himself distinguished the concentrated spectacle, which involves the "magical identification with a leader," from the diffuse spectacle of consumerism with which he was primarily concerned. The spectacles of the Roman arena would belong to the category of the concentrated spectacle, and the particular material I am dealing with, poetry written about the spectacles in the early imperial period, speaks about the power of spectacle and the spectacle of power as it celebrates the divinity of the emperor made manifest in his amphitheater.[11] Submission to the emperor is submission to the spectacle and vice versa. And yet, Martial's celebration of these imperial spectacles displays strategies that anticipate the modern spectacle as Debord has described it.

I will be discussing two related aspects of spectacle as it is understood by contemporary spectacologists. First, the omnivorousness of the spectacle—its claim to recast the world as spectacle and so to erase the distinction between inside and outside. The spectacle is an overwhelming *presence* in which everything takes its place. Martial's epigrams represent the amphitheater and its spectacles as a new order of object, space, or event, which is adequate to represent, rather than compete with, whatever lies outside it, so that everything comes into its own in this reassembled "world." The other topic I will be discussing is the transformation of the image from something that refers to another reality into something that replaces that reality, a copy without an original (a "simulacrum").[12] Here we are concerned primarily with the dissolution of the power and authority of the original and of the past, together with the transformation of their exemplary potential into an object of consumption.[13]

## SPECTACLE AND WORLD: MARTIAL ON THE FLAVIAN AMPHITHEATER

Martial begins his book by hailing the Flavian amphitheater as a new wonder of the world.[14] The pyramids, Babylon, the temple of

Artemis at Delos and the Mausoleum can no longer give their respective countries cause to boast:

> omnis Caesareo cedit labor Amphitheatro,
>    unum pro cunctis fama loquetur opus. (*Spec.* 1.7–8)

> Every work cedes precedence to Caesar's amphitheater, and
> fame will speak of one work in the place of all.

The rhetoric seems straightforward: all the wonders of the world will be eclipsed by this latest prodigy, which will leave posterity with only one subject.[15] But if we put pressure on the last line, there is room for more than one reading of the phrase *unum pro cunctis*: "one instead of all others," certainly, but also "one on behalf of all others." In the mouth of posterity, the Flavian Amphitheater (Colosseum) will come to stand for all wonders, not so much eclipsing as representing them. The amphitheater is not just one wonder among others, the seventh and newest; it also replaces all others as the very medium of wonder. As Debord puts it, "The oldest social specialization, the specialization of power, is at the root of the spectacle. *The spectacle is thus a specialized activity which speaks for all others.* It is the diplomatic representation of hierarchic society to itself, where all other expression is banned. Here the most modern is also the most archaic" (my emphasis).[16]

In the following poem, Martial turns from the status of the Colosseum on the international, world-historical stage to the Colosseum in its Roman context:

> Hic ubi sidereus propius videt astra colossus
>    et crescunt media pegmata celsa via,
> invidiosa feri radiabant atria regis
>    unaque iam tota stabat in urbe domus.
> hic ubi conspicui venerabilis Amphitheatri
>    erigitur moles, stagna Neronis erant.
> hic ubi miramur velocia munera thermas,
>    abstulerat miseris tecta superbus ager.
> Claudia diffusas ubi porticus explicat umbras,
>    ultima pars aulae deficientis erat.

reddita Roma sibi est et sunt te praeside, Caesar,
deliciae populi, quae fuerant domini.

Here where the shining colossus takes a closer look at the
stars, and tall scaffolds rise in the middle of the street, the
odious halls of that savage king used to spread, and one house
alone then stood in the entire city. Here where the august
mass of the amphitheater rises and is seen from afar, were
Nero's lakes. Here where we admire the hot baths, swiftly
bestowed and built, the arrogant estate robbed unfortunates
of their homes. Here where the Claudian portico extends its
spreading shade was the limit where the palace finally gave
out. Rome is returned to itself and under your tutelage, Caesar, the master's pleasures have become the people's.

The siting of the Flavian Amphitheater on the ruins of Nero's
Golden House was a propaganda masterstroke, and Martial milks
it skillfully, beginning with the colossal statue of Nero, remodeled
by Vespasian into a statue of the sun.[17] The burden of the poem
is that what had been stolen from the Roman people for his own
private pleasure by Nero has been returned to them by the Flavian program of public works. Nero's appropriation of the center
of Rome recalls the rhetoric of the previous poem, but to different
effect: "A single house now stood in all the city" (*unaque iam tota
stabat in urbe domus*, 4) just as a single work will speak for/re-
place all others for posterity. But if we map the ambiguity of the
word *pro* at the end of the last poem onto the structure of this
poem, we can see that the two senses have now been placed in
sequence: where Nero built a palace that displaced the people of
Rome (one in place of many: *abstulerat miseris tecta*, 8) the Flavians have built an edifice that was for their benefit (one for the
sake of many: *deliciae populi*).[18] There is still one colossal building in the middle of Rome, and Martial makes no claim that the
dwellings Nero expropriated have been reinstated. Instead "Rome
has been returned to itself." Again, there are two meanings to be
teased out of this phrase, and specifically the word *reddita*, both
"given back" and "reflected"; the latter sense is supported by the
reflexive *sibi*. Nothing need actually be given back or handed over,

since it is through the amphitheater and its god that Rome reflects itself, achieves unity, and grasps itself as such, a point made by the following poem, as we shall see.[19]

Martial's first two poems are related chiastically: the first moves from all to one and the second from one to all. But in both cases the opposition between one and all is smudged, and the chiasmus contributes to this smudging. The third poem continues the process by moving from multiplicity to unity, and as it does so it erodes the distinction between foreign and Roman. At first, though, it seems to contradict the claim that Rome has been returned to itself:

> Quae tam seposita est, quae gens tam barbara, Caesar,
>   ex qua spectator non sit in urbe tua? (*Spec.* 3, 1–2)

> What people is so remote, so barbarous, Caesar, that it does
> not have a spectator in your city?

*Spec.* 3 will broaden the concept of Rome, both a city and the metropolis of an empire, and so it starts with the foreign visitors attracted to the spectacles. This time it is the word *spectator*, both "tourist" and "spectator," that is doing the work, for Rome is not merely one attraction among others to be gazed at, but the place whose main attraction is now the amphitheater to which people come from all over the world to be spectators.[20] The amphitheater is not merely a sight—one of the wonders of the world that a tourist might visit—but the site of spectatorship itself.

In the amphitheater, the spectator/tourists who have come from all over the world find themselves constituting a world that can be synoptically surveyed:[21]

> venit ab Orpheo cultor Rhodopeius Haemo,
>   venit et epoto Sarmata pastus equo,
> et qui prima bibit deprensi flumina Nili,
>   et quem supremae Tethyos unda ferit;
> festinavit Arabs, festinavere Sabaei,
>   et Cilices nimbis hic maduere suis.
> crinibus in nodum torti venere Sicambri,
>   atque aliter tortis crinibus Aethiopes.

vox diversa sonat populorum, tum tamen una est,
　　cum verus patriae diceris esse pater. (*Spec.* 3.3–12)

> The farmer of Rhodope has come from Orpheus's Haemus,
> and the Sarmatian fed on the blood of horses, and the one
> who drinks at the discovered source of the Nile, and he who
> is battered by the wave of farthest Tethys; the Arab has hur-
> ried here and so have the Sabaeans, and the Cilicians have
> been drenched by their own showers. The Sygambrians with
> their hair tied in a knot, and the Ethiopians with their hair
> twisted otherwise. The varied voice of the peoples sounds,
> which then is one, when you are hailed true father of the
> fatherland.

Martial's amphitheater is a miniature world, where races that are
widely separated can experience the unity that otherwise escapes
them, becoming one instead of many. Sygambrian and Ethiopian,
from the North (Germany) and South (Africa) respectively, are
juxtaposed, their contrasting hairstyles signifying the geographic
poles. In the amphitheater, the Egyptian who drinks the Nile
and the Briton from the farthest edge of the Ocean come under
the same awning as the Cilicians who are drenched in "their own
showers" (8). The "showers" are the saffron with which a generous
emperor sprinkled the audience, and the reference allows Martial
to allude to the arena's capacity for reconstructing various ecolo-
gies.[22] But if the Cilicians' saffron has found its way to the Roman
arena, it is most emphatically no longer "their own." The amphitheater returns to the Cilicians their own in the same sense that it
returned Rome to itself in the previous poem: not as possessors, but
as consumers of a spectacle in which everything, and everybody,
finds its proper place. One only has to compare the Elder Pliny's
description of imperial Italy to see the ideological implications of
Martial's spectacle:

> (terra) numine deum electa quae . . . sparsa congregaret imperia rit-
> usque molliret et tot populorum discordes ferasque linguas sermonis
> commercio contraheret ad colloquia et humanitatem homini daret,
> breviterque una cunctarum gentium ut toto orbe patria fieret.

> (a land) chosen by the gods to gather together the scattered realms
> and to soften their customs and unite the discordant and wild tongues
> of so many peoples into a common speech so they might understand
> each other, and to give civilization to mankind; in short, to be a single
> fatherland to all the races throughout the world. (*NH* 3.39)

The arena is not the most obvious example of Rome's softening of customs, but otherwise the picture fits, down to the play on words that has the Romans providing humanity access to its own nature. Pliny's *humanitatem homini daret* is a grander version of the Cilicians coming to Rome to be drenched by "their own" saffron. His unification of discordant tongues in a "common speech" has its equivalent in Martial's closing couplet, where the babel of foreign tongues dissolves into the single language of acclamation, the unified chants that were a feature of all kinds of public spectacles from the late Republic on.[23] Ring composition marks the conclusion of Martial's opening sequence as the amphitheater provides the universal language, just as it had at the end of the first poem, where fame need only speak of the amphitheater to speak of all wonders.[24]

After this preface, the description of the games themselves begins with *Spec.* 4 and 5, on the display of the *delatores*.[25] Titus, in a goodwill gesture, inflicted upon them the very exile that they brought upon others, and so deprived himself of the profit from confiscations: "You can chalk that up to the emperor's expenses" (*Spec.* 5.2). These exiled *delatores* continue the circulation between native and foreign begun in the previous poem, where foreigners became Romans in and through the amphitheater: the opposite is now the case. Furthermore, the exiled Romans, for whom the arena comes to represent the deserts and beaches (*arenae*) to which they will be relegated, are the inversion of the Cilicians whom the amphitheater drenches with the "showers" of their native land:

> Turba gravis paci placidaeque inimica quieti,
>     quae semper miseras sollicitabat opes,
> traducta est +getulis+ nec cepit harena nocentis:
>     et delator habet quod dabat exilium. (*Spec.* 4)

> The crowd, threatening to peace and enemy of tranquil sleep,
> which constantly harassed unfortunates for their wealth,
> was handed over to the [???] and the arena could not hold the
> guilty. The informer received the exile he imposed.

The amphitheater is the world, but the world rearranged, so that foreigners become Romans and Romans become foreigners. As Erik Gunderson puts it in a different connection, "The sand itself can be read as a symbolic space functioning to represent a select, idealized version of the empire to the audience. As far as geography was concerned, Rome was a small point at the center of a vast empire. This physical relationship was inverted, however, on the day of the shows: an orderly construct of Roman society ringed its own empire, contained, controlled and choreographed."[26] In *Spec.* 4, the peoples who have assembled from all over the empire to achieve unity out of the noisy diversity of their cultures (*vox diversa sonat*, 3.11) now expel those who had disturbed the peace into the arena, which represents the remote wastes of the empire. The amphitheater, then, is the place that stands for all others (*unum pro cunctis*); the place where spectators are given (back) what is their own (*reddita Roma sibi; nimbis . . . maduere suis*), and where malefactors receive what they gave (*habet quod dabat exilium*); it is a place that simulates a just (re)distribution. Being the place for all places, the amphitheater has no outside. As Debord says of the spectacle, it is "a specialized activity that speaks for all others." Martial's opening sequence realizes this capacity in epigrammatic form by playing with reversible conceits: outside becomes inside, and vice versa; one stands for all and all become one.

## SPECTACLE AND MYTH:
## PERPETUATING THE EPHEMERAL

The parading of *delatores* receives a second epigram (*Spec.* 5) in which Martial turns a clever compliment to the emperor, who has sacrificed the income derived from the victims of delation. But there is something familiar about the first line of this couplet:

> Exulat Ausonia profugus delator ab urbe:
> haec licet impensis principis adnumeres.

> The informer, a fugitive, is banished from the Ausonian city:
> you can chalk that up to the emperor's expenses.

Next to the epic *Ausonia*, *profugus* must conjure up the second line of the *Aeneid*, where its hero is described as *fato profugus*.[27] But isn't Aeneas, who *carried* his father to safety from captured Troy (*defero*, *OLD* 1), also the most famous *delator* in history?[28] As we shall see, it was not unusual for punishments and executions in the arena to be staged as mythological events, but in this case Martial has made his own, irreverent, connection between myth and spectacle. The informer figures as an anti-Aeneas, reversing the direction of the Trojan's exile and inverting his *pietas*. It is the emperor who shoulders the pious burden (*impensis*, 2). In the context of the opening of the new dynasty's most conspicuous monument, Martial's appropriation of the *Aeneid* for Titus's display of good government may have a polemical edge. These spectacles, emphasizing an overwhelming and all-inclusive presence, serve as a substitute for the historical depth to which the Julio-Claudians, with their illustrious mythical and divine ancestors (including Aeneas himself), could lay claim. In what follows I will be examining the status of these events as Martial celebrates them, and in particular their relation to the world of myth and legend.

We are able to identify the games that Martial celebrates as those given by Titus in 80 because of accounts in Suetonius (*Titus* 7ff) and Dio (66.25); but the difference between Martial's version and theirs is revealing. Martial gives us no statistics, no overview, and few grand events, but rather a selection of cameos, stressing the unusual, the irregular, and even the unscheduled occurrence.[29] Certainly he is showing off the abilities that this debut collection is recommending to potential patrons, including the ability to make an imperial compliment from the most unpromising material; in the process he cleverly remolds topoi of the Greek epigram of wonders to the Roman event that has made them real.[30] But Martial's focus on the particular also serves to make a case for the epigram as the form that is best suited to celebrate a new kind of event: the games are represented as a succession of epiphanies, in which the divinity of the emperor flashes up, often unexpectedly, in the sudden elations of the audience. In this respect, Martial's epigrams belong to the same world as Statius's *Silvae*, of which Carole Newlands has observed that "swift poems, supposedly dashed off in the heat of the moment, are part of a culture of wonder of an empire that tried to sustain the myth that any obstacles to its dominion could be swiftly and easily overcome."[31] The poet speaks as a member of the astonished audience, sometimes exclaiming on behalf of a "we," sometimes addressing the audience himself, and often turning to the emperor in an act of homage to the beneficent power that presides over this miraculous world.

Kathleen Coleman situates these poems in the context of pictorial representations of particular spectacles whose aim is to "perpetuate the ephemeral."[32] I want to take this paradoxical formulation seriously, and ask how Martial might go about perpetuating the ephemeral. A suggestive parallel from the visual arts of our own time is drawn by Jean-Marie Pailler (1990), who speaks of Martial's epigrams as snapshots (*instantanées*), a useful analogy if we reflect on the way that a snapshot conceives of the event it captures. By contrast with an oil painting, which transforms the ephemeral into the permanent, the snapshot finds an angle on the event—not the timeless truth, but an aspect of the event's spontaneity. The snapshot acknowledges that there are many possible ways of capturing the same event, and provides a fruitful analogy with Martial's epigrams to the extent that Martial sometimes commemorates a single event with more than one epigram. It is fitting, then, that this book of snapshots, which makes of a single event a series of discontinuous apparitions, should be bedeviled with problems of division. Different editions have different numbering, and just where to draw the line between one poem and the next is a problem that is sometimes destined to produce arbitrary answers. As Susan Sontag remarks in her book on photography, "In a world ruled by photographic images, all borders ("framing") seem arbitrary. Anything can be separated, can be made discontinuous, from anything else: all that is necessary is to frame the subject differently. . . . It is a view of the world which denies inter-connectedness and continuity, but which confers on each moment the character of a mystery."[33] Martial uses the discontinuity of the epigram form to exaggerate the instantaneous as a mode of the divine, but this exaltation is accompanied by a deflation that is also characteristically epigrammatic. Pailler's comparison of Martial's poem to snapshots is followed by two important points: "In this series of thoroughly specific visual snapshots of the world of the arena, the sacral reality of the scenes and objects represented is vindicated so emphatically, even at the expense of the myth that serves as their pretext, only because it exalts the memory of an ephemeral moment."[34] Martial exalts the memory of an ephemeral instant by recalling the exaltation of the ephemeral. He also plays off the reality of these ephemeral events against the status of the myths they so often recall.

Though he must have had ample opportunity to do so, Martial is not interested in celebrating technological miracles.[35] In Pailler's words, these poems express "the nostalgia for an illusion."[36] Martial's suppression of backstage mechanics, and his lack of interest in technological wonder, mean that it is hard to tell how much of a given show was scripted and how much happened spontaneously. When a pregnant sow is killed in a *venatio*, and gives birth to its brood as it expires, Martial has a field day, ringing the changes on the themes of life in death and of the doubleness of Diana, huntress and goddess of childbirth.[37] If the event was engineered, Martial has no interest in telling us so: his sequence of three poems on this event begins and ends with puns, double readings of the event that conjure up the effect of illusion. In the first of these puns a divine epiphany emerges out of an initially unobtrusive phrase, and in the other just the opposite occurs: an exclamation at the wonder of the event is deflated into banality. The sequence begins:

> Inter Caesareae discrimina saeva Dianae
> fixisset gravidam cum levis hasta suem,
> exiluit partus miserae de vulnere matris.
> o Lucina ferox, hoc peperisse fuit? (*Spec.* 14.1–4)

During the savage crises of Caesar's hunt, a light spear
pierced a pregnant sow. The offspring leapt from the womb
of its unfortunate mother. Fierce Lucina, was this, then,
childbirth?

The sequence opens with a periphrasis that serves, at first, simply
to locate the event in the "perils" (*discrimina*) of "the emperor's *venatio* (Diana)," but it mutates retrospectively into an expression of
the difference (*discrimina*) between the two Dianas at the end of
second poem:

experta est numen moriens utriusque Dianae,
   quaque soluta parens quaque perempta fera est. (*Spec.* 15.5–6)

Dying she experienced the godhead of both Dianas, who delivered her as mother and killed her as beast.

Diana is truly "Caesar's Diana" insofar as Martial's periphrasis for
the emperor's *venatio* comes to express the ambiguous nature of
Diana herself.

The poems in the sequence become progressively shorter, but in
the last line of the series it is the sheer fertility of the event that is
celebrated: *o quantum est subitis casibus ingenium* ("how much genius there is in sudden chances"), exclaims Martial.[38] *Casibus* is a
pun: as the sow fell (*cadente*, 16.4) she gave birth and her young ran
off. But *ingenium*, whose root is *gigno*, "bring to birth," is also a pun,
or rather two.[39] Furthermore, *subitis* (sudden) can be understood as
the past participle passive of *subeo*, "undergo." So we could read the
line "how much birthing there is when falls are undergone"—not so
much a reflection *on* the event as a reflection *of* it. The exclamation
simultaneously elevates and banalizes, enriches and impoverishes
the event, reflecting an elation as intense and as evanescent as a fire-
work. The moment of illusion, which flashes and is gone, is perpetu-
ated *as ephemeral* in the flickering of meaning, the optical illusion
that comes in and out of focus. This sequence of ever-shorter epigrams on the same event moves to an epigrammatic epiphany of the

arena's wonder at the same time as the arena provides the occasion for an epiphany of the epigrammatic form as simultaneously full and empty.

## SPECTACLE AND MYTH:
## THE DISSOLUTION OF AURA

Myth is omnipresent in Martial's *Liber de spectaculis*. While some of the poems celebrate mythical charades staged in the arena, others glorify the arena as the place where the divine emperor outdoes the marvels of a mythical time.[40] But it is not just that the arena outdoes the marvels of myth, for quite as frequently we are told that the spectacles confirm or realize a fabled story.[41] Emblematic of this is the emperor's resolution of the combat between the gladiators Priscus and Verus (*Spec.* 31) by bestowing victory on both: the ancient has been reconciled with the true! Where the arena is said to confirm the stories of old we can see that the second of Pailler's insights holds, and that the reality of the arena exists *at the expense* of the mythical world it purports to confirm. The arena, as Pailler elaborates, is the realization, outdoing, and replacement of myth: "replacement (*substitution*) to the extent that the myth, made visible and transcended by the representation in the arena, finds itself devalued, reduced to the status of *fama*, of the mere 'they say.'"[42] For instance, the dialectic between glorification and banalization that we found in the final couplet of the slain sow sequence recurs with respect to myth in the final couplet of the first poem in the sequence (*Spec.* 14):

> quis negat esse satum materno funere Bacchum?
> sic genitum numen credite: nata fera est. (7–8)

> Who denies that Bacchus was born at his mother's death?
> Believe that a god was born thus: a beast was.

We are asked to believe in the miraculous birth of Bacchus a fortiori: since a beast can do it, there is no reason why a god could not. But then what is special about a trick that, as we are all in a position to confirm, even an animal can perform? In becoming a credible event, the birth of Bacchus has been removed from the realm of belief altogether, and so deprived of its aura. What happens in the arena, far from acquiring status by association with divine myth, dissolves the special status of that myth. Martial is more direct about the effect of credibility on belief when he celebrates a *venatio* featuring women hunters (*Spec.* 8); this prompts a reference to Hercules' slaughter of the Nemean lion, a feat that has now been duplicated for the arena's audience, and duplicated "by female hands" (*haec iam feminea vidimus acta manu*, 4). *Prisca fides taceat* (4), he exclaims: "Let ancient testimony [or the belief accorded to what is ancient] be silent."[43] There is no need to believe, since we've seen. Here again, it is not so much that the wondrous events of myth have been outdone as that the *venatio* witnessed by the audience dissolves the aura of *fides* radiated by the ancient.[44]

When "Pasiphae" mates with the bull in the arena, we are told to believe the ancient story, which has now been confirmed. But there is more:

> Iunctam Pasiphaen Dictaeo credite tauro:
> vidimus, accepit fabula prisca fidem.
> nec se miretur, Caesar, longaeva vetustas:
> quidquid fama canit, praestat harena tibi. (*Spec.* 6)

> Believe that Pasiphae coupled with the Dictaean bull! We've seen it, the ancient myth has been confirmed. Hoary antiquity, Caesar, should not marvel at itself: whatever Fame sings of, the arena presents to you.

The weighty authority of the word *prisca* (2) is drained in the second couplet to produce *vetustas*, which has some of the same connotations, but might also imply decay, a possibility reinforced by *longaeva*. Antiquity becomes a superannuated Narcissus, still laboring under the delusion that it is worthy of its own admiration, until Caesar, firmly wedged in the middle of the line (3), breaks in. Since Caesar allows us to *see* what Fame has *sung,* antiquity changes its mode of being: no longer veiled in the aura of distance, or installed as the object of *fides*, it is like an ancient building that has survived, shabby with old age, to compare unfavorably with the spectacle in its shiny new arena. As with the end of *Spec.* 14 (*sic genitum numen credite: nata fera est*), the apparent confirmation of myth has become its dethronement.[45] The arena indeed "makes good on" (*praestat*) the wonders recounted by poetry, just as it gives credence to the story of Bacchus's birth, but it does so by "serving them up" to the emperor (*praestat tibi*); the last word, *tibi*, effects a subtle shift in the meaning of *praestare* and a decisive shift in the relation between *fama* and arena. No more does the arena confirm the truth of what *fama* has sung as having happened long ago, in some other world; rather the arena supplies to the gaze of emperor and people what *fama* merely sings. So the arena refers to the world of myth neither to confirm nor to outdo it, but to replace it: as copy becomes original, *fama* is reduced to a promissory note on which the arena now delivers.

A similar relation between the past and its replica has been observed in connection with epic movies that recreate in their pristine novelty a historical world surviving otherwise only in crumbling monuments or yellowing photographs and engravings. Maria Wyke cites a *Bioscope* review of Enrico Guazzoni's 1913 film of *Quo Vadis?*: "It is a spectacle far surpassing that which any modern tourist may see on an actual visit to the city and it realizes the past for us as it has never been realized before. If the cinematograph had been invented a thousand years ago [presumably the author means two thousand years ago], and the film taken then had been preserved, we should have no more fascinating and invaluable possession than this picture."[46] Not only does the cinema's recreation outdo *vetustas*, but it renders the past itself otiose, for even if we could have filmed the past, that film would be no more valuable than this one. Vivian Sobchak makes a similar point about the press material that accompanied the release of the 1962 Cinerama epic *How the West Was Won*. In the press booklet, engravings from the Bettmann Archives were juxtaposed to color stills from the movie not only as authenticating documents but also as pale models of the movie itself.[47]

It is hard here not to think of the line of theory about the modern spectacle that concerns the relation of the copy to the original, a line stretching from Benjamin's famous essay, hailing mechanical reproduction as a technique that would destroy the aura of the original work of art, to the gloomier prognostications of Baudrillard, who, with a mixture of awe and disgust, celebrates the spectacle's precession of simulacra, copies without (and before) originals.[48] Benjamin, whose "Work of Art in the Age of Mechanical Reproduction" is one of the founding texts of the theory of the spectacle, welcomed the loss of the original's aura in the availability and dissemination of cheap copies. As he saw it, the physical uniqueness, distanced presence, and limited accessibility of the original work of art gave it a mystical authority that was destroyed by handy availability. Strictly speaking, there is no original of which Martial's mythical charades are copies, not, at any rate in the sense that there is an original painting the aura of whose physical uniqueness and presence is destroyed by its mechanical reproduction. But one aspect of Benjamin's "aura" is "the unique phenomenon of distance, however close it may be." He continues: "If, while resting on a Summer afternoon, you follow with your eyes a mountain range on the horizon or a branch which casts its shadow over you, you experience the aura of those mountains, of that branch."[49] In the Roman context, we might cite the beginning of Catullus's *Peleus and Thetis* (c. 64), where the distant age of heroes (*optato saeclorum tempore*, 22) that the poet conjures up (*compellabo*, 24) with his song, and gazes at, is richly endowed with aura.[50] By contrast, in Martial the amphitheater's copy dispels the aura of *fabula prisca*, an aura which stems from the fact that it demands belief. No longer. It is the visible here and now of the imperial arena in which wonder resides.

If I were to speculate on the political context of this strategy, I would point to the word *Caesar* that sits in the middle of the line about antiquity's self-admiration (*nec se miretur, Caesar, longaeva vetustas, Spec.* 6.3), a word that marks both continuity and discontinuity between the first and the second dynasties of Rome. Martial cunningly places it not only in the middle of the line, but immediately after the caesura, so that the intervention of Caesar into the self-admiration of antiquity reminds us of the historical break that has changed the meaning of the word. Ovid made this same play on words in his exile poetry with lines like *bellaque pro magno Caesare Caesar obit* (and Caesar undertakes wars for great Caesar, *Tristia* 2.230), where the two Caesars are Augustus and Tiberius respectively.[51] But with Martial the wordplay has new implications. The relation of the Flavians to the Julio-Claudians was more than that of successor to predecessor. This was the first change of dynasties in the history of the Principate, and as such it effected a decisive change in the *notion* of the Principate. True, it had taken another civil war to bring the Flavians to power, but the issue of that war was not whether Rome would continue to be a Republic. This was a repetition without the angst and trauma of the original break, for the Principate was by now an established institution. When Vespasian was hailed as "Caesar," a family name became a title, whose bearer need have no connection to the original Julius Caesar.[52] Augustus made much of the legendary characters and divinities from whom his family claimed descent; his successors of the Julio-Claudian dynasty had been able to claim their own participation in the carefully constructed myth of Augustus. Nero had identified himself with various mythical characters on the stage.[53] But for the Flavians, members of a new aristocracy which could not plausibly claim descent from Venus, a different approach was required.[54] Martial's flattening of the historical dimension, his substitution of the copy for the original, would not have been inappropriate to the ideological needs of his Flavian patrons, the new Caesars; however much they alluded to Augustus as their model, they could only draw attention to the fact that they were different.[55] That Martial had dynasties on his mind in this book is confirmed by the poem which probably closed the original collection (*Spec.* 34); it begins with Augustus and ends with Nero, the first and last emperors of the Julio-Claudian dynasty, both of whom have been outdone by Titus's *naumachia* (*Augusti labor . . . Caesaris nostri . . . pars est quota?* 1–3; *taceantur stagna Neronis*, 11).

## SPECTACLE AND MYTH: EXECUTING THE PAST

The Pasiphae poem may refer to what Coleman has dubbed a "fatal charade," a punishment or execution staged as a mythical event.[56] As Coleman argues, it is certainly part of the purpose of these charades to humiliate and mock the criminal by having him or her incarnate some revered or heroic figure. The decking out and mocking of Jesus as "king of the Jews" is a familiar example of this,[57] and Martial's couplet on the "Daedalus" charade (*Spec.* 10) amounts to a sadistic laugh: "Daedalus, now that the Lucanian bear has got his teeth into you / how you wish you had your feathers." But this is not the usual focus of Martial's poems on punitive charades, nor do these poems offer much encouragement to the Foucauldian model which would see in the "spectacle of the scaffold" the sovereign's reply to the challenge flung at him by the crime.[58] In fact, Martial makes very little reference to the crimes of the condemned, but instead emphasizes that the emperor confirms the myth, makes real what was fable, makes present what was rumored, or turns ancient glory into present play. It would not be inappropriate to paraphrase Foucault and say that Martial represents these spectacles as the reply of the sovereign to the challenge represented by *fabula* or myth, and that this is the object of the violence that displays the emperor's power.[59] The real target of these acts of violence, as Martial represents them, is not the criminal but the past itself, whether historical, mythical, or legendary—the past as something that is done, unchangeable and unsurpassable, repository of authority and exemplarity and object of awe.

In another "fatal charade" (*Spec.* 24) the condemned man was cast as Orpheus. The arena displayed for the emperor "whatever Mt. Rhodope is reputed to have watched in the Orphean theater" (*Quidquid in Orpheo Rhodope spectasse theatro . . . dicitur*, 24.1): rocks slithered, trees scampered, and all manner of animal surrounded the musician, while above his head "hung a lot of birds" (*multa pependit avis*, 6). But Orpheus himself lay savaged by an ungrateful bear. "This was the only inaccuracy" (*haec tantum res est facta par'historian*, 8), Martial comments. But the phrase *par'historian*, recovered by A. E. Housman's brilliant emendation of the nonsensical *ita pictoria*, is Greek, and it intrudes into the Latin poem rather as the Roman execution intrudes on the Greek myth.[60] *Par'historian* is a phrase found in ancient commentaries when a scholiast points out that the author has deviated from the standard version.[61] Martial slyly adopts the tone of a finger-wagging pedant reminding us that the Philistine Romans have got it wrong again. But who's going to complain, knowing what happened to "Orpheus"?

A subtler violence is done to the myth of Orpheus by the first line of Martial's poem, which pictures the original event in terms of its own duplication in the arena. Mt. Rhodope, identified as a spectator in the Orphean theater, represents the emperor sitting in the imperial box at the amphitheater.[62] Furthermore, the distinction between mythical event and reenactment is flattened out to the distinction between theater and arena, drama and charade.[63] The inspiration for Martial's *Orpheo . . . theatro* was surely the Orpheus episode in Ovid's *Metamorphoses* (11.20–28), in which Orpheus's death is compared to an event in the arena:

> ac primum attonitas etiamnum voce canentis
> innumeras volucres anguesque agmenque ferarum
> Maenades Orphei titulum rapuere theatri.
> inde cruentatis vertuntur in Orphea dextris
> et coeunt, ut aves si quando luce vagantem
> noctis avem cernunt structoque utrimque theatro
> cum matutina cervus periturus harena
> praeda canum est; vatemque petunt et fronde virentes
> coniciunt thyrsos non haec in munera factos.

> First the Maenads attacked the swarms of birds, the snakes,
> and the throng of beasts, depriving Orpheus of his theater's
> pride. Then they turned on Orpheus with their bloody hands,
> converging as birds when they see an owl abroad by day, or
> when in the amphitheater the doomed stag in the morning
> show falls prey to the dogs; they go for the bard and cast their
> leafy thyrsi that were not made for these tasks [shows].

The Maenads perversely transform the spectacle of Orpheus's enchantment of the beasts into a *venatio* and so rob his theater of its *titulum*, the animals that are its "claim to fame," as the usual interpretation of *titulum* goes. But *titulum* could also be a placard that announces what is currently playing—the Maenads have broken in on the scene and given it a different "title."[64] Not only that, but they themselves have strayed from a different scene, with *thyrsi* that "were not made for these displays (*munera*)."

In the context of the arena, it is the emperor who is the true Orpheus. For Ovid to cast the shadow of the amphitheater and its *venatio* over the story of Orpheus is not inappropriate in view of the long tradition associating the divinity of the monarch with power over animals, and it is in precisely such terms that Martial celebrates the emperor in many of his poems.[65] As the only natural object that is not moved by Orpheus's performance, Martial's Mt. Rhodope points to the emperor ensconced in his box as the true Orpheus, and his power over animals is in this case manifested by the executors of his punishment. It is interesting that Martial does not choose to cast the *sparagmos* of his "Orpheus" in terms of the well-known end of the original, though the manner of the unfortunate criminal's death would remind some of the tragic end of Orpheus himself.[66] To call it *par' historian* is to deny the parallel to Orpheus's *sparagmos* by the maddened Bacchants, a parallel that would have less than flattering implications for the emperor.

In other poems on mythological charades Martial does not, or cannot, shy away from identifying the criminal with heroic victims. The criminal, mocked by the insertion of his ignominious execution into the heroic world, threatens to come into his fifteen minutes of fame as a real hero.[67] Does Martial contribute to this subversive possibility? Frederick Ahl has argued that this is the case with Martial's poem on the criminal crucified as the robber Laureolus (*Spec.* 9).[68] Laureolus had been the subject of a mime, notable for its gory special effects, in the time of Caligula (Suetonius, *Caligula* 57.4), so the punitive charade in the amphitheater was the enactment of a dramatization of a historical execution, bringing the wheel full circle.[69] Martial ends with a characteristic celebration of the arena's transcendence of the past: the criminal outdid the crimes of ancient fame (though the precise nature of his transgression is unclear), and in his case what had been a play became a punishment (*in quo quae fuerat fabula poena fuit*, 12). Since crucifixion was a lengthy business, a bear had been sent in to speed the execution. The pseudo-Laureolus attacked by a bear suggests to Martial the figure of Prometheus, chained to the rock and exposed to the eagle's beak:

> Qualiter in Scythica religatus rupe Prometheus
> adsiduam nimio pectore pavit avem,
> nuda Caledonio sic viscera praebuit urso
> non falsa pendens in cruce Laureolus.

> Just as Prometheus, shackled to the Scythian rock, fed the
> persistent bird on his all too great heart, so Laureolus offered
> his entrails to the Scottish bear, hanging on a real cross this
> time.

There is an interesting chiasmus here, for as the Laureolus mime
becomes reality, the criminal who realizes it is removed from reality into the world of heroic myth, and more specifically the myth of
the great benefactor of humanity who defied the supreme authority.
Obviously Martial's comparison of the criminal to Prometheus has
inconvenient implications if we think of the execution in Foucauldian terms: the emperor's answer to the challenge flung at him by
the criminal has cast that criminal as the archetypal heroic rebel
against an oppressive power. The example of Pompey's elephants reminds us that the audience's sympathy could go in the wrong direction; Cicero (*ad Fam.* 7.1.3) tells us that as the crowd watched them
die in the arena it was moved to pity; feeling arose that there was
something human about these magnificent beasts.[70] Martial's poem
is not a record of the audience's reaction, of course, but the volatility
of the Promethean comparison may reflect an element of unpredict-
ability or ambiguity in that reaction.

To compare the criminal to Prometheus is both inappropriate
and appropriate. Inappropriate because the bear that finishes off
"Laureolus" is actually sent in to speed up his death, not to expose
him to the prolonged agonies of Prometheus. Where Prometheus
had too much *pectus*—"breast," but also "spirit" (cf. Horace *Ep.*
1.4.6)—the mangled Laureolus has "no body in all his body," (*inque*
*omni nusquam corpore corpus erat*, 6), a horrific distinction between the vision of heroic suffering conjured up by the myth and
the gory mess of the execution. In fact, Martial's paradox reminds
us that the criminal being executed is all (and only) body. But, if
we take seriously the fact that Martial calls the victim of this fatal charade Laureolus, and bear in mind that the Romans did not

use inverted commas, then there is a rationale for the comparison between the prolonged sufferings of Prometheus and the execution of Laureolus. Laureolus, the executed criminal, is brought back to life, yet again, like Prometheus's reconstituted liver, to suffer again. We are reminded of one of his earlier incarnations, in the mime, by the words *non falsa pendens in cruce Laureolus* (4)—it's the same Laureolus, but this time (like the first time) on a real cross. And this needn't be his last appearance. The bear may be shortening the torment of this particular "Laureolus," but its attack is only one episode in the constantly renewed suffering of Laureolus the role.[71]

On one level, then, the comparison is wrong and on another it is apt, depending on whether Laureolus is taken to be the criminal impersonating the figure of the bandit or the self-renewing figure itself. A new kind of Prometheus is being created by the theatrical medium, with its potential for endlessly reanimating its roles, and this new Prometheus empties out the exemplary content of the mythical figure. Martial's comparison is potentially subversive, and perhaps deliberately so, since the specter of heroic defiance is conjured up only to be exorcised as the defiant hero becomes merely entertaining. I would suggest that what is happening here is the familiar spectacular process by which the potentially subversive is turned into an object of consumption, and so defused, a process to which Jonathan Crary alludes when he speaks of "the spectacle as a new kind of power of recuperation and absorption, a capacity to neutralize and assimilate acts of resistance by converting them into objects or images of consumption."[72]

## WATCHING MUCIUS SCAEVOLA

Martial continued to celebrate events in the arena throughout his oeuvre. There is a notable cycle of epigrams on the spectacle of the hare and the lions in Book 1, which will concern us in the next chapter. The three poems with which I will end all describe a single event, but they are spread across different books. Nevertheless, I hope to show that they are related in significant ways and, when considered as a cycle, provide an interesting study of Martial's perspective on the spectacles.[73]

In the case of the Laureolus charade it is the poet who makes the potentially subversive comparison of the criminal's sufferings to those of Prometheus. The poems which I will consider now concern a punitive charade that itself cast the criminal in the role of one of the great exemplary heroes of the early Republic. Just how advisable was it for an emperor to have a criminal replicate the heroic display of Mucius Scaevola, given that Mucius's heroism was exercised in defence of the newly Republican Rome against Porsena's attempt to foist an Etruscan monarchy upon it again? How is the contemporary Roman viewer to consume this icon of Republican virtue without making awkward connections to the present moment of history?[74]

One possibility would be to contrast oneself with Porsena, who was unable to bear the sight of Mucius's self-mutilation. Part of the Roman military virtue of which Scaevola was such a conspicuous example was the ability to endure the sight of other people's wounds, and in this connection the arena had an educative role to play.[75] Livy's account of King Antiochus's introduction of games in the Roman style provides an interesting parallel to the story of Mucius Scaevola:

> Gladiatorum munus, Romae consuetudinis, primo maiore cum terrore hominum, insuetorum ad tale spectaculum, quam voluptate dedit; deinde saepius dando et modo volneribus tenus, modo sine missione, etiam familiare oculis gratumque id spectaculum fecit, et armorum studium plerisque iuvenum accendit. (Livy 41.20.11–13)[76]

> (King Antiochus) gave a gladiatorial show, of the Roman kind; at first it was received by the spectators with more terror than pleasure, since they were unused to this kind of spectacle. But then, by staging the shows more frequently, and at first only to first blood, then without quarter, he succeeded in making the sight familiar to the eyes and pleasing, and he encouraged the love of arms among many of the young men.

On the one hand, the Roman public congratulates itself on being able to watch the spectacle that Porsena couldn't endure, and celebrates its descent from the virtuous Mucius who provided it; but on the other hand, since it is a criminal who impersonates the would-be assassin Mucius before emperor and people, the audience is put in the position of the Etruscan enemy rather than of Mucius's compatriots. A further complication ensues from the political context of this glorious deed. How can the spectator, subject of an emperor, claim descent from this attempted regicide? Is this spectacle a representation of ancestral virtue to be claimed proudly by the Roman spectator, or is it a repetition of the same drama, with the spectator once again shamed by the criminal he had sought to humiliate? The charade raises the question of how it is to be consumed, and it is this problem that lies behind Martial's three poems, published over a broad swathe of his career.[77]

The full story of Mucius Scaevola, as Livy recounts it (2.12–13.5), makes for particularly interesting connections with the reproduction. Andrew Feldherr has argued that Livy uses internal spectators within his narrative to provide a model for his readers as they contemplate the spectacle of Roman history and take up their own position within it.[78] In this case, however, the internal spectator is an enemy. Porsena is in the position of the Greek subjects of Antiochus who at first could not bear the sight of gladiatorial combat, and the Roman spectator here differentiates himself from the internal spectator, who, as we shall see, ends up by wishing that Mucius were one of his own. But let us examine Livy's narrative from the beginning.

Livy tells us that the young noble C. Mucius considered it disgraceful that the Roman people, never besieged while "enslaved" under the kings, now found itself besieged by the Etruscans, whose armies it had often defeated. He intends to redeem the disgrace with some great *facinus* ("deed," but also "crime"). But Mucius fears that his plan to penetrate the enemy's camp might be misinterpreted: "There was a risk, if he attempted this without anybody's knowledge and without the authorization of the consuls, of being arrested by the guards as a deserter—a charge only too plausible, conditions in Rome being what they were" (2.12.4). He explains to the senate that he is planning to enter the enemy camp, but not as a brigand (*praedo*, 2.12.5), for he has a greater *facinus* in mind. It will be quite appropriate, then, that Titus's charade will cast a criminal as the

Mucius who insists he is no brigand and fears he might be taken for a deserter.[79] The theme of mistaken identity in Livy's narrative persists when Mucius mistakes an official (*scriba*) for the king. Mucius comes upon the royal entourage when the troops are being paid, and the official, dressed in much the same way as the king, is the center of the action. Failing to distinguish underling from master, Mucius kills the wrong man and is apprehended and brought before the throne of the king. But "more to be feared than fearing" (*metuendus magis quam metuens*, 2.12.8) he boasts that he is a Roman citizen ("*Romanus sum" inquit "civis*," 2.12.9) and no less ready to die than to kill.[80] Let the king beware, for there is a long line of Romans waiting for the same honor. This indifferentiation, in which Mucius displays a virtue of which there are innumerable other exemplars, equally threatening to the king, is Mucius's way of appropriating the confusion that led to his killing the wrong person: now it is Porsena who does not know whom to kill. He threatens to burn Mucius alive unless he reveals the secret of the conspiracy. But Mucius turns the tables on his captor by making the fire with which the king threatens him serve as a prop in his own demonstration. Thrusting his right hand into the fire prepared for a sacrifice he says, "Look . . . and know how cheap the body is to those who set their sights on great glory" (*En tibi . . . ut sentias quam vile corpus sit iis qui magnam gloriam vident*, 2.12.13). This is too much for the astounded Porsena (*prope attonitus miraculo*, 2.12.13), who orders Mucius removed from the fire, and addresses the Roman hero with the words "Go free, now, for you have dared to make war on yourself more than on me. I would bless you, if that courage of yours were at the disposal of my country."[81] By making war on himself, and so causing the king to wish Mucius were one of his own, Mucius becomes the deserter he feared he might have appeared, but in a very different sense.

Martial's first poem on the charade (1.21) focuses on the notion of *felix culpa* that permeates Livy's narrative.

> Cum peteret regem, decepta satellite dextra
> ingessit sacris se peritura focis.

> sed tam saeva pius miracula non tulit hostis
> et raptum flammis iussit abire virum:
> urere quam potuit contempto Mucius igne,
> hanc spectare manum Porsena non potuit.
> maior deceptae fama est et gloria dextrae:
> si non errasset, fecerat illa minus.

Aimed at the king, but deceived by an attendant, that right hand laid itself, doomed to perish, upon the sacred hearth. But the kindly foe could not endure a prodigy so cruel and ordered the warrior to go free, rescued from the flame. The hand which, scorning the fire, Mucius endured to burn, Porsena could not endure to behold. The fame and glory of that right hand is greater because it was deceived; had it not erred, it would have achieved less.

There is no explicit mention of the punitive charade in this poem, nor of the fact that it is a criminal who is impersonating the great representative of Republican virtue, but Martial draws out the spectacular implications of Livy's account: Porsena cannot bear to look at (*spectare*, 6) the hand that Mucius could bring himself to burn. Enemy and Roman exchange identities, the latter displaying the savagery of the barbarian (*saeva miracula*, 3; cf. Livy's *prope attonitus miraculo*) and the former the *pietas* that the descendants of Aeneas claimed for their own (*pius . . . hostis*). Paradoxically, the failure of Mucius's mission made possible his triumphant demonstration of *virtus*, and the name Scaevola not only alludes to the fact that he was gloriously left-handed but also reminds us that he had a tendency to make the wrong choice (*scaevus*, "instinctively choosing what is wrong, perverse, contrary, misguided," *OLD* 3). The error of Mucius (*errasset*, 8) fuses with the transgression that brought "Mucius" to impersonate Rome's great hero, so that the same paradox covers the action of both hero and criminal. This punning relation between original and replica serves to dissipate the "aura" of the original.

But there is a further level of relevance to Martial's final epigrammatic point. The emphasis on deception, on getting the wrong man, could be referred to by the illusion of the punitive spectacle itself, which is so complete that this poem makes no mention of it, except to cast the original event in terms that rhyme with that illusion. The spectator echoes parodically the glorious mistake of Mucius when he is deceived (or deceives himself) into feeling that he is witnessing the heroism of Mucius, taking a criminal for a hero, just as Mucius took the scribe for a king; this analogy is supported by Martial's choice of the word *satelles*, which has overtones of criminality ("henchman," also "accomplice"). Of the credulous spectator it could indeed be said that if he had not made the mistake (entered the illusion), he would have done less. While the historical content of the charade threatens to assault the spectator with a shaming image of defiance against a king, Martial's first poem allows the spectator as consumer to identify himself with Mucius by virtue of a pun.

In the next poem (8.30), the quasi-Mucian virtue of the spectator who enters the illusion is made more explicit, but it is connected with a revealing analogy between the Roman past and the criminal past of "Mucius."

> Qui nunc Caesareae lusus spectatur harenae,
>     temporibus Bruti gloria summa fuit.
> aspicis ut teneat flammas poenaque fruatur
>     fortis et attonito regnet in igne manus!
> ipse sui spectator adest et nobile dextrae
>     funus amat: totis pascitur illa sacris;
> quod nisi rapta foret nolenti poena, parabat
>     saevior in lassos ire sinistra focos.
> scire piget post tale decus quid fecerit ante:
>     quam vidi satis hanc est mihi nosse manum.

What now is watched as entertainment in Caesar's arena was in Brutus's days their chiefest glory. You see how the hand grasps the flame and relishes its punishment, and bravely reigns amid the astonished fire! He is his own spectator and admires his right hand's noble death; his hand feeds on the whole sacrifice. Had not that penalty been denied, against his will, his left hand, fiercer still, was ready to approach the sated hearth. I care not, after such a feat, to know what it had done before; enough for me to have known the hand I saw.

The first couplet contrasts now and then on the historical plane, and the last projects the same contrast onto the story of the criminal. Could it be that Martial needs to block out knowledge of the historical past quite as much as he needs to ignore what the criminal may have done before enacting this glorious scene? In order to enjoy this spectacle of courage as cultural icon, rather than awkward *exemplum*, Martial the imperial panegyrist must forget, or screen out, not only what the criminal "Mucius" (ingloriously) did to deserve this punishment but also what the legendary Mucius was (gloriously) attempting to do before he was apprehended, namely to kill an enemy king and redeem Rome from a shame it had not suffered even when "enslaved" under the kings itself. The ambiguity of the opening couplet makes it a moot point whether the emperor's arena has outdone the times of Brutus or merely degraded *gloria* into *lusus*. Is it Martial himself who is playing with fire? In fact, Martial has superimposed one contrast between *gloria* and *lusus* on top of another: the glory achieved by Mucius as he lay his hand on the fire has become the mockery (*lusus*) inflicted on the unfortunate criminal forced to play Mucius; at the same time, the glorious ornament of Republican virtue (*gloria*, OLD 3b) has become an entertainment (*lusus*) to be watched in the arena. What is it that is being degraded by this charade: "Mucius" the criminal or "the times of Brutus"?

Martial's juxtaposition of the names Caesar and Brutus traces a potentially ominous line from the early to the late Republic and on to the present moment. But for Rome's second imperial dynasty the name *Caesar* was symbolic rather than familial, *lusus* rather than *gloria*, so to speak.[82] This shift in the significance of a glorious name is symmetrical with the reduction of Mucius to his logo: "It is enough for me to have known the *hand* I saw" (10). So perhaps Martial risks the dangerous associations of Brutus's name only to render them impotent.[83]

The poem's description of the charade prepares us for this exclusive focus on the hand which it is enough for Martial to have known. Livy's scene is sucked into a tight close-up that suspends the drama on a moment of attention and reshuffles the roles: his "thunderstruck" (*attonitus*) king becomes the astonished fire (*attonito igne*, 4), but it is Mucius's hand that "rules" in (*regnet*, 4) and feeds on the fire, a fire that now represents the flickering continuity of the surrounding audience's attention. "Mucius" himself stands outside the close-up, which represents in miniature the exchange between himself and the *cavea*; he has become a superspectator. In the arena, then, hand, fire, and criminal all become forms of the spectator, as well as objects of fascination in themselves. If Laureolus-as-Prometheus became a figure for the theatrical, here the scene of Mucius thrusting his hand into the fire generates figures of spectatorship. In Martial's poem, protagonist and spectator merge to consume what is now purely spectacle, not an event in history or a ritual, but a *scene*, abstracted from its context and representing its own fascination. The detachment of Livy's Mucius from his own sensations (*velut alienato ab sensu . . . animo*, 2.12.13) as he provides an example of Roman endurance finds a debased echo in Martial's refusal to know what the criminal has done; such is the "sacrifice" he makes in order to maintain an exclusive focus on this icon of Roman virtue, the hand burning in the fire.

In Martial's diminution of this glorious scene from exemplary drama to fascinating spectacle (and spectacle of fascination) we can see a foreshadowing of an aspect of our own cinematic culture, with its tendency to reduce history to a period "look," as Fredric Jameson has observed.[84] In the genre of the period film, history is reduced to a collection of objects and costumes together with a cinematographic style that not only ignores, but actually screens out, the human and historical context of these surroundings. Further, in the case of the nostalgia movie, the historical referent is frequently not so much the period in which the movie is set as the style of entertainment—television, movies, or radio—that is associated with that period.

To move from descendant to precedent, we find that Lucan too links Mucius's detachment from his own pain to the detachment of the spectator. In the ninth book of *Bellum Civile*, the remnants of the defeated Republican army in Africa are having a hard time with snakes, of which one of the nastiest is the basilisk:

> quid prodest miseri basiliscus cuspide Murri
> transactus? velox currit per tela venenum

invaditque manum; quam protinus ille retecto
ense ferit totoque semel demittit ab armo,
exemplarque sui spectans miserabile leti
stat tutus pereunte manu. (9.828–833)

What good is it that the basilisk has been skewered on
wretched Murrus's spear? The swift poison courses along
the weapon to attack his hand, which he strikes with drawn
sword and severs in one stroke, arm and all; and watching
the pathetic model of his own death he stands in safety while
his hand shrivels.

Murrus is, quite literally, detached from the suffering of his hand,
which he contemplates from a pleasing security, more Epicurean
than Stoic. Matthew Leigh, who reads Lucan's epic as a sustained
reflection on the ethical consequences of spectatorship, argues convincingly that in this passage the exemplary courage of Mucius has
been crossed with the spectator's comfortable enjoyment of the peril
and death *of others* in the arena.[85] For Martial to *become* Scaevola
he need only exercise the virtue of spectatorship, which can now be
detached from the unpleasant prerequisites of the original's own
unshaken gaze. Martial too, like Livy's Mucius, can say *En tibi, ut
sentias quam vile corpus sit iis qui magnam gloriam vident*, only
he means something different: "What a cheap body it is [viz. the
criminal's] to those who watch great glory." Whereas Mucius holds
his body cheap and so proves that he has glory in his sights, Martial
is able to see great glory even in a mean body, and so proves that
he has an *eye* for virtue. For Mucius, to be a Roman was to offer a
display that other citizens might duplicate; for Martial, it is to recognize, and be moved by virtue's logo, wherever it might appear.

Martial's third epigram on this charade (10.25) is quite different
in tone, and introduces into the scene that has been examined in
such minute close-up some of the context that had been excluded—
not the wrongdoings of the criminal, but rather the backstage ma-
chinery of the spectacle:

In matutina nuper spectatus harena
Mucius, inposuit qui sua membra focis,

> si patiens durusque tibi fortisque videtur,
>     Abderitanae pectora plebis habes.
> nam cum dicatur tunica praesente molesta
>     "ure manum," plus est dicere "non facio."

> If Mucius, whom recently in the morning show you saw lay
> his hand on the fire, seems enduring to you, unflinching and
> strong, you have all the brains of Abdera's rabble. For, when,
> with the flaming tunic in the wings, you're told "Burn your
> hand" it's braver to say "I will not."

To be a Roman spectator is now neither to prove oneself able to endure the sight that Porsena could not, nor to focus on the *decus* of this hand to the exclusion of all else, but rather to be sophisticated enough not to behave like a gullible rube from Thrace (Abdera was proverbial for the stupidity of its natives).[86] This "Mucius" was merely saving his skin, as Livy's Mucius feared that the uninitiated might think *he* was doing. To be in the know, like the senate to which Livy's Mucius entrusted his plans, is in this case to recognize the charade of virtue. If the first of Martial's poems cast the legendary event in terms that assimilated it, via a pun, to the charade itself, the third suggests the conditions under which the charade might actually revive the legendary event: the criminal could become Mucius by refusing to play Mucius. But he doesn't, and once again the exemplarity of this hero is held at bay.

In its wording, the end of the third poem reverses the end of the first: "It is more to say 'I won't do it'" recalls "if he had not erred, he would have done less." "He could have done *more*," "he would have done *less*" and, in the middle poem, "it is *enough* for me to know the hand I saw." "Less," "more," "enough"—Martial is, so to speak, adjusting his set. All three of these words imply difference, and yet they allow Martial to reconstitute, through that difference, a simulation of the Roman virtue of Mucius. Martial experiments with different ways of tuning in to this scene, of exercising a virtue *of spectatorship* by entering into the illusion. Or not entering, for in the final poem, he vindicates his Romanness by proving that he's no dupe, and with the closing words, *non facio*, he assimilates his own refusal to be fooled to the virtue that this "Mucius" might have exercised (but didn't). With this assimilation, he replays the end of the first poem (*fecerat illa minus*), where to make an error of identification turns out to be a *felix culpa* for the spectator, as well as for Mucius. Livy's Mucius had declared *Romanus sum civis* as he defied a king in the glorious days of Brutus. Martial, who comes not to bury a Caesar but to praise one, must find other ways to be a Roman citizen. Here we can return to Crary's description of the spectacle as "a new kind of power of recuperation and absorption, a capacity to neutralize and assimilate acts of resistance by converting them into objects or images of consumption." Is this not what Martial has done to the *exemplum* of Mucius?

In the next chapter, which deals with the first of Martial's numbered, and miscellaneous, books, we will be following up his equivocal celebration of earlier *exempla virtutis*. As in these poems on punitive charades, Book 1's epigrammatic celebration of Republican and early Imperial icons will resituate them in a contemporary context. But our attention now shifts from the simulated world of the emperor's all-encompassing arena to the urban world of the first of Martial's numbered books of miscellaneous epigrams.

# CHAPTER THREE

# WHAT·IS·A·BOOK·OF·EPIGRAMS?
# (MARTIAL'S·BOOK·1)

What is it to interpret a book of miscellaneous epigrams? I am choosing Book 1 as my laboratory not only because it is Martial's masterpiece but also because it questions the status of the book of epigrams both explicitly and implicitly. The book of epigrams is a problematic notion in itself, as we have seen in chapter 1, but in the particular case of Martial's epigram books it is not only the status of the book as a unit that is in question but also the relation between the book and the world in which it circulates. At one point or another Martial will stress the permeability of the book to its surrounding world or affirm the boundaries that mark it off from that world. As a literary artifact, the book is the abstract entity that survives to this day, but it was also an object that could be bought, given, or passed around, a public place for a dedication or a possession to be plagiarized. Martial's books have a distinctive presence to their world and, to the extent that they are part of the very world they describe, their peculiar status shines light on the social relationships dealt with in the book. Both material and immaterial, for sale and not, the presence of the book serves as an irritant to which the various relationships described in the book must respond. In what sense, for instance, does an author own his book, given that anyone can plagiarize or purchase it? That depends, to a certain extent, on the range of available senses in which a thing, or person, can be owned; at the same time, the special sense in which a book is owned by its author serves as a point of comparison for other kinds of possession.

One way in which an author might assert his ownership of his book is to deny the wrong kind of reader access to it. But can he do that? At what point and under what conditions does the reader enter the book? Once he has raised this question in the preface to Book 1, Martial proceeds to repel some potential interlopers at the entrance to the book, and this chapter will begin by examining how Martial makes an issue of the crossing of thresholds as we embark on our reading of the book. One kind of unwanted interloper is represented by the figure of Cato Uticensis, who introduces a succession of exemplary figures from the past. The first half of this chapter will concern the status of the exemplary past in the present of Martial's book. This brings us back to some of the concerns of the previous chapter, especially since entertainment, both public and private (arena and dinner), will be an important context throughout. The book of epigrams, as Martial stresses, is a mixed bag (1.16), and it is this that allows him to relate the macropolitical to the social, arena to dinner. Furthermore, Martial will use the fact that heterogeneous epigrams within the book are made to speak to one another to echo and reflect on the asymmetrical exchanges that link patron to poet. In the second half of the chapter I will examine the way in which the book itself, as a compound entity with a complex relation to its author, plays a role in, and reflects, the social relationships that characterize its world. Slavery, a subject that is in many ways emblematic of the genre itself, will perform an important role in linking the various agendas of the book. I hope to show that the book has a coherence (though not a unity), which emerges from the overlapping themes of the book as they constellate in their shifting configurations. Here Martial makes a claim for the epigram as a form adequate to its world , but in a way that is distinct from what we have seen in the previous chapter.

## FIRST THINGS

The first thing to notice about Martial's first book is the profusion of first things. We begin with a prose preface, described by Martial as an epistle, in which the poet makes some disclaimers about himself and his genre: he is innocent of malice and he will claim the privilege of the genre to "speak plain Latin."[1] But is the preface really the first thing in the book? In the course of this preface, Martial refers to the title as the first point at which the (wrong sort of) reader might, or should, decide to read no further.[2] The *titulus VALERIUS MARTIALIS LECTORI SUO* appears in some of the manuscripts, and it may well be genuine, since in all of Martial's other epistles (introducing books 2, 8, 9, and 12) there is an addressee.[3] The preface undermines its own *pre*fatory status by debouching into a four-line epigram, the first poetry in the book, but still the end of the "epistle" rather than the beginning of the book of epigrams. When we cross over into the book itself (1.1), Martial introduces himself as the poet who is (already) known "the world over"; in 1.2 we discover that he is in fact introducing a reissue of Book 1 in codex form.[4] With 1.3 we have moved back in time, and Martial finally sends Book 1 out into the world in its original (book roll) form. Now, by contrast with 1.1, he professes nervousness about the reception that it may receive from the fastidious audience of "mistress Rome" (*dominae Romae*, 3). As we cross one threshold after another we are invited to reflect not only on the status and nature of the book, but also on the terms under which we enter it.

But who are "we"? Martial offers a range of arbiters of the book's fate, for "mistress Rome" in 1.3 is replaced in 1.4 by the "master of the earth" (*terrarum dominum*, 2) the emperor himself. Poem 1.5 and (by implication) 1.6 also concern the reception of the book by Domitian, celebrated in his capacity as the *editor* and *auctor* of the games. So, the mass audience suggested by the games is subordinated to the superreader himself. In addition to the book's main dedicatee, there are also secondary, "mortal" dedicatees, celebrated in 1.7 (Stella) and 1.8 (Decianus) respectively.[5] The first seven poems in the book, then, introduce a succession of interested readers, from the "fan" (*lector studiosus*, 1.1) of Martial the international sensation, to the hypercritical Roman public of the debutant in 1.3, to the potentially censorious emperor and superpatron in 1.4, 1.5 and 1.6, and finally to the two lesser, but still major, patrons praised in 1.7 and 1.8. The prefatory material of the book closes here, and the first satirical epigram follows immediately. By the time we get to this point we have crossed various thresholds and have been made acutely conscious of the interrelated parties who share our interest in its production, circulation, and consumption.

Let us now have a closer look at the preface, which acts as the gatekeeper of the book and conjures up two potential interlopers.

## ON THE THRESHOLD: ENTRANCES AND EXITS

Under the preface's standard satiric protestations that (a) no personal malice is displayed or intended, and (b) straight speaking (obscenity) cannot be taken amiss in this particular genre, we can detect an anxiety about interlopers: "If there is anyone so ambitiously severe that in his presence no page can speak plain Latin, he can be content with the epistle, or rather the title."[6] Even to read the *title* is to understand the terms of entry, Martial reminds us. The "ambitiously severe" reader now takes on the form of Cato: "Epigrams are written for those who are in the habit of watching the *Florales*: let Cato not enter my theater, or if he does, let him watch."[7] The preface ends with a four-line epigram in which Cato's conspicuous entrance and exit from the lascivious spectacle of the *Florales* (on being alerted to the fact that his presence was inhibiting the audience's pleasure) is subjected to a devastating critique (see below).[8]

The ancient Cato has a more deadly, living counterpart in the "malicious interpreter" (*malignus interpres*) who infiltrates Martial's book; as Cato made himself the focus of the show at the *Florales*, so this reader seeks to be witty in another's book, attaching names to Martial's epigrams: "Let the malicious interpreter keep away from my straightforward jokes and desist from giving them a title: it's a dirty trick to be clever in someone else's book."[9] As far as the "ambitiously grim" Cato and his descendants are concerned, it is enough for the poet to declare that the entering reader accepts an implied generic contract; if he doesn't accept it, he should read no further than the letter (preface), or even the title. But the *malignus interpres* is a more insidious figure, who reminds us that in the end the author of a book of epigrams has no control over the reception of his work, which is porous to the interpretations, imputations, and depredations of the world in which it circulates.[10]

Another difference between the two interlopers is that Cato is dead, whereas the *malignus interpres* is very much alive. Cato, the Republican *exemplum*, will be diminished at the threshold of this eminently Imperial work as his exit from the *Florales* melts into that other more famous and definitive exit of his, the suicide at Utica.[11] To read this book, as we shall see, is to read the past through the present, and not vice versa. The very opening sentence of the preface distinguishes between Martial's policy of respecting persons and the practice of the *antiqui*, who "did not shrink from abusing true names, and even great ones." "I would not have fame at such a price," claims Martial.[12] Behind those *antiqui* looms the figure of Lucilius, emblem of Republican *libertas*. Roman satire was haunted by the fearless example of Lucilius's naming of names, and Juvenal (1.1150–71) will apologetically cite political motives for not naming the living.[13] As though to preempt Juvenal, Martial substitutes ethical for political considerations: the old poets were not so much fearless as lacking in respect (*reverentia*), and he adds "Let fame come to me at a lesser price, and may cleverness be the last thing I am approved for."[14] In place of true names (*nominibus veris*), Martial offers us "the playful truth (*veritatem*) of words," that is, "speaking plain Latin" (not shrinking from obscenity), a lesser *libertas* to be sure. If the ghost of Lucilius hovers behind all protestations that names will be spared, then he is the first in a series of *exempla* of Republican *libertas* who will be subjected to revisionary scrutiny in this book. Epigram speaks for the present, and even the exemplars of the past whom Martial cites as precedents for his plain speaking (Catullus, Marso, Pedo, Gaetulicus) are identified as authors who are still read from cover to cover.[15]

The specter of the Republic is most definitively exorcised by the four-line epigram that stands before the threshold of the book proper. Turning from prose to verse, Martial engages Cato on the poet's own turf and ends the preface with a poem. If the poet breaks into the prose of the preface, his intrusion, unlike Cato's, is legitimate (*videor mihi* meo iure *facturus si epistulam versibus clusero*):

> Nosses iocosae dulce cum sacrum Florae
> festosque lusus et licentiam vulgi,

cur in theatrum, Cato severe, venisti?
an ideo tantum veneras, ut exires?

Since you knew the rite of playful Flora, the festive sport and
license of the crowd, why, grim Cato, did you come into the
theater? Did you enter only in order to leave?

This Cato, far from holding up the show, is an exhibit in Martial's
gallery of rogues and impostors; it is he who is exposed, not the
mimes. And he is not only exposed for a calculated display of virtue
at the *Florales*, for the insinuation that is so devastating to Cato's
"ambitious" exit from the theater attaches itself inevitably to his
suicide, making his whole life into an opportunity for the leaving of
it. Political suicide will feature prominently in Martial's first book,
with its parade of Republican and early Imperial martyrs, and the
topic is anticipated by this phrase, which transfers itself from the
*Florales* to the crowning event of Cato's life. Rather like the attribu-
tions of the *malignus interpres*, who is clever in another's book, the
phrase infiltrates its wit into an alien context, turning the tables on
the figure representing all who would make Martial's book into an
arena for displaying their own virtue. But this poetic exorcism of
the spirit of Cato at the threshold of the book could also be taken as
an introduction to (and of) the epigram. For it could truly be said
of the epigram, as Martial shaped it, that it begins in order to end.
Exit Cato, enter Martial.

## POET AND AUDIENCE

It is Martial who greets us as we cross the threshold into the book of
epigrams proper, and a Martial who is very much alive:

Hic est ille, quem requiris,
toto notus in orbe Martialis
argutis epigrammaton libellis:
cui, lector studiose, quod dedisti
viventi decus atque sentienti,
rari post cineres habent poetae

Here he is, the one you ask for/after, Martial, known the whole world over for his witty books of epigrams. To him, my fan and reader, you have given such glory while alive and conscious as few poets have received after their death.

If *hic est* conjures up the epitaph, which is the epigrammatic form par excellence, it does so only to cover it with the *hic est* which might accompany the act of pointing someone out in a public place.[16] In the here and now, Martial takes the place of Cato, and enters *his own* theater (*theatrum meum*, praef.); not for him the posthumous fame to which other poets aspire.[17] As the poet we read and ask for (or after), he is the object of current demand. Poet and reader, then, are bound together, each supplying what the other wants—a very different transaction from that between Cato and the audience at the *Florales*. If we have crossed the threshold of the book, we have accepted the contract of the genre and have been absorbed into the category of "fan and reader" (*lector studiosus*).

Poems 1 and 2 introduce a codex edition (*membrana*, 1.2.3), possibly containing more than one book (*libellos*, 1.2.1), whereas poem 3 introduces a book roll (*scrinia*, 1.3.2). The difference in tone between the confident boast of 1.1 and the diffident launching of the book on its public career in 1.3 indicates that this book has already had a history, and a history that we read in reverse. The same book has different moments, but it also provides different models of its own consumption. The reader of the codex edition, which can conveniently be toted around, is cast as a private consumer in 1.2, but in 1.3 reading is again related to public entertainment, as in the preface. Martial the nervous debutant addresses his book roll as a rambunctious slave, eager to leave the safety of the house for the big city and its stage (echoing Horace *Ep.* 1.20):[18]

> Argiletanas mavis habitare tabernas,
> cum tibi, parve liber, scrinia nostra vacent.
> nescis, heu nescis dominae fastidia Romae:
> crede mihi, nimium Martia turba sapit.
> maiores nusquam rhonchi: iuvenesque senesque
> et pueri nasum rhinocerotis habent.

audieris cum grande sophos, dum basia iactas,
ibis ab excusso missus in astra sago.
sed tu, ne totiens domini patiare lituras
neve notet lusus tristis harundo tuos,
aetherias, lascive, cupis volitare per auras:
i, fuge; sed poteras tutior esse domi.

You prefer, little book, to inhabit the shops on the Argiletum, though there's room for you in my cylinders. You do not know, alas, how demanding mistress Rome can be: believe me, the crowd of Mars is all too knowing. Nowhere are the snorts louder: young and old have the nose of a rhinoceros. Just when you hear the big "bravo," while you're blowing kisses, you'll fly to the stars propelled by the shaken blanket. But, so you won't have to undergo the frequent erasures of your master and the reed/cane won't mark your play, you, mischievous creature, want to flit through the ethereal breezes. Go, flee, but you could have been safer at home.

The book-as-slave is here an actor appearing before a treacherous public, but in the next three poems Martial goes over the head of this audience to acknowledge, or claim, the emperor as the ultimate arbiter of his fate. In the first, Martial asks that if the book should reach his notice, the emperor should accord its harmless play (*lusus*, 1.4.7; cf. 1.3.10) the same license he does to the actors in the mime or to the ribald troops at a triumph. As the book that escaped from the safety of its master's home reaches the attention of the emperor, the significance of its *lusus* and *lascivia* changes; now these terms refer not to the book's ill-advised desire to have done with correction and fly the nest (1.3.9–10), but rather to the risqué nature of its contents, which might attract the disapproval of the *censor*/emperor (1.4.6–7). Similarly, as the judging audience of the book shifts from Rome to emperor, *nasum* (nose), the fastidiousness of the Roman audience (1.3.6), has become *supercilium* (1.4.2), the divine "nod." In this context, Martial reminds the emperor that his page may be playful but he himself is not (*lasciva est nobis pagina, vita proba*, 1.4.8), which is all the more convincing for the fact that *lascivia* was what drove the book to detach itself from Martial in the previous poem (*aetherias, lascive, cupis volitare per auras*,

1.3.11). In the next poem (1.5), Domitian speaks back with a witty, and ominous, complaint that he gives Martial a sea battle, but only gets epigrams in return: evidently, Martial wants to swim along with his book! Behind the intimacy assumed by the uneasy humor of this exchange lies the terrible punitive power of the emperor, on display in the arena. But the arena also features displays, and figures, of the emperor's clemency, and Martial goes on to celebrate such a figure in the following poem, the first of six poems in this book on the spectacle of the lion and the hares. Here the lion that picks up hares in its mouth without harming them is compared to the eagle of Zeus abducting Ganymede, and the poem concludes "which is the greater miracle? The supreme *auctor* is responsible for each: the latter is Caesar's, the former Jove's" (*quae maiora putas miracula? summus utrique / auctor adest: haec sunt Caesaris, illa Iovis*, 1.6.5–6). Not only does this provide a more hopeful model of the emperor's power, but it reminds us that it is the emperor, not the Roman public, who is the ultimate arbiter of the book's fate.

We have so far been presented with two different models of Martial's readership. The *lector studiosus* of the codex edition is introduced by poems 1 and 2 as an isolated reader whose favor has made Martial famous, and who buys a Martial to carry around with him; as a generic figure, he comes to stand for a readership, but without being part of an audience. By contrast, the Roman readership to which Martial addresses his first book is figured as an audience at a performance. The slave/book is warned that the Roman public is known for its snorting derision: young and old have the nose of a rhinoceros (*maiores nusquam rhonchi*, 1.3.5). The book is imagined as a performer who is tossed to the stars in a blanket just as he acknowledges the applause (1.3.7–8).[19] In the context of public entertainment, the Roman public's "nose" looks more sinister, for, as we know from Martial's *Liber spectaculorum* (*Spec.* 11; 26), rhinoceroses had tossed bulls and other animals at the games celebrating the opening of the Flavian amphitheater.[20] But the introduction of the arena to figure the place where Martial performs has the advantage that it is not *domina Roma* which presides there but the *terrarum dominus* himself. How much better to deal with the emperor's playful lion (1.6) than the Roman people's rhinoceros!

In the opening sequence of the original book roll, then, Martial uses the arena as one way of imagining the relation between himself and two heterogeneous arbiters of his reputation (*domina Roma* and the *terrarum dominus*), putting them all into the same space. But in the two poems that introduce the codex, poet and reader relate only through the act of reading and the fame that is its correlative: Martial is "the one you read" (*quem legis ille*, 1.1.1) and the reader is addressed in 1.1.2 as "you who want to have my books always with you." We are presented with two models for the relation between poet and audience: on the one hand, the dangerous excitement of live mass entertainment, overseen by political power, and on the other the anonymous exchange between book-buying public and popular author, mediated by demand and desire.[21] As the book progresses, the dinner will emerge as a third model for the relation between reader and poet, and the relation between the microlevel and the macrolevel of Martial's world will be expressed by the connection between the dinner and the arena as forms of entertainment. But before we take up this connection we must pick up another strain of the book's thematic, a strain that was introduced when the ambitiously severe Cato was stopped at the threshold of the book, namely the question of how the exemplary past is to be accommodated to this book of the present.

## PAST AND PRESENT

After acknowledging Domitian as superpatron, Martial rounds off the opening sequence with two poems recognizing lesser patrons, Stella and Decianus respectively. Like the poem which brought the preface to a close on the threshold of the book proper, each of these poems at least appears to downgrade great exemplars of the past: Catullus in 1.7; Thrasea and Cato in 1.8. The dedicatee of 1.8 is a man who can be praised before his death, like his contemporary, Martial (1.1.5–6), and that gives him the edge over his own heroes:

> Quod magni Thraseae consummatique Catonis
> dogmata sic sequeris salvus ut esse velis,

> pectore nec nudo strictos incurris in ensis,
> quod fecisse velim te, Deciane, facis.
> nolo virum facili redimit qui sanguine famam,
> hunc volo, laudari qui sine morte potest. (1.8)

Because you follow the precepts of great Thrasea and of the perfected Cato, and keep your will to live; and because you do not rush onto drawn swords with bared breast, you do what I would want you to do, Decianus. I don't want a man who buys an easy fame by shedding his blood. I want the man who can be praised without having to die first.[22]

The praise of Stella in 1.7 is a little more complicated, but here again an admired figure from the past provides a foil:

> Stellae delicium mei Columba,
> Verona licet audiente dicam,
> vicit, Maxime, Passerem Catulli.
> tanto Stella meus tuo Catullo
> quanto passere maior est columba. (1.7)

The Dove, my Stella's plaything, has surpassed Catullus's Sparrow, and I can say that, Maximus, in Verona's hearing. My Stella is greater than your Catullus by as much as a doe is greater than a sparrow.

"My friend Stella's is bigger than your friend Catullus's," to put it in the language of the schoolyard, or the locker room. The comparison based on the respective sizes of the birds that have given their names to the collections (or poems) is aggressively literal-minded, and brings more than a suspicion of double entendre. In place of the teasing ambiguity of Catullus's *passer*, whose eroticism stems precisely from its ambiguity, we are presented with a crude joke; as we shall see in chapter 6, this kind of banalization is typical of Martial's reception of Catullus.[23] In the final two lines of 1.7, Martial alludes to the last two lines of the earlier poet's much-disputed poem of thanks to Cicero (*tanto pessimus omnium poeta / quanto tu optimus omnium patronus*, c. 49.6–7). It is impossible to be certain that Catullus's extravagant praise of Cicero is ironic and impossible not to suspect that it is. My own view is that Catullus is putting the fulsome style of Cicero to the test of the slender lyric, where it comes across as pompous.[24] If Catullus parodies Cicero's style to tease the great orator, Martial alludes to Catullus's poem to banalize his great forbear's poetry, and quite possibly to tease Stella with a hint that this praise is not to be taken too literally. Furthermore, what the *passer* is to Catullus, suicide is to Cato, so that the synecdochic bird of Catullus's corpus is juxtaposed to the synecdochic event in Cato's life, to similarly banalizing effect.[25] Once again, at the threshold of the book, understood now as the end of the honorific dedicatory material, Martial establishes the terms on which the great exemplars of the past will be allowed to enter.

## HETEROGENEITY AND SUSPICION

The opening sequence comes to an end with the praise of Decianus, completing the book's preliminary acts of deference and recapitulating the mockery of Cato at the end of the preface. It is followed by the first satirical epigram of the book. But as we cross yet another threshold we do not leave Cato and Decianus behind, for this poem is addressed to a certain Cotta, a Cato with the vowels reversed:

> Bellus homo et magnus vis idem, Cotta, videri:
> sed qui bellus homo est, Cotta, pusillus homo est.

You're an elegant chap, Cotta, and you want to be thought of as a great man too. But an elegant chap, Cotta, is a puny chap.[26]

What are we to make of this in the light of the previous poem, or rather, what are we to make of the previous poem in the light of this? Decianus follows the precepts of great Thrasea and of Cato, but without the showy death. Is he, then, a Cotta rather than a Cato, failing not only to end like Thrasea, but also to be *magnus*? Does Martial's *sic* (*magni Thraseae . . . / dogmata* sic *sequeris salvus ut esse velis*, 1.8.1–2) sit awkwardly with the following poem's insistence that you can't be both *bellus* and *magnus*? Or does this poem serve to show that Martial knows the difference between the merely self-serving and the prudently virtuous? This structural analogy demands an interpretive choice of a kind that we will frequently be called upon to make. For some, the suspicious reading will always be stronger, an irresistible infection. But we will later have reason to believe that Martial sometimes poses us the difficult task of resisting just such an infection. In this case, the boundary between introductory material and book proper is both stressed and put at issue by the infection that might or might not spread across it.

The repercussions of the Cotta poem for what has preceded it ramify. Cotta wants to be *great*, but can only appear paltry; Decianus follows the precepts of *great* (*magni*) Thrasea, but in such a way as to survive, and Stella is as much a better poet than Catullus as the dove is *greater* (*maior*) than the sparrow, as Martial tells his friend *Greatest* (*Maximus*). Clearly, the three poems (1.7, 1.8, and 1.9) are connected by a common theme.[27] Are we expected to appreciate the difference between a conspiratorial tease (Martial's praise of Stella) and a truly satirical unmasking (of Cotta), just as we should understand the difference between Decianus's prudence and Cotta's contradictory pretensions? What is it to be *magnus*? Are there different spheres of application, each with its own criteria, or does one usage cast an ironic light on the other? In the heterogeneous world of Martial's epigram book, the question of whether infection spreads from one poem to another or whether each poem is closed off from the next is a question that cannot be answered once and for all; it is, rather, as much part of the experience of reading Martial as deciding at what point we begin to read Book 1.

## FURTHER SUICIDES

Toward the end of the book, Martial celebrates a suicide of his own time, but once again he manages to make the comparison with Cato, and again to the advantage of his own contemporary.[28] The suicide of Festus in 1.78 is not political: he resolved to die in the old Roman manner because he was suffering from a wasting and deforming illness. But it is in the last couplet that Martial returns to his critique of heroes of the past, and to his systematic unraveling of Cato's image:

> hanc mortem fatis magni praeferre Catonis
> fama potest: huius Caesar amicus erat. (1.78.9–10)

> This death fame can prefer to the fate of great Cato. He was
> Caesar's *friend*.

Cato, Martial implies, had nothing to lose after the defeat of the Republican cause, whereas Festus, an "amicus Caesaris," was leaving a life that still had much to offer. The final hemistich engineers a brilliant clash of worlds, as the name-become-title *Caesar* confirms that Julius Caesar inaugurated just what Cato feared he would. Furthermore, by Martial's time the phrase *amicus Caesaris* is almost equivalent to a rank, and that because the cause of those who were enemies of Julius Caesar failed.[29] Festus is blandly judged a success by a standard that Cato died rather than acknowledge, and yet there is just enough truth to the insinuation that Cato had nothing to hope for from a world governed by the original Caesar to take some of the shine off his glorious death.

If the exemplary status of Cato, anti-imperial suicide, is debunked in 1.8 and 1.78, what are we to make of the epigrams celebrating the glorious suicides of Arria (1.13) and Porcia (1.42), epigrams that appear to be straightforward in their admiration for these *exempla* of womanly fortitude?[30] Porcia, the wife of Brutus, was Cato's daughter, and Arria was the mother-in-law of Thrasea Paetus, who is mentioned along with Cato in 1.8 as another anti-imperial suicide. Arria's husband, Caecina Paetus, had taken part in an unsuccessful revolt against Claudius and had resolved on suicide. When, at the last moment, he hesitated, Arria snatched his dagger, stabbed herself and gave the dagger back with the words *Paete non dolet*.[31] The Arria poem is one of Martial's most celebrated and most imitated.

> Casta suo gladium cum traderet Arria Paeto
> quem de visceribus strinxerat ipsa suis
> "si qua fides, vulnus quod feci non dolet," inquit,
> "sed tu quod facies, hoc mihi, Paete, dolet." (1.13)

> When Arria handed over to Paetus the sword she had herself
> drawn from her vitals, she said "If you believe me, Paetus,

> the wound I made does not hurt, but the one that you will make, that hurts me."

Martial expands Arria's famous utterance to produce a complete couplet, and some have found his phrase *si qua fides* a wordy betrayal of her laconic severity.[32] Certainly Martial's expression takes the *exemplum* in a different direction from the "original," which almost admonishes Paetus to be a man. Martial's final couplet, by contrast, alludes to the tenderness and understanding between husband and wife. In the next poem but one (1.15) the phrase *si qua fides* is echoed as Martial prefaces his advice to Iulius Martialis with a reference to their long friendship: "If long trust and venerable oaths have any power . . ." (si quid *longa* fides *canaque iura valent*, 2). This poem is a variation on the well-worn, and vaguely Epicurean admonition to live for the day: in spite of his nearly sixty years, Martialis has few days he can call his own; he should remember that now is the time to live. Where Arria had handed Paetus the instrument of his death, Martial urges his namesake to live, or rather to "live," for the poem concerns precisely the difference between being alive and *living*. Not only does this poem make life, not death, the fruit of a long relationship and of the *fides* that it has accumulated, but it modulates the gory details of Arria's self-wounding into the metaphorical. A version of Arria's *quem de visceribus strinxerat ipsa suis* reappears in Martial's figure for the transience and elusiveness of joys, which "slip from the bottom of the pocket and flow away" (*saepe fluunt imo sic quoque lapsa sinu*, 10): Martial asks Martialis not to let pleasures fall from his pocket (or lap, *sinus*), while Arria draws from her own vitals the sword with which Paetus is to put an end to his life. Arria's dying words to her husband distinguish between past (*quod feci*), present (*non dolet*) and future (*quod facies*); Martial urges that tomorrow is too late and Martialis must live today (*vivam*, 11; *vive hodie*, 12). Between them, 1.13 and 1.15 furnish a contrast between the unbending icons of a heroic past and a more accommodating present, a contrast similar to that in 1.8. The political context of that contrast is supplied by the intervening poem, 1.14, another celebration of the arena's lion and hares, in which a tame lion picks up the hares in its mouth and then lets them go without harm.[33] Clearly this is an allegory of the emperor's *clementia*, and implicitly it points out that the story of revolt and death under Claudius, which is the background of the previous poem, is no longer pertinent under the current regime. Arria is, in a sense, a wonder analogous to the tame lion. Her behavior goes magnificently against the natural order as she proves more manly than her husband and at the same time displays her wifely tenderness by (of all things) passing the knife. This sequence of three poems, each of which belongs to a quite different epigrammatic type, constitutes a subtle argument in which the glorious *exemplum* of Arria is subjected to an ironic confrontation with the concerns and character of the present age: Martial's words to Julius are more appropriate than Arria's to Paetus because this emperor is not the Claudius against whom Paetus revolted, but rather the clement Domitian, in whose reign the prodigies are entertainments, not suicides.

We return to the late Republic in 1.42 for another famous suicide, that of Cato's daughter, Porcia, who refused to survive the defeat of her husband (Brutus) at Philippi. Poem 1.42 celebrates this suicide, producing a companion piece to the poem on Arria as well as another appearance of Cato:

> Coniugis audisset fatum cum Porcia Bruti
> et subtracta sibi quaereret arma dolor,
> "nondum scitis" ait "mortem non posse negari?
> credideram fatis hoc docuisse patrem."
> dixit et ardentis avido bibit ore favillas.
> i nunc et ferrum, turba molesta, nega!

When Porcia had heard of the death of her husband Brutus, and in sorrow looked for the weapons that had been removed from her, she said "haven't you yet grasped that death can't be refused? I would have thought my father proved that with his death." So she spoke, and greedily gulped down burning ashes. Go on, deny her steel, you meddling rabble.

Porcia alludes to her father when she swallows hot coals, outwitting the *turba molesta* that has denied her access to a weapon. But, as with the Arria poem, a perfectly straight celebration of an act of Republican heroism is somewhat undermined by its context. This poem about Porcia, wife of Brutus (*Porcia Bruti*, 1), is followed by one of Martial's many poems on a stingy host, beginning, "We were six hundred for dinner, Mancinus, and all you gave us was a boar (*aper*)." The boar encourages us to read *Porcia Bruti* literally, as "Piggy, wife of Brute."[34] There are further connections. Both Porcia and the stingy host Mancinus produce unconventional meals: while Porcia gulps down live coals, the boar that Mancinus serves is not only diminutive and unaccompanied by side dishes, but it is not even served, merely displayed (*tantum spectavimus omnes*, 11). Porcia resorts to her greedy meal (*avido ore*, 5) when she is deprived of weapons (*subtracta . . . arma*, 2); the killing of Mancinus's boar needs no weapons; it is so small that an unarmed dwarf in the arena could have dispatched it (*a non armato pumilione*, 10). This reference to the arena is expanded to bring 1.43 to a close:

> et nihil inde datum est; tantum spectavimus omnes:
> ponere aprum nobis sic et arena solet.
> ponatur tibi nullus aper post talia facta,
> sed tu ponaris cui Charidemus apro.

And none of it was served to us. We all just watched. That's how the arena regales us with boar. May you never be served boar after such behavior, but instead be served up to the same boar as was Charidemus.

The huge crowd of guests is imagined as an audience at the arena, taking vengeance on the host who had treated them as spectators only. It is he who is served up for their pleasure, a real crowd-pleaser (Chari-demus).

In each of these poems, a single figure confronts a crowd. Poem 1.42 ends with an address to the *turba molesta* and 1.43 begins with the six hundred guests.[35] The defiant Porcia of 1.42 becomes the host Mancinus, who is served up, in the imagination, to a crowd in the arena. In the one case, it is the isolated exemplary figure who is the bearer of value, in the other, the poetic voice identifies with the crowd that is being humiliated by the solitary host. So, what has changed? As we move from the Republic to Principate, and from the literature of *exempla* to Martial's world of patron and client, the solitary, isolated figure mutates from *exemplum virtutis* to the *rex*—patron or emperor—who despises his guests or subjects. Here, the allusion to the arena tells us that this particular emperor is a better host than Mancinus. In the opening sequence of this book, Domitian's presidency of the games had allowed Martial to appeal to a higher authority than *domina Roma*; now the good emperor, as editor of the games, allows Mancinus's guests to conceive of vengeance against the solitary host. This makes a particularly appropriate connection, given that the solitary host is a potential figure for the bad emperor.[36]

Earlier in the book there is another sequence in which the same concatenation of themes appears. A poem on a stingy host (1.20) is juxtaposed to a poem about an illustrious suicidal hero of the past (1.21), and this is followed by a celebration of the hares and lion display in the arena (1.22). The poem on Mucius Scaevola (1.21) which we have come across in a different context in the previous chapter probably refers to a punitive charade in the arena.

> Cum peteret regem, decepta satellite dextra
>     ingessit sacris se peritura focis.
> sed tam saeva pius miracula non tulit hostis
>     et raptum flammis iussit abire virum:
> urere quam potuit contempto Mucius igne,
>     hanc spectare manum Porsena non potuit.
> maior deceptae fama est et gloria dextrae:
>     si non errasset, fecerat illa minus.

Aimed at the king, but deceived by an attendant, that right hand laid itself, doomed to perish, upon the sacred hearth. But the kindly foe could not endure a prodigy so cruel and ordered the warrior to go free, rescued from the flame. The hand which, scorning the fire, Mucius endured to burn, Porsena could not endure to behold. The fame and glory of that right hand is greater because it was deceived; had it not erred, it would have achieved less.

In the previous poem, Martial deplores Caecilianus's hospitality:

> Dic mihi quis furor est? turba spectante vocata
>   solus boletos, Caeciliane, voras.
> quid dignum tanto tibi ventre gulaque precabor?
>   boletum qualem Claudius edit, edas. (1.20)

> What's this madness, tell me? You invite a crowd and, while
> it watches, wolf down mushrooms all on your own, Caeci-
> lianus. What can I wish on you to match such a stomach and
> gullet? May you eat a mushroom such as Claudius ate.

The spectacle of Caecilianus eating his mushrooms in splendid isolation, while the crowd of invitees looks on, provides a burlesque
counterimage to the lone Mucius in the enemy camp, not stuff-
ing his guts but burning his hand. The enemy king whom Mucius
had attempted to assassinate is unable to bear the sight (*spectare*,
1.21.6) of these *saeva miracula* and orders his captive to go free. By
contrast, on behalf of the spectator-guests (*turba spectante*, 1.20.1),
Martial wishes his host would die by the same poisoned mush-
room that dispatched Claudius. Caecilianus and Mucius are both
reduced to body parts: in the one case a glorious right hand, which
received its just deserts (*gloria dextrae*, 1.21.7), and in the other a
stomach and gullet whose owner deserves the very assassination
that Mucius was attempting. Poem 1.20 ends with a reference to the
assassination of an emperor, and 1.21 begins with Mucius's failed
attempt on a king. In the final poem of the group we are in the
arena implied by the "watching crowd" of 1.20 (*turba spectante*, 1)
and by the punitive charade that probably lies behind 1.21:

> Quid nunc saeva fugis placidi lepus ora leonis?
>   frangere tam parvas non didicere feras.
> servantur magnis isti cervicibus ungues
>   nec gaudet tenui sanguine tanta sitis.
> praeda canum lepus est, vastos non implet hiatus:
>   non timeat Dacus Caesaris arma puer. (1.22)

> Why, hare, do you now flee the savage jaws of a lion? They
> have not learnt to grind such small beasts. Those claws are

reserved for great necks, nor does such a thirst rejoice in
mean blood. A hare is the prey of dogs, it doesn't satisfy the
vast maw: the Dacian boy need have no fear of Caesar.

Between 1.20 and 1.21 one kind of defiance is measured against another, but, as in 1.42 and 1.43, a change of context has altered the
meaning of the lone figure who is the cynosure of all eyes.[37] Again,
the solitary banqueter (1.20), emblem of the tyrant, is contrasted
with the good emperor as *editor* (1.22). In 1.22 the spectacle of the
lion and the hares makes its second appearance in the book, and this
time the emphasis is on the haughty lion's *disdain* (to eat the hares), a
modulation of the theme of 1.20, retaining some of its terms but with
different values (compare *tanto . . . ventre gulaque*, 1.20.3, to *tanta sitis*
and *vastos . . . hiatus*, 1.22.4, 1.22.5). Again, the drama is presented in
terms of body parts (*servantur magnis isti cervicibus ungues*, 1.22.3),
but the crowd that watches *this* scene is reassured rather than in-
sulted. Domitian is the emperor as good host, serving up for all to
enjoy a spectacle that reassures his invitees that he will not have them
eaten, a possibility of which we will be reminded when the host of
1.43, who serves up a boar merely as a spectacle, is told that he deserves to be served up *to* a boar in the arena, just like Charidemus.

What are we to make of the collocation of (Republican) *exemplum*, dinner and arena? On the face of it, the juxtaposition is
grotesque, and it works very well as such. Connors (2000.511) has
remarked that "again and again in the literature of leisure [during
the Flavian period] the public story of historical transformation is
called down to a private story of dining." These juxtapositions are
good examples of her observation, but, as I have suggested above,
there is a logic to this collocation, insofar as the arena mediates
between prodigious historical *exemplum* and the smaller world of
private hospitality. The wonders of this imperial age are not the exemplary figures who resisted tyrants, but the displays with which
the emperor regales his people; the emperor who puts on the shows
and invites his people to them is the generous host par excellence.
His antithesis, or rather the emblem of the bad emperor, is the solitary diner who insults his guests, and it is about this figure that the
social and the political axes of Martial's world, the micro- and the

macropolitical, can pivot. Martial's juxtapositions also emphasize the historical shift in the significance of the defiant, isolated figure as we move from Republic to Principate. The very company that this model of republican *virtus* is made to keep in the book serves to relativize his, or indeed her, status. However iconic the event celebrated by the individual epigram may be, it must take its place in a context to which it cannot remain impermeable.

## MIXTURE AND THE BOOK

The groupings that I have pursued in the previous section must not be thought of as self-contained units. Add a poem before or after the group, and new configurations may appear. I want to return now to 1.42 (Porcia's suicide) and 1.43 (Mancinus the host who invites guests to watch him consume a boar) and expand the context a little. In the Mancinus poem, the bad host is a negative version of the emperor. But in the course of the book Martial uses the dinner host as analog to another important figure, namely the poet himself. A good example of this analogy is provided by the two poems that follow 1.43. These poems both address a potential complaint from a reader to the effect that Martial is repeating himself, and specifically with his poems on the spectacle of the lions and the hares.

> Lascivos leporum cursus lususque leonum
>     quod maior nobis charta minorque gerit
> et bis idem facimus, nimium si Stella, videtur
>     hoc tibi, bis leporem tu quoque pone mihi. (1.44)

If it seems excessive, Stella, that my larger and my smaller page bear the frisky scamperings of the hares and the play of the lions, and that I do the same thing twice, then go ahead yourself and serve me twice with hare.

The lion and the hares are celebrated seven times in Book 1 (6, 14, 22, 48, 51, 60, 104). On the last occasion before this poem (1.22) we saw Martial draw the spectacle into connection with the theme of dining (via analogies and proximity to poem 1.20). Now it is the poet, not the emperor, who is the metaphorical host. Being a host, it appears, is both like and unlike being a poet, for Martial the guest would be only too happy to get a double helping of hare, even if Stella the reader complains.[38] Vengeance requires that like be returned for like, but this turns out to be a case where the same thing is not the same, a strategy that is repeated in the following poem, which takes up Stella's complaint again:

> Edita ne brevibus pereat mihi cura libellis
> dicatur potius *ton d'apameibomenos.* (1.45)

So that my work should not go for nothing published in short books, let me say "he in answering spake."

The phrase from Homer not only exemplifies the repetitive formulaic style of epic but also alludes semantically to the fact that Martial is engaging in a dialogue with his reader.[39] We might paraphrase either "let me repeat myself (like Homer)" or "let me reply to objections (to my repetitions)." Martial is "padding" his oeuvre not just by repeating but also by including in the book responses from his readers, and his own replies to those responses.[40] The Homeric tag draws our attention to one of those features that distinguish Martial's epigram from epic, a genre where the reader doesn't get the opportunity to talk back. As in the previous poem, a paradigm of sameness (there revenge, here the Homeric formula) produces a mark of difference.[41]

From the first poem of the book, where the reader asks for his Martial and gives the poet glory in return, exchange features as an important theme. "Domitian," for instance, reckons he is getting a bad bargain in the exchange of sea battle (*naumachia*) for epigrams (*epigrammata*, 1.5), a good example of the way that the things exchanged are both differentiated and assimilated (*naumachia* and *epigrammata* are both Greek words). Is the book, in all its variety and miscellany, like the meal for which it is exchanged? Martial does not explicitly makes the comparison of book to meal in Book 1, though he does elsewhere.[42] The nearest he comes in this book is the more interesting collocation between a poet mixing poems and a host mixing wines. Poem 1.16, one of several in this book about the *book* of epigrams, makes a typically deprecatory statement about Martial's genre:

> Sunt bona, sunt quaedam mediocria, sunt mala plura
> quae legis hic: aliter non fit, Avite, liber.

> Here you read some good ones, some middling, and more
> that are bad: a book, Avitus, is made no other way.

This distich is closely followed by one of Martial's attacks on a stingy host (1.18):

> Quid te, Tucca, iuvat vetulo miscere Falerno
> in Vaticanis condita musta cadis?
> quid tantum fecere boni tibi pessima vina?
> aut quid fecerunt optima vina mali?
> de nobis facile est, scelus est iugulare Falernum
> et dare Campano toxica saeva mero.
> convivae meruere tui fortasse perire:
> amphora non meruit tam pretiosa mori.

> What good does it do you, Tucca, to mix with aged Falernian
> must that has been stored in Vatican casks? How have these
> dreadful wines put you so in their debt? Or what harm have
> the good wines done you? Never mind about us, it's a crime
> to slaughter Falernian and mix savage poison with Campan-
> ian. Maybe your guests deserved to die. But such a valuable
> jar did not.

Tucca is doing with his wines what Martial is doing with his po-ems, but mixing doesn't work as well with wines. Or does it? The bad wine, after all, is improved, just as any epigram may acquire new meaning next to another. As we reflect on what it is about a mixed bag of epigrams that is or isn't like a bottle of good wine mixed with bad, or vice versa, we are engaged in the process of en-riching one epigram by association with another. As far as mixing is concerned, poems are not like wines: to mix them, it seems, is always to their advantage.

Later in the book, Martial will describe one circumstance in which the mixing of good epigrams with bad does involve contamination of the kind perpetrated by Tucca. One of the themes that runs through Book 1 is plagiarism, or literary theft. As we learn right from the start, however, a poet's work can be stolen by addition as well as by subtraction.[43] In the preface, the wit who is *ingeniosus in alieno libro*, attaching names to Martial's generic targets, is such a thief. In 1.53 Fidentinus has gone further, and circulated a collection of Martial's poems as his, but he hasn't been able to resist mixing in a page of his own productions. Ironically, it is his own page that identifies him as a thief.[44] Since Martial proceeds now to use one of his trademark lists—a paradigm of the heterogeneity that informs his oeuvre—to exemplify Fidentinus's deception, he seems to undermine his own rhetoric of contamination. The list progresses from the realistic detail to the literary topos, from low to high (1.53.4–10): Fidentinus's interpolated page is like an oily cloak that contaminates fancy garments, cheap earthenware that disfigures rock crystal, a black crow among white swans, and a magpie whose chattering jars with the "Cecropian laments" of nightingales in their grove (*multisona . . . Atthide lucus*, 8). The language ranges from the vulgar and barbaric *bardocucullus* ("cowl," 5) to the mythological allusion (*Atthide*, 8) and the epic (*Cecropias querelas*, 10). Fidentinus's failed attempt to make his own poems pass in their alien context is taken by Martial as an opportunity to display his own ability to put diverse matter together, one of the glories of his oeuvre. Both the black crow amid white swans and, more clearly, the magpie chattering in the grove of nightingales are figures for poetic rivalry.[45] The offending page interpolated into Martial's book by the thieving Fidentinus, then, becomes Fidentinus himself, outclassed by the poems among which he raises his voice.

But hasn't Martial already said that a book necessarily consists of good, bad, and indifferent? Isn't the list itself a reminder of the heterogeneity that is a constitutive element of the book? Might not the page marked by the hand of Fidentinus in time find a way to mix with the poems of Martial, as the high and the low mix in Martial's list? The following poem offers us an analogy for this latter possibility, and in the process wards it off:

Si quid, Fusce, vacas adhuc amari—
nam sunt hinc tibi, sunt et hinc amici—
unum, si superest, locum rogamus,
nec me, quod tibi sim novus, recuses:
omnes hoc veteres tui fuerunt.
tu tantum inspice qui novus paratur
an possit fieri vetus sodalis. (1.54)

If, Fuscus, you still have time for a friend—for you have
friends wherever you look—I ask for one place, if there's one
left. Don't refuse me because I'm new to you: all your old
friends were new. Just take a look and see if the new friend
you're making can become an old companion.

Here Martial urges his worthiness to join the circle of Fuscus's
friends and clients.[46] At the moment, he is a misfit by virtue of being new, but that, unlike Fidentinus's poetic talent, can change. In
1.53, Fidentinus inserts one page of his own among Martial's poems
(una *est . . . pagina*, 1–2), and in 1.54 Martial seeks to occupy one
more place among the friends of Fuscus (unum *si superest locum
rogamus*, 3). The implied metaphorical relation between the social (collections of friends) and the poetic (collections of poems)
is underpinned by a metonymical relation between them: poetry
is an aspect of sociality, and collections of poems are one of the
ways that poets make new friends. We can spell out the relation between these poems in two different ways, depending on whether we
make one consequent on the other or read them in parallel. Either
Fidentinus's failure to make his poems pass for Martial's proves
that Martial is fit to join the circle of Fuscus's *amici*. Or the fact
that Fidentinus's poems could never mix into Martial's oeuvre, as
Martial *can* in time become an old friend of Fuscus, proves that
poetry transcends its social world. On various levels, the oscillation
between embeddedness and transcendence is one of the constitutive issues of Martial's books, and the question of how the book
relates to the world in which it circulates is echoed by the questions
of how, and whether, neighboring poems within the book relate to
each other, given that they are so emphatically closed in form and
heterogeneous in content. The boundary between the book and its

world is reflected by the boundary between consecutive poems. Furthermore, the book, both embedded in the exchange between patron and client and freely available for sale at bookstores, situates the poet's authorship (the sense in which it is "his") within a network of related but heterogeneous possessive relations.

## POSSESSION

Martial wants to become Fuscus's (cf. 1.54.4–5: *nec me quod tibi sim novus recuses / omnes hoc veteres tui fuerunt*), whereas Fidentinus wants Martial's poems to become his own, and vice versa. Possession, in its various dimensions, is a running theme in this book, as throughout Martial's oeuvre. Starting with the preface, Martial conducts a subtle investigation of the sense in which a poet does or does not own his poems, and particularly of the conditions under which they may be alienated. Clearly, the most important realities behind this concern are the commercial, or at least professional, status of Martial's poetry and the threat of plagiarism, particularly acute in a world in which copyright protection did not exist.[47] But these are not all, and the very first instance of this theme, in the preface, has to do with the question of whether a sceptic epigram does or does not attach to a particular individual. The wit who identifies the butt of epigrams that, as Martial insists, are not directed at individuals, is described as "witty in another's book" (*ingeniosus in alieno libro*) and threatens to make himself into the author of Martial's poem (*nec epigrammata mea [in]scribat*). Martial is suggesting that in a very real, and potentially dangerous, sense he cannot control the meaning of his book, nor can he prevent others from making his poems into the expression of their own wit. Later, he will raise this possibility in a different context and with less anxiety. In 1.38 Fidentinus has been reciting Martial's poems as his own:

> Quem recitas meus est, o Fidentine, libellus:
> sed male cum recitas, incipit esse tuus.

> The book you're reciting, Fidentinus, is mine; but when you recite it badly it begins to be yours.

Behind this facetious insult lies a deeper point, I think. Modern disagreements about the interpretation of particular epigrams do not always stem from insufficient information about the ancient context. Many of the epigrams leave us struggling to articulate the point: secondary points may lie beneath primary ones; double entendres may be featured, or their presence merely insinuated. Often Martial presents the reciter with the problem of deciding how to read the written text as a sally of wit, and of deciding which potential point to realize. Even for silent readers such as ourselves, the act of reading may involve a conflict between the ambiguity of the written text and the need to imagine an effective spoken realization.

Let me give as an example of this ambiguity another poem about ownership. In 1.29 Martial addresses Fidentinus again:

> Fama refert nostros te, Fidentine, libellos
> non aliter populo quam recitare tuos.
> si mea vis dici, gratis tibi carmina mittam:
> si dici tua vis, hoc eme, ne mea sint.

> Rumor has it, Fidentinus, that you are publicly reciting our books no differently than you do your own. If you want them to be called mine, I will send you poems free. If yours, then buy this, that they be not mine.

Here Martial characteristically plays with two kinds of possession.[48] If Martial's poems are for sale, then isn't he allowing other people to own them? Does Fidentinus have the right to call the poems his own once he has bought them? Yes and no. The meaning of the final line is disputed by the two modern editions of Book 1. Mario Citroni has *hoc* refer to the book, but Howell rejects this in favor of a *hoc* that anticipates *ne mea sint*. "Buy this book, and make them mine no longer" (not!); or, "Buy this—namely, that they not be called mine." Martial has left it up to the reader to grasp this double meaning and its implications, and to the reciter (in the reader) to realize the epigram more or less richly. Possibly the ambiguity in the last line is a response to Fidentinus's own prevarication when he publicly recites Martial's books "no differently than his own." Here we would like to know more about the protocols of recitation: what were the conventions of attribution when you recited poems other than your own, or mixtures of the two? Could Fidentinus imply that he had written Martial's poems without actually claiming so? This, at any rate, is what Martial's wording would lead us to understand, and the wording of his response is appropriately ambiguous.

How could Fidentinus "buy this: that they not be mine"? At first, we might think that Martial is describing an impossibility: some things just can't be bought, and that's the point. But in 1.66 he makes a suggestion. The poem addresses a plagiarist who mistakenly thinks that he can make Martial's poems his own by buying them. The status of poet cannot be bought that cheaply, he replies. But at the fourth line the poem takes a surprise turn as the plagiarist is urged to buy poems that haven't yet been published. "A known book cannot change master" (*mutare dominum non potest liber notus*, 9), comments Martial, recalling the comparison of book to slave in earlier poems.[49] What the plagiarist needs to buy is the poet's silence (12–13), which means, first of all, his promise not to claim the unpublished poems as his own, and then, more radically, his silence as a poet, insofar as he has no longer written these poems. Just what is, or can be, for sale if a poet lives by his poetry? In what senses can (or can't) poetry be sold?[50] Can authorship be transferred?

Publication itself raised difficult questions about ownership in Rome. Roman authors not only received no royalty for the published book but were also unprotected by laws of copyright. Nevertheless, publication was a useful defence against plagiarism insofar as it made public the author's claim to the poems.[51] Pliny advises a friend as follows: "Some of your verses have become known and, without your permission, broken out of their confinement. If you don't drag them back into your collection, sooner or later, like truant slaves [*errones*], they will find someone who'll call them his own."[52] It is striking that Martial, Pliny's contemporary, uses the same figure from slavery, with the difference that the *erro* has become the *libertus*:

> Commendo tibi, Quintiane, nostros—
> nostros dicere si tamen libellos

> possum, quos recitat tuus poeta—:
> si de servitio gravi queruntur,
> adsertor venias satisque praestes,
> et, cum se dominum vocabit ille,
> dicas esse meos manuque missos.
> hoc si terque quaterque clamitaris,
> impones plagiario pudorem. (1.52)

I consign my books to you Quintianus—if I can indeed call mine the books that your poet recites. If they complain of a burdensome slavery, may you come as their vindicator and stand security for them; and, when he calls himself their master, may you declare that they are mine and have been set free. If you call this out three or four times, you will make the kidnapper ashamed.

*Plagiarius* (kidnapper) is used of literary theft only here in Latin literature. Our "plagiarism" comes from this poem via the fifteenth-century humanist Lorenzo Valla, who imitates Martial in the preface to his *Elegantiarum latinae linguae*, where he accuses someone of "plagiarizing" his work.[53] Martial's "plagiarist" has re-enslaved the poems that the poet manumitted. Like the freedman, the poems bear Martial's name and, like the freedman, they have been let go. So, manumission stands for publication, and the freedman figures the relation between the author and the work that is now public property—unprotected by copyright, and yet, somehow, still Martial's. Here we run into an asymmetry, for Martial does not say that when the poet claims to be the master of these poems Quintianus should answer that Martial is their master, but rather that they are Martial's (*meos*) and have been manumitted. We expect something like "If I can call mine the poems that he recites as his"; instead we have "If I can call mine the poems that your poet recites."[54] As *adsertor*, Quintianus is saying that the poems are free and no longer *belong* to anyone, though in some sense they remain Martial's (like a freedman?).[55] Author and published poems stand to master and freed slave in a figurative relationship, but how does the figure of slavery attach to the relation between author and Quintianus, or Quintianus and plagiarist (*tuus poeta*, 1.52.3)? In context, 1.52 can be seen to combine the two kinds of possession treated, respectively, in 1.53 (Fidentinus's thieving interpolations) and 1.54 (Fuscus's circle of friends). The possessives applied to poetry in 1.53 (your page, my book) and that applied to friends/clients in 1.54 (your old friends: *veteres tui*) are combined in 1.52. Martial's asymmetrical contrast between *nostros libellos* and *tuus poeta* suggests that we compare the way that an author's poems are his to the way that a patron's *amici* belong to him, and that we do so through the metaphor of slavery, which figures the condition of the poet/*cliens* throughout his work.[56] Certainly it would be more natural for Quintianus's poet to complain of a "grave *servitium*" than for the poems to do so. At any rate, the crossing of two kinds of possessives reminds us that Martial's ownership of his poems may *depend* on Quintianus's influence over the thieving poet who is his client, as well as on Quintianus's patronal relationship to Martial.[57] In these three poems, the oscillation between metaphorical and metonymical relations (comparison and combination) offers us both a socially embedded and a transcendent account of Martial's authorship, a conflict nicely encapsulated in the contradiction between 1.53.11 (*indice non opus est . . .* ) and 1.52.5 (*assertor venias*): Martial's authorship speaks for itself, or, quite the contrary, it needs to be vindicated and enforced.[58]

The book of epigrams is at the same time authored text, commercial object, and focus of a client-patron relation. It serves, among other things, as a point about which to assemble the possessive relations in Martial's society. At the same time, the peculiar status of the book with respect to possession serves to problematize those relations. In this case, the book is as much a figure for the freedman as vice versa.

## SLAVERY

When Martial declares that he has manumitted his poems in 1.52 he picks up a thread that can be traced back to the opening sequence, where the figure of slavery looms large. Martial may own his poetry, but that poetry is also for sale, and furthermore it is (and in some senses isn't) "Martial." The poet addresses an anonymous public which knows him only as his book, and yet a relation of mutual benefaction exists between poet and audience: the author produces the books that the public craves, while the public bestows fame on its beloved author. Both are abstractions to the other, and the relationship between them takes place, if anywhere, at the bookstores through which readers could bypass the aristocratic circles that served as the gatekeepers of refined culture.[59] These mediated, partially commercialized relations, in which an object that is for sale can serve as proxy for a person, are aptly figured by slavery.

Object and person are conflated in the first word of the first epigram of this book: Hic est... *ille Martialis* (1–2). The demonstrative is ambiguous. Does it refer to Martial the individual or to a codex "Martial"? Insofar as Martial is identified as "the one you read," he *is* a book for his anonymous public. But then he isn't identical with his books, since he is known *for* his witty books of epigrams (*notus ... argutis epigrammaton libellis*, 2–3), the source of the individual Martial's fame. Do we then "ask after" Martial (*quem requiris*, 1), eager to have the man behind the book pointed out to us, or do we "ask for" a Martial, keen to read it again? *Requiris* allows for both possibilities. The burden of the poem is that Martial will not need to *become* a book in order to aspire to the fame granted posthumously to other poets. And yet, as we shall see, it is important for the flesh-and-blood Martial that his books can substitute for him. If in the first poem Martial is the object of reading, in the second he is an object to be acquired:

> Qui tecum cupis esse meos ubicumque libellos
> et comites longae quaeris habere viae,
> hos eme, quos artat brevibus membrana tabellis:
> scrinia da magnis, me manus una capit.
> ne tamen ignores ubi sim venalis et erres
> urbe vagus tota, me duce certus eris;
> libertum docti Lucensis quaere Secundum
> limina post Pacis Palladiaeque forum. (1.2)

You who want to have my books with you wherever you go, and who are looking to have them as companions on a long journey, buy these, which the parchment confines within small covers: give cylinders to the great, one hand can hold

me. That you should not be ignorant of where I am on sale
and wander aimlessly over the whole city, with me as your
guide you will be certain: look for Secundus, the freedman
of learned Lucensis, beyond the threshold of the Temple of
Peace and the Forum of Minerva.

As in 1.1, there is at first confusion as to whether the speaker is the
poet (*meos . . . libellos*, 1) or the book itself (*me manus una capit*, 4).
By the end of the poem it is clear that the poet has merged with his
book, which, in its codex form, is a convenient way for the man in
the street to have the poet accompany him as companion (*comes*),
just like a proconsul embarking on a term of office with his entourage (*comites*). There could hardly be a better illustration of the observation of Starr (1987.223) that the spread of bookstores allowed
access to a literary culture that had previously been the exclusive
province of elite literary circles.

Thanks to the "eager reader" of poem 1.1, Martial's fame had
spread through the whole world; but now, compressed into a
"handy" edition, he is brought back as an imported slave (*venalis*,
1.2.5).[60] The worldwide fame bestowed by an expanded readership is
but the other side of the commodification of literature implied by
the metaphor of the book as slave. As a commercial object that can
be acquired and can then stand in for the poet as *comes*, the codex
has advantages for the reader. As a mobile proxy that both is and
isn't the poet, the book has advantages for Martial, who can use it
to perform, virtually, the duties that Martial the client would rather
not perform in person. Furthermore, the book's ambiguous relation to its author also allows Martial to disclaim its *lascivia* since,
as ambitious slave, it has its own intentions (1.4). These two aspects
of the book as its author's slave reflect the two intertexts of 1.3, in
which Horace's reluctant envoi to the book as slave, eager to leave
the nest and prostitute himself at the booksellers' shop against
his master's advice (*Ep.* 1.20), is conflated with Ovid *Tristia* 1.1, in
which the little book (*parve . . . liber*, 1) is figured as a slave who is
free (*liber*) to go where the exiled master is not.

The material conveniences of the fact that his book both is and
isn't Martial prove themselves in 1.70, which begins with a sharp

contrast to the reluctant dismissal of the book in 1.3 (*i, fuge, sed poteras tutior esse domi*, 12):

> Vade salutatum pro me liber: ire iuberis
> ad Proculi nitidos, officiose, lares.

Go, book, in my stead to perform the morning greeting. You are commanded, dutiful servant, to go to the elegant house of Proculus.

Sending his book in his stead, to Proculus's *salutatio*, Martial elaborates the allusions to Ovid's *Tristia* in 1.3.[61] In its new context, these allusions make more sense, and they are followed by ten lines of directions capped by a flattering reference to Proculus's accessibility and Muse-friendliness.[62] The poem concludes:

> Si dicet "quare non tamen ipse venit"
> sic licet excuses: "quia qualiacumque leguntur
> ista salutator scribere non potuit." (1.70.16–18)

If he says "But why doesn't he come himself?" you can make your excuses as follows: "Because what you're reading, such as it is, could not have been written by a (the?) *salutator*."

This final couplet is particularly complex. We could think of it, first of all, as another version of "what you are reading is not me." But, in addition to the contrast between the spoken (*salutator*) and the written (*leguntur, scribere*), there is also a contrast between the single *salutator* and the broader public implied by the indefinite passive (*leguntur*, 17): this poem, as *salutatio*, will enhance Proculus's prestige more than the appearance of one more *salutator* at his house, for Martial can deposit a whole busload of readers at Proculus's doorstep. Insofar as the *salutator*/book is identified as a slave or freedman (*ire iuberis*, 1), Martial's point is that what we have just read could not have been written by a *salutator*; not only would its author have been occupied by this task, but the virtual *salutatio* performed in the book is the work of a free man.[63]

The book as *salutator* reappears in 1.108, where Martial complains that his friend Gallus lives too far away for him to perform the morning greeting. It makes little difference to Gallus to be deprived of one *salutator*, but it makes a great difference for Martial to be deprived of himself (7–8). He will greet Gallus at dinnertime; in the morning his book will do the greeting in his stead (*dicet havere liber*, 10). In 1.117 Martial plays a variation on this theme, with the roles redistributed. Lupercus has been asking the poet if he can send round a slave to pick up a copy of his book, which he will return once he's read it. "Don't bother the slave," says Martial. "I live far away, up three flights of stairs; but you could pick up a copy yourself at the bookstore of Atrectus, who will give you a Martial for five denarii. 'You're not worth that much,' you say? You're wise, Lupercus."[64] Here, the public availability of the book will spare Lupercus's slave a journey, whereas in 1.70 and 1.108 the fact that the book serves as a proxy for its "master" spares Martial a journey.[65] In all three cases, the peculiar status of the book plays a role in the drama of social relations between poet and addressee. Lupercus is mocked because he wants to engage neither in relations of gift-exchange between patron and client (for he will borrow and return the very same thing, and without actually encountering Martial), nor in relations mediated by the bookstore and by cash. But in 1.70 and 1.108 Martial wants to claim that the absence of personal contact between patron and client will work to everyone's advantage. The same feature can be given a negative or a positive interpretation.

As we have seen, Lupercus's slave is materialized out of metaphors of slavery that have been used to characterize relations between author, book, and others at several points in this book. Two epitaphs for slaves in the latter half of the book involve a similar materialization, though these slaves never quite emancipate themselves from the role of figuring their master's books. At the beginning of this book Martial very emphatically wrote a nonepitaph for himself: he has achieved fame during his life such as few poets receive after death (1.1). The epitaphs for slaves later in the book allow Martial to have his cake and eat it, both imagining his own posterity and uncoupling it from his death. Instead of the author himself, it is his

slaves who die and live on, in Martial's book. Demetrius (1.101) is a
scribe, whose handwriting was known even to Caesars:

> Illa manus quondam studiorum fida meorum
>     et felix domino notaque Caesaribus,
> destituit primos viridis Demetrius annos:
>     quarta tribus lustris addita messis erat.
> ne tamen ad Stygias famulus descenderet umbras,
>     ureret implicitum cum scelerata lues,
> cavimus et domini ius omne remisimus aegro:
>     munere dignus erat convaluisse meo.
> sensit deficiens sua praemia meque patronum
>     dixit ad infernas liber iturus aquas.

> Once the faithful hand of my studies—lucky for his master
> and known to Caesars—here is young Demetrius, who has
> laid aside his early years. A fourth harvest had been added to
> three five-year *lustra*. When the wretched disease held him
> burning in its grip, I saw to it that he should not go to the
> Stygian waters a slave, and gave up all rights of a master over
> the sick man: he was worthy to have recovered with my gift.
> On his deathbed he was conscious of his reward and called
> me *patronus* as he was on the point of departing for the wa-
> ters of the underworld, a free man.

Here, toward the end of the book, Martial rewrites his envoi, as
again he reluctantly lets a slave go. But Demetrius is not headed
for the *aetherias . . . auras* (1.3.11) through which the book-as-slave
wanted to flit; his destination is instead the *infernas . . . aquas* (10).
It is an appropriately closural reversal, and if Martial's chiding
of the reckless impatience of the book-as-slave carried, and off-
loaded, some of the anxieties of the debutant poet, the farewell to
the scribe suggests that here, at the end of his first book, Martial is
no longer writing juvenilia.[66] Furthermore, with the death of the
scribe, his poetry is now relinquishing its mortal parts. Literaliz-
ing the figure of slavery brings with it an increase in confidence on
Martial's part. We may contrast 1.52, in which the figure of manumission expressed the tenuous, or paradoxical, claim of the poet
over the poetry that he has released into the public sphere. There

are no such anxieties in the epitaph for Demetrius, whose last words acknowledge Martial, once and for all, as his *patronus*. For the dying Demetrius, freedom may be a poignantly empty gift, but not only is he going to the underworld *liber*, for what it is worth, he is also going into a *liber*, where he will live on. The fragility of the exchange between slave and master on the threshold between life and death serves to accentuate Demetrius's installation in Martial's book, and this contrast in turn makes a powerful claim that the book of epigrams transcends its own elements.

Epitaphs for favorite slaves, and other celebrations of these precious possessions, are a significant element of Martial's panegyrical poetry, in which they often attest to the taste, culture, and humanity of their masters.[67] Slaves also feature prominently in his satirical or invective poetry, being close to, or a part of, the secret world of their masters and mistresses. Poems on slaves, then, can be synecdochic for Martial's genre, and the social status of slaves is analogous to the generic position of the epigram, at the bottom of the ladder. Martial's epitaph for his slave Alcimus (1.88) adapts a familiar metapoetic topos to a new purpose. The living garden in which he has buried his slave is contrasted with marble monuments that are prone to fall, an adaptation of a topos that usually contrasts the crumbling of tombs to the immortality of poetry.[68] By contrast with the toppling marbles (*Pario nutantia pondera saxo*, 3), the shade and greenery of the garden is light (*faciles buxos et opacas palmitis umbras*, 5). It is conventional for epitaphs to ask, or declare, that the earth lie(s) lightly on the deceased, but this motif has a more material significance in the case of a slave, for whom an easygoing (*facilis*) master might mitigate some of the burdens (*pondera*) of slavery. Of course, Martial's contrast between the unstable weight of Parian marble and the *faciles* ["easily procured"] *buxos* also implies a contrast between the heavier and the lighter genres. In this case, one could just as easily say that the language of the literary agenda is being applied figuratively to the relation between master and slave as vice versa. "This tribute" (hic *tibi perpetuo tempore vivet* honor, 8), at any rate, alludes both to the garden and to the epigram book: the monuments of Martial's grief (*nostri monimenta doloris*, 7) that the slave is to receive are also those of the epigram itself. It comes as no surprise to learn that Martial himself will want to be buried in the same way (place?) when his time is up (*cum mihi supremos Lachesis perneverit annos, / non aliter cineres mando iacere meos,* 9–10). With the slave Alcimus, whose memorial is and isn't in the book, and whose death is and isn't the poet's, we have come full circle from 1.3, where the figure of the slave is used to elaborate some of the ways in which the book is and isn't Martial. The slave, figure or individual, stands at the center of a connected set of themes having to do with the relation between the poet and his poems, collected in a book that circulates as a commodity under his name.

The ambiguous relation between book and author is but one aspect of the relation between book and world explored in Book 1. Another strain I have pursued is that of exchanges, symmetrical and asymmetrical. Under this heading we can bring together the exchanges between patron and poet—of dinners and poems, or epigrams and sea-battles—with the broader issue that is implicitly raised again and again, namely whether the poetry of Martial is embedded in or transcendent of its world. I have argued that this question is sometimes posed at the level of connections, or exchanges, between adjacent poems, and that here too we are faced with decisions about embeddedness and transcendence. Is there a common coin through which the cautious greatness of Decianus can be converted into the paradoxical ambition of Cotta to be both *bellus* and *magnus*, or are the two as noncommensurable as poems and dinners (sometimes are)? The traffic between poems echoes that between things exchanged socially, and it invites us to ask analogous questions. But the two issues are connected, for the value of a panegyrical poem is inevitably affected by the company it keeps in the book.

The issue of embeddedness and transcendence arises again in connection with the commodification of the book, available to all and sundry for a fixed price at a bookseller. The book is just like any other thing you can buy. Or is it? In a rather unusual way, the book remains Martial's even when another has acquired it, and that is one of the curious properties of poetry. However, it is one of the distinguishing marks of epigrams that they can be attached to people for whom they were not intended, and so, by acquiring a specific target, acquire a new author (*nec epigrammata mea [in]scribat,* praef.).

Because they are quintessentially poems that circulate, epigrams are up for grabs, and the book that contains them may have boundaries that are difficult to police. Furthermore, because they are both emphatically closed and yet short enough to jostle each other in the reader's mind, epigrams collected in a book, especially a book that is thematically heterogeneous, will pose for the reader the question of how to observe the boundaries between them. The problematic boundary between book and world is echoed by the problematic boundary between epigrams. Are the individual poems, and their diverse themes, to be isolated in noncomparable worlds, or are their terms to be transferred across the boundaries between them? One form that this question takes is whether the glorious past, memorialized and marmorealized in a celebratory epigram, can be revised by the present into which it has been inserted.

Perhaps the most threatening figure that Cato has to contend with when he breaks into Martial's book is the poet himself, whose fame is not attendant on his death. In the opening sequence of this book we are introduced to one of Martial's most important themes, namely the relation between committed but unknown reader and the author he makes famous, a relation mediated by the public availability of the book. But the commodification of the book and the concomitant relation between anonymous readership and famed poet does not simply replace the more traditional social ties between poet and patron; the two systems coexist. If this produces awkward tensions it also brings new opportunities: not only can the poet-*cliens* perform his duties virtually, through the book, but the book can lay claim to stand at a nodal point in the structure of its changing world. One of the most significant features of that world is a relatively new political system in which one man claims the right to be *auctor, editor,* and *censor* and communicates with his own anonymous public via huge and hugely popular entertainments. The analogy between emperor and author is there to be made, and in later chapters we will see Martial explore some of its possibilities. This is not solely a matter of competitive relations between poet and prince. It is rather a matter of new patterns of association and relation for which the book of epigrams will provide a valuable laboratory, as we shall see in the next chapter.

CHAPTER·FOUR

# JUXTAPOSITION: THE·ATTRACTION·OF·OPPOSITES

Juxtaposition, as I suggested in chapter 1, is the most useful term for describing the environment of Martial's books, and the effect of juxtaposition is one of the main constituents of Martial's epigrammatic world. I will begin this chapter by considering a very broad type of juxtaposition which strongly affects the character of Martial's books, namely that of panegyric and scoptic. The second half of this chapter will deal with juxtapositions of different, in fact contrasting, forms of social status. The two categories are not unconnected, insofar as Martial's adoption of the scoptic or of the panegyrical mode affects his social pose and establishes different relations of power between him and his world.

Scoptic and panegyric are Martial's most common modes, and they relate as polar opposites, but what effect do they have on each other when juxtaposed? At the very least we may ask how the same poet who strips away surfaces so ruthlessly can then "lay it on with a trowel" without batting an eyelid. Coming at it from another perspective, we can ask what kind of an environment such juxtapositions create for the reader. The reader who expects a book of Martial to interleave different kinds of material must learn to switch between registers and, to a certain extent, isolate them from each other. At the same time, once a spark has jumped between two opposed but juxtaposed registers, the reader will be on the alert for more.

My other topic in this chapter is Martial's use of juxtaposition to analyze aspects of the structure of his world. I will be primarily concerned with two statuses that, like sceptic and panegyric, form polar opposites. Emperor and slave are two of the most significant presences in Martial's poetry but they are also two exceptional beings, each of whom raises problems of juxtaposition individually. Can a book that contains obscenity accommodate an emperor as well? Are slaves, who are always *next* to the free, also *part* of their lives? I hope to show that in the case of these two problematic figures Martial's juxtapositions often have a wit that is analytic as well as irreverent.[1] Finally, I will consider a relation that will be taken up more fully in the next chapter, namely that between emperor and author.

I WILL BEGIN with a juxtaposition that belongs to neither of my categories but provides a useful methodological introduction to the chapter since it concerns a poem that seems to form part of a mini-cycle in its book. It has long been noticed that individual books of Martial contain "cycles" of poems on the same theme, sometimes grouped together but also scattered through a given book.[2] I want to read this poem (4.71) against its "cyclical" context by proposing a juxtapository reading that works across heterogeneous subject matter in neighboring poems.

> Quaero diu totam, Safroni Rufe, per urbem,
>  si qua puella negat: nulla puella negat.
> tamquam fas non sit, tamquam sit turpe negare,
>  tamquam non liceat, nulla puella negat.
> casta igitur nulla est? castae sunt mille. quid ergo
>  casta facit? non dat, non tamen illa negat.

For a long time, Safronius Rufus, I've been searching all over the city for a girl who says no: no girl says no. You'd think it were sinful or disgraceful to say no, or simply not allowed, but no girl says no. So, is no girl chaste? Thousands are chaste. What then does a chaste girl do? She doesn't give, but she doesn't refuse.

Is there something intermediate between giving and refusing, and if so, what?[3] Ten poems later (4.81), Martial complains that Fabulla, having read his epigram, now refuses his advances. "I asked you to refuse, not to flatly refuse (*pernegare*)," he jokes. This would seem to settle the question of what is meant by the final words of 4.71: the chaste girl is being asked to refuse, rather than keep her suitor dangling. Poems 4.71 and 4.81, then, constitute a miniature cycle and between them echo a poem earlier in the same book in which Martial tells Galla to refuse him: torment in love keeps it alive, but not forever . . . (4.38; cf. 1.57).

But the figure who neither gives nor refuses crops up in another context in Martial's oeuvre. When it comes to financial transactions, the torment of being kept in suspense is not quite so sweet, and Martial tells a dithering Phoebus to go ahead and refuse him the loan he's been asking for (*iam, rogo, Phoebe, nega*, 6.20.4). Cinna, behaving much like the chaste girls in 4.71, is castigated for his indecision over a loan or gift in similar terms in 7.43. A convenient pun on the word *dare* allows Martial to bring the sexual and the financial incarnations of this figure together, and a nameless old woman who wants to be fucked for free is told "that's absurd, you want to 'give' and not to give" (*res perridicula est: vis dare nec dare vis*, 7.75.2). Generosity in this context is not always laudable, and in 2.56 Gallus is reassured that the rumors about his wife's greed are baseless: "She doesn't take at all. What then does she do? She gives." Reversing the gender positions, Martial turns the same joke on himself when he protests to the grasping Atticilla that he has given her all she asked for and more: "Whoever refuses nothing, Atticilla, is a fellator" (*quisquis nil negat, Atticille, fellat*, 12.91.4; cf. 4.12). Again the sexual and the financial are conflated, this time with a play on *negare*. In the light of this we might consider an alternative interpretation of the punch line of 4.71. The chaste girl doesn't refuse, but doesn't offer it for free, either, which is how she manages to stay chaste (for a similar idea, see 3.54). This interpretation would be supported if we read 4.71 not with the poem that refers to it (4.81) but instead with the poem that follows it, which features a very different kind of relationship:

> Exigis ut donem nostros tibi, Quinte, libellos.
> non habeo, sed habet bibliopola Tryphon.

"aes dabo pro nugis et emam tua carmina sanus?
non" inquis "faciam tam fatue." nec ego. (4.72)

> You demand that I make you a gift of my books, Quintus. I
> don't have any, but the bookseller Tryphon does. "Shall I give
> money for trifles and would I be sane to *buy* your books? I
> won't be so idiotic," you say. Neither, Quintus, will I.

In effect, Quintus can have Martial's books, but not for free. The
parallel between *non habeo sed habet bibliopola* and "non dat, non
tamen illa negat" suggests that, if we apply 4.72 to 4.71, the chaste
girl neither refuses sex nor gives it away free.[4] In order to solve the
riddle of 4.71 we must pass from one sense of *dare* to another: according to one system, giving is opposed to refusing, whereas according to the other, it is opposed to selling. Like the "chaste" girls
of Rome, Martial is readily available, but not necessarily for free.
Another reason to connect these two juxtaposed poems is that 4.72
also features a quibble on "giving," since what Quintus really wants
is a dedication (cf. *cui dono . . .?* Catullus c. 1.1), but Martial pretends not to understand and takes him literally.[5] But if the riposte
to Quintus helps to solve the riddle of the previous poem, then what
does the model of venal sex do for the relation between Quintus and
Martial? With this juxtaposition, Martial takes up the dominant
metaphor of Horace's envoi to *Epistles* 1 (1.20), in which the book is
eager, against the poet's wishes, to be off and prostitute itself at the
booksellers'. But in Martial it is not the reluctance to make public
what is private that has the poet reaching for the sexual analogy.
Quintus is presuming on a friendship that the poet does not acknowledge, and the poet, neither refusing nor giving, maintains his
"chastity." In fact, Martial manages to make Quintus the one who
mentions money, though whether he will "give" (dedicate) his book
to Quintus depends on whether Quintus will give money for trifles.
Juxtaposed to a poem about the chastity of women who neither give
nor refuse, this too becomes a poem about ambiguous, even disingenuous, relationships. It is as though Martial had heard the anxiety in Horace's figure of prostitution, and instead of warding it off
had diverted it into a subtle commentary on the maneuverings of

literary patronage. Martial's performance flaunts a lack of anxiety that puts him at the opposite pole to his contemporary Pliny, always concerned to scotch possible misinterpretations of his behavior. Pliny, for instance, is anxious that if he recites his own work he will seem a creditor, not a listener, at the recitations of others, storing up obligations to be cashed in when his own turn comes to recite (1.13.6). The financial metaphor is to be disclaimed at all costs. Martial's juxtapository wit often has an irreverent edge, but he is not shy of turning this irreverence on himself, since he has no image to protect. This same lack of anxiety about his image characterizes Martial's juxtaposition of mockery and flattery, as we shall see.

## PRAISE AND BLAME

The most common principle of *variatio* in Martial is polarity. Book 14 (*Apophoreta*), for instance, is explicitly constructed as an alternation between rich and poor (*divitis alternas et pauperis accipe sortes*, 14.5).[6] Martial likes to juxtapose polar statuses, but he also likes to cast *himself* alternately in dominant and subordinate positions. One aspect of this would be the alternation between Martial the poet of satire and invective and Martial the panegyrist. There is nothing necessarily contradictory about this combination. For one thing, the judicious mixing of flattery and abuse was a skill that distinguished the welcome dinner guest at the tables of the rich and powerful.[7] More broadly, in the ancient world (and perhaps not only there) it was an essential corollary of the fact that certain people were to be praised that others should be blamed. The poet of invective and the panegyrist may be in opposite positions relative to their objects, but the activities are complementary. To praise everybody is not to praise anyone, as Martial himself points out (12.80), and besides, no ancient Roman could tolerate unbroken praise of others. We readers are prompted to recognize our own envy in a poem that explicitly comments on the reception of its panegyrical predecessor.[8] Epigram 1.40, which follows a poem of fulsome praise for Decianus, turns on the jealous reader who takes no pleasure in the praise of another (*Qui ducis vultus et non legis ista libenter, / omnibus invideas, livide, nemo tibi*).[9] Perhaps it is the humiliation of the putatively envious reader which helps *us* to swallow the praise of Decianus, in which case we are not so far removed from that envious reader ourselves. Martial leaves it to us to identify (with?) the *lividus.*

Sometimes praise emerges from blame in a single poem, and Martial tucks in a compliment to a friend while lambasting an enemy.[10] It is part of the wit of these poems that we have to reassess our assumption about the poem's subject. "You'll never get a good word out of X, even if you are as virtuous as Y, as clever as Z . . ." (5.28); "Malisianus is as impudent as if he were to . . . recite elegiacs in the house of Stella" (4.6). Such supportive relations between praise and blame occur between poems as well. For an obviously complementary pair, we could take 8.78 and 8.79. The first celebrates the splendor of Stella's games for the emperor's triumphant return from the Sarmatian war: the gods themselves would have been happy to receive such a celebration, but all the splendors of the games were surpassed by the honor of having Caesar himself as spectator (*omnia sed, Caesar, tanto superantur honore, / quod spectatorem te tua laurus habet,* 8.78.15–16). The following poem accuses Fabulla of making herself beautiful by surrounding herself with old and ugly friends (*Omnis aut vetulas habes amicas / aut turpis vetulisque foediores,* 8.79.1–2). The emphatic *omnia* that introduces the last couplet of 8.78 is picked up by the *omnis* with which 8.79 opens. But this echo only accentuates the difference between these structurally analogous situations. Fabulla shines at the expense of her friends (*sic formosa, Fabulla, sic puella es,* 5), whereas Caesar and Stella mutually enhance each other's prestige. The greater the emperor appears, the greater those who are associated with him, which is quite the opposite of the way beauty works for Fabulla.[11]

While praise and blame can be seen as complementary activities that mutually support each other, the situation changes if we look more carefully at the forms in which they appear. A great many of the invective poems could more precisely be described as unmasking: "You see that man who poses as a Stoic *sapiens,* well really he . . ."; "Why does X do A? The real reason is . . ." Here we may see a tension, rather than a complementarity, between the hyperbolic encomiast and the suspicious debunker. How are these two aspects of the work to coexist in the mind of the reader, and do they undermine each other? Just how suspicious should we be? Suspicion, of course, is the stock-in-trade of the contemporary critic and subversiveness the prerequisite of critical respect. Nobody wants to work on a poet who can be described as a pusillanimous jester who upsets no one, as Bramble (1982.115) said of Martial. And indeed if Martial had wanted to be subversive in an environment as dangerous as that of Domitian's reign, then juxtaposition would be the most deniable way of going about it. Whether Martial deliberately indulges in hidden criticism of the emperor, or whether what could be taken as critical or irreverent is intended to be so taken, are thorny questions, which, in my opinion, cannot be answered.[12] Rather than focus narrowly on this unfruitful issue I would prefer, first of all, to examine the range of attitudes or responses that such juxtapositions might bring into play and, secondly, to examine how Martial's juxtapositions might serve to position the emperor in his world.

## IRREVERENCE AND THE EMPEROR

In the preface to Book 8 Martial rather neatly explains that, though this book is particularly assiduous with its *pietas* toward the emperor, he has varied the brew with some jests, so as not to overburden a modest emperor with his own praises. At the same time he protests that he has moderated the generic lewdness of the epigram because "only people purified by religious lustration should approach temples" (*non nisi religiosa purificatione lustratos accedere ad templa debere*).[13]

Book 8, like the similarly emperor-centric Book 5, is notable for its relative lack of obscenity.[14] But what of the jests that leaven the emperor's praise? How do they interact with the imperial panegyric? Let us take as an example the joke that interrupts the opening sequence of imperial panegyric in Book 5. It features Myrtale, who habitually stinks of wine and disguises the smell by chewing laurel.

> Fetere multo Myrtale solet vino,
> sed fallat ut nos, folia devorat lauri
> merumque cauta fronde, non aqua miscet.

> hanc tu rubentem prominentibus venis
> quotiens venire, Paule, videris contra,
> dicas licebit "Myrtale bibit laurum." (5.4)

Myrtale usually stinks of all the wine she's drunk. But to
fool us she wolfs down leaves of laurel and mixes her wine
not with water but the protective frond. So Paulus, whenever
you see her approaching, with red face and bulging veins,
you can say, "Myrtale has drunk laurel."

On one side of this squib is a poem on the visit to Rome by the
brother of the Dacian king, Decebalus: Degis congratulates himself on being able to come so close to the god whom his brother
must worship from afar. On the other side is a request to Sextus,
Domitian's librarian, who is greeted as "you who enjoy the god's
genius at close quarters" (*ingenio frueris qui propiore dei*, 5.5.2). Better to be close to the emperor than to the wine-bibbing Myrtale!
The theme of proximity, particularly pertinent to a court society,
pervades the opening panegyrical sequence of this book, and this
is not the only theme that links the Myrtale poem to the neighboring panegyrics.[15]

From the opening poem in which the book is sent off to Caesar,
residing in one of his villas, the poet's separation from the godly
Domitian is set against scenes of intimacy. Martial may not know
in which of the emperor's villas his book may reach him, but he
imagines the emperor enjoying intimate commerce with the "truth-
telling goddesses" (*veridicae . . . sorores*, 5.1.3) to whom he *teaches*
oracular responses. The second poem of the book ends with a cozy
scene in which the new book jokes with the master of the world
and he, in turn, reads it in the presence of Minerva; thanks to the
modesty of the book, he can do this without blushing. Degis, in 5.3,
contrasts his own closeness to the godly Domitian with his brother's separation. The librarian Sextus, addressee of 5.5, is close to the
emperor, but Martial himself doesn't aspire to have his own poems
located next to Domitian's in the library (that privilege belongs to
Vergil). In 5.6, Parthenius is asked to choose the right moment to
present his book to Domitian, since he of all people knows the emperor's private moods (9–11); but the emperor will ask for Martial's

*libellus* himself (18–19), recognizing that it is a work of literature, rather than a common petition (*libellus*).

Not only is Myrtale, in 5.4, someone you do *not* want to be close to, but the final joke about her laurel-chewing turns her into a comic version of the Delphic priestess undergoing the presence of Apollo, which parodies a theme of the imperial panegyric that surrounds it (cf. especially 5.1.3 and 5.2.7–8). The studied flattery of Martial's tableaux in which Domitian gives responses to the goddesses (5.1.3) and reads to Minerva (5.2.7–8) is matched by the mockery of the abundantly inspired "laurel-bibbing" Myrtale, whose ruddy complexion (4) recalls, and contrasts with, the unblushing decorousness of Domitian's intimacy with Minerva (*ore non rubenti*, 7).[16] We may feel that the dignity of the "proximity to a god" motif, applied to Domitian, has been compromised, but it is just as likely that the mocking of Myrtale enhances the praise of Domitian; that these two versions of the same thing mark the distance between high and low. Juxtaposition, which supplies no conjunctions, leaves it up to us to decide.

One of the consequences of Martial's juxtapositions is that praise and blame, or panegyric and invective, can seem to be two versions of the same thing. Martial ends his squib on Myrtale with the words "whenever you see Myrtale advancing on you, you may say [*dicas licebit*, 6] 'Myrtale has drunk laurel.'" Imperial panegyric, with its baroque compliments, extravagant figures of speech, and mythological paraphernalia, is also the realm of the "you may say," and Martial takes equal pleasure in the witty nonsincerity of the clever insult and the well-turned compliment.[17] On the one hand, the bizarre world of Myrtale drinking laurel; on the other hand (or is it?), the paradoxical world where Domitian inspires the oracles (5.1.3) and reads Martial to his friend Minerva (5.2.7–8). Courtliness and insult are both opposite and analogous.[18]

The nonsincerity of Martial's compliments and insults should be distinguished from insincerity, where we either cover up real feelings or profess to have feelings we don't, as well as from theatricality where, as Bartsch (1994) describes it, subordinates perform to a script as the superior watches, scrutinizes, and judges the convincingness of their performance. The nonsincerity of the "you could say" does not put real feelings at issue; instead, all concerned are involved in a conspiracy to enjoy a well-turned compliment, or insult.[19] As we move from mockery to flattery in Martial's books, we are asked to exercise a rapid switching of attitudes. The sceptic element of Martial's poetry demands that we be suspicious, constantly on the qui vive, and ready to unmask, deflate, and debunk; at the same time, we must be prepared to relax our suspicion, to indulge permissively and pleasurably in the hyperboles of flattery. It is often said, in a rather self-congratulatory way, that imperial panegyric is the aspect of Roman literary culture that is most difficult for us to appreciate, most alien to our tastes and experience, and it is certainly true that the hyperbolic deference of Martial's panegyric is hardly suited to the sensibilities of a democratic society.[20] But if we are imagining how we would feel about an epigram addressed to the president in which he dines with the gods, we are looking for the comparatum in the wrong places. Let me suggest a more appropriate analogy to the nonsincerity of Martial's panegyrico-scoptic world in the environment of advertising. Is there not a contemporary equivalent of the rapid switching of attitudes I have described in the ability of a now very sophisticated public to enjoy advertisements which invite us to congratulate ourselves on belonging to the circle of the nonduped? "Buy me—I'll change your life" declares an ad for a London department store during the post-Christmas sales. We will buy this product, so the logic of the ad goes, because we don't "buy" ads, or because it pleases us, now, to "buy" this one, suspending our disbelief in the promise of consumerism even as we congratulate ourselves on that same disbelief.

The arbitrariness of whether we choose to "buy it" or not is thrust in our face by the following juxtaposition from Book 6.

> Iurat capillos esse, quos emit, suos
> Fabulla: +numquid ergo, Paule, peierat?+[21] (6.12)

> Fabulla swears that the hair she buys is her own. Is she then perjured, Paulus?

> Quis te Phidiaco formatam, Iulia, caelo,
>     vel quis Palladiae non putet artis opus?
> candida non tacita respondet imagine lygdos
>     et placido fulget in ore decor.
> ludit Acidalio, sed non manus aspera, nodo,
>     quem rapuit collo, parve Cupide, tuo.
> ut Martis revocetur amor summique Tonantis
>     a te Iuno petat ceston et ipsa Venus. (6.13)

Julia, who wouldn't think you were shaped by the chisel of Phidias, or the work of Athena's art? The white Lygdian marble answers me with an image that speaks, and beauty shines in your calm visage. She plays, but her hand is not hard, with the Acidalian girdle, which she took from your neck, little Cupid. If the love of Mars and that of the supreme thunderer are to be won back, let Juno, and Venus herself, ask for your *cestos* ("bra").

The elaboration of 6.13 pits itself against the insinuating and deadly brevity of 6.12. We cannot help but notice, and revel in, the expansive volubility of the panegyrical, its cavalier dismissal of suspicion, and its reckless artificiality. The crucial interrogatives that characterize both poems' address (*numquid* in 6.12; *quis . . . non* in 6.13) measure the thickness of the wall between them, the radical switch of attitudes they require of us. Fabulla's claim bounces back to her off the poet's deadpan sarcasm, whereas Julia receives an unsolicited confirmation of a boast her statue seems to imply. The echo of the aspirated *p*'s of 6.13's first line (*Phidiaco, formatam*) in the unaspirated *p*'s of the second (*Palladiae, putet, opus*) emphasizes the satisfying responsiveness of the first couplet. By contrast the two lines of 6.12 are effective because they stop short, leaving us to complete the thought.

Paradoxically, the very comparability of the poems, the fact that we can see connections between them, enhances the deliberate shift in attitude we must make in moving between them. The final conceit of 6.13, on Domitian's deified niece Julia, has Martial reformulating a familiar literary scene in typical fashion: Hera borrowed the *cestos* from Aphrodite to seduce Zeus in the Homeric *Dios Apate* (*Iliad* 14); now, both Hera *and* Aphrodite must borrow

Julia's *cestos* if they would deceive their husbands again. This high-cultural exchange of symbolic beauty aids between women of the highest standing contrasts with the disguised and disavowed purchase by Fabulla of another woman's hair. Fabulla's hair is her own in a manner of speaking, and therein lies the disgrace, but there seems to be no such problem with the circulation of the talismanic *cestos*. In one case it is complimentary, and in another accusatory, to say that a woman's beauty is enhanced by something that is not her own. These are two sides of the same coin, two reflections of a world in which the emperor can give a freedman the insignia of a knight or declare a man to be father of three by imperial fiat. The burlesque version of the Julia poem in the Fabulla squib reminds us of the attitudes we must suspend in order to participate in the world of courtly compliment.

In the case of Julia's statue, artificiality is positively flaunted: as a statue, Julia may be more artificial than Fabulla with her wig, but she's "pretty as a picture" and that's high praise. However, in the following four lines the opposite point is made, of the statue: the thrice repeated *non* protests, against an imaginary objection, that the statue pulls off its deception (as Fabulla does not); it is like Julia and, what's more, it's good enough to be the real thing, not just a Roman copy (*Phidiaco, Palladiae artis*). Whether Julia is like a statue or the statue is like her, in her case it is good *not* to appear to be what you are (*Julia* could be a statue; *it* could be flesh). This parade of artifice is underlined by the pun on *caelo* ("chisel," but also "heaven") in the first line: Julia's divinization is a matter of the sculptor's art, and the heaven she inhabits is "Phidian." Unlike the play on *suus* in the previous poem, this is no debunking pun, but simply another component of the artifice which enhances Julia's status. The interrogatives (*numquid . . . ? Quis . . . non?*) remind us of our own part in the effectiveness of praise or blame. We must play the appropriate role in relation to the poet's "couldn't you say?"

The five poems which follow this pair diffract its themes through a variety of genres. Not only do they continue the contrast between the suspicious poet of invective and the expansive panegyrist, but they embed this in a metapoetic reflection on the epigram form.

Versus scribere posse te disertos
adfirmas, Laberi: quid ergo non vis?
versus scribere qui potest disertos,
non scribat, Laberi, virum putabo. (6.14)

You claim, Laberius, that you can write elegant verses: so
why do you not want to? If a person who can write elegant
verses doesn't write them, I'll think he's a real man.

Dum Phaethontea formica vagatur in umbra,
implicuit tenuem sucina gutta feram.
sic modo quae fuerat vita contempta manente,
funeribus facta est nunc pretiosa suis. (6.15)

While an ant wandered in the shade of Phaethon's tree, a
sticky drop (of amber) enfolded the little creature. So the being that was just now despised while life remained has now
been made valuable by its death.

Tu qui falce viros terres et pene cinaedos,
iugera sepositi pauca tuere soli.
sic tua non intrent vetuli pomaria fures,
sed puer aut longis pulchra puella comis. (6.16)

You who terrorize men with your sickle and pathics with
your penis, guard these meager acres of secluded soil. So
may no old thieves enter your orchards, but a boy or a girl
with long hair.

Cinnam, Cinname, te iubes vocari.
non est hic, rogo, Cinna, barbarismus?
tu si Furius ante dictus esses,
Fur ista ratione dicereris. (6.17)

You tell us, Cinnamus, to call you Cinna. I ask you, Cinna,
is this not a barbarism? If your name had originally been

Furius, you would by that reasoning now be called Fur (Thief).

------

> Sancta Salonini terris requiescit Hiberis,
>     qua melior Stygias non videt umbra domos.
> sed lugere nefas: nam qui te, Prisce, reliquit,
>     vivit qua voluit vivere parte magis. (6.18)

The sacred shade of Saloninus rests in Spanish earth. No better sees the halls of Styx. But it is wrong to grieve: for, Priscus. he who left you lives on in the part of him he would most wish.

Martial's ant in amber (6.15) is usually taken as an emblem of his genre: not only does it recall the wonders of Hellenistic epideictic epigram, but this miniature reflection of the story of Phaethon, expressed with comically grandiose periphrasis, makes an apt figure for the genre that locates itself at the opposite end of the generic spectrum to epic: the ant wanders in the shade, whereas Phaethon drives headlong with the chariot of the sun. The *objet* itself, which makes precious what is insignificant, might stand for the aspiration of the genre, and certainly the theme of life and/in death alludes to its epitaphic associations.[22] But this condensation of the epigram genre itself is embedded in a sequence of poems which refracts, elaborates, and bring to life its implications.

Preceding the ant in amber is the squib on Laberius, a man who claims to be a poet but never puts himself to the test. He is an antitype of Phaethon, whose story of overreaching and tragedy is summoned up by the lumbering adjective with which the ant poem begins (*Phaethontea*, 15.1). But Laberius fails even to be the inversion of Phaethon, and in the second half of that poem Martial holds up for our contemplation and wonder the true inversion: the man who *can* write but chooses not to. Laberius produces no eloquent verses himself, but at least he occasions them, and, like the ant who becomes a precious object in death, he is nicely skewered in Martial's poem. So the ant in amber is made to represent the way the sceptic poem makes a silk purse of a sow's ear. In 6.16 Priapus is introduced to figure a different aspect of the sceptic genre. Richlin (1992) has shown how the satirist casts himself as the ithyphallic scourge of thieves, and this Priapean poem emphasizes the potential pleasures of the guardian god's revenge. The *sic* that announced the transformation of the straying ant in 6.15 (sic *modo quae fuerat . . . nunc*) now articulates a wish that Priapus may only have to exercise his duty on attractive girls and boys (sic *tua non intrent . . . sed*)—Priapus's custodial duties are their own reward! In isolation, each of these two poems is a simple genre piece; an epideictic epigram is followed by a Priapean, and we might think nothing more of it. But in the environment that Martial has given them, each points to a different aspect of Martial's poetic activity: on the one hand, the satisfaction of the object produced and on the other the pleasures of aggression itself.

That Priapus, scourge of thieves, should be a figure for the sceptic poet is confirmed by the poem which follows, in which Martial unmasks Cinnamus as a thief. The *Furius/Fur* joke is not just a clever analogy, for Cinnamus's shortened name steals something to which he is not entitled, namely freeborn status (normally, a freed slave would retain his slave name as a *cognomen*). Since this theft of a syllable is castigated by Martial as a *barbarismus*, a category of grammatical error (Quintilian *Inst. Or.* 1.5.10), Cinnamus is tied to his condition by an unbreakable chain: his change of name merely confirms his status as a (barbarian) slave.[23] Priapus's victims trespass in order to thieve, while Martial's Cinnamus is a man whose theft constitutes an act of trespass, for by stealing a syllable from his name he lays claim to a freeborn status to which he is not entitled.

Characteristically, Martial follows this sceptic epigram with a flattering celebration of two friends, whose conceit recalls the very procedure that had been mocked in the previous poem. Saloninus's death is not to be mourned, for he survives in his friend Priscus, living on as the part of himself he would most wish to be. But didn't Cinnamus aspire to live on as a part of himself too? The analogy is, perhaps, not as metaphysical as it seems—Farouk Grewing suggests that Saloninus is also a freedman.[24] At any rate, as Saloninus is to Priscus, so Cinnamus is to Cinna, the one name being foreign and the other impeccably Roman. Saloninus achieves what Cinna failed to bring off, and what Saloninus achieves is not unlike the elevation accorded to the ant that strays into amber, and so becomes more precious in its death.

This particularly dense sequence of interrelated but heterogeneous poems thrusts in our face the arbitrary power of the poet to interpret a given figure of speech positively or negatively. The phenomenon of people who manage, or pretend, to be something other than themselves comes in satiric and panegyrical versions. It is introduced by Fabulla, who provides Martial with the opportunity for one of his favorite wordplays, on *suus*.[25] The other butts are Laberius (6.14), who is not the poet he claims to be, and Cinnamus, whose name is Cinna only by the theft of a syllable (6.17). The despised ant is transformed into a valuable object on its death in 6.15, but something similar is the case with the objects of the two panegyrical poems: Iulia is preserved, like the ant, as a durable object (6.13) and Saloninus (6.18) survives in his friend Priscus, the part of him he would most want to be.

## JUXTAPOSITION AND THE STRUCTURE OF MARTIAL'S SOCIAL WORLD

Invective and flattery are not only two opposed but analogous manners of speaking, they also position the poet quite differently in relation to his world. Not infrequently Martial juxtaposes two poems that cast him in a superior and an inferior position respectively: the satirist and the panegyrist rub shoulders, but with a particular emphasis on the relative social and status positions of speaker and addressee.[26] Poems 11.56 and 11.57 provide a typical example. The first is a satirical poem about an impoverished Stoic with a generic name, the second a flattering invitation poem addressed to a rich patron. So: rich and poor, high and low, flattery and insult, anonymous (or generically identified) and named. Very much the kind of *variatio* we would expect.[27]

> Quod nimium mortem, Chaeremon Stoice, laudas,
>     vis animum mirer suspiciamque tuum?

hanc tibi virtutem fracta facit urceus ansa,
    et tristis nullo qui tepet igne focus
........................................
rebus in angustis facile est contemnere vitam:
    fortiter ille facit qui miser esse potest. (11.56.1–4, 15–16)

Because you praise death endlessly, Stoic Chaeremon, do
you expect me to wonder at your courage and respect it?
This virtue of yours is the product of a jug with a broken
handle and a sad hearth warmed by no fire. . . . In straight-
ened circumstances it's easy to despise life: he is brave who
can endure misery.

Miraris docto quod carmina mitto, Severe,
    ad cenam cum te, docte Severe, vocem?
Iuppiter ambrosia satur est et nectare vivit;
    nos tamen exta Iovi cruda merumque damus.
omnia cum tibi sint dono concessa deorum
    si quod habes non vis, ergo quid accipies? (11.57)

You wonder that I send you poetry, poet Severus, when I invite you to dinner? Jupiter is stuffed with ambrosia and lives
on nectar, and yet we give him raw entrails and unmixed
wine. Since, by the gift of the gods, all things are given to
you, if you then don't want what you already have, what will
you accept?

Here, as elsewhere, Martial plays on the names in these juxtaposed
poems.[28] The grim Stoic has a name that quite inappropriately suggests rejoicing; it is the cultured diner, Severus, who has the "Stoic"
name, again, quite inappropriately.[29] The contrast between the high
life and beggary is elaborated at some length in 11.56.3–12, where
Martial juxtaposes the details of Chaeremon's wretched life with
those of a life of luxury. This is condensed in 11.57 into the paradox
that we give Jupiter raw offal and undiluted wine even though he
dines on ambrosia and nectar (3–4). Martial neatly uses the analogy
with which he justifies his poetic invitation to allude to the invitation itself, for Severus, like Jupiter, is invited to dinner. Thematically,

these poems are by no means unique in the corpus. From the introduction of Cato in the preface to Book 1, Stoics have been cast as prime antagonists to Martial and, starting with 1.8, Martial has ostentatiously refused to be impressed by Stoic suicide. It is also common for Martial to allude to his patrons' own poetic practices, even suggesting that he is carrying coals to Newcastle in writing poems for them (7.42). These, then, are themes that are likely to meet, but what happens when they do?[30] The repetition of the verb *miror* in the first couplet of each poem might be a place to start:

> Quod nimium mortem, Chaeremon Stoice, laudas,
>  vis animum *mirer* suspiciamque tuum? (11.56.1–2)

> *Miraris* docto quod carmina mitto, Severe,
>  ad cenam cum te, docte Severe, vocem . . . (11.57.1–2)

"You expect me to wonder at you, when . . ." and "You wonder that I . . ." Is this merely a verbal echo? Certainly the word that is echoed is relevant to the Stoicism of Chaeremon, and both poems respect the injunction *nil admirari*. Beyond this, we might say that the Martial who marks his superiority in the first poem by withholding his admiration is cast in a subservient position in the next, where Severus wonders at his gall. But the reversal of Martial's position is accompanied by a surprising analogy between the miserable Chaeremon and the richly blessed Severus. "You are forced to despise life by your poverty (and you can't expect me to admire you for that)" / "I am forced by your blessings to give you what you already have (and you can't wonder at that)." We will later be looking at some other ironies of power, other points where highest and lowest converge in Martial's world, but before we get to that we must introduce a figure who always complicates power relations in the Roman world, namely the slave.

## SLAVERY

The contrast between the impoverished philosopher who has nothing and the glorious patron who has everything in 11.56 and 11.57 is smudged in the next poem by a third possibility, the slave-favorite (*delicatus*) who has everything *and* nothing.

> Cum me velle vides tentumque, Telesphore, sentis,
> magna rogas—puta me velle negare: licet?—
> et nisi iuratus dixi "dabo," subtrahis illas,
> permittunt in me quae tibi multa, natis. (11.58.1–4)

> When you see that I want it, Telesphorus, and that I'm stiff,
> you make demands—suppose I want to deny you, could I?
> And until I've promised and said "I'll give," you deny me
> those buttocks which give you power over me.

This third, paradoxical, position is emblematic of that human exception, the slave, and it complicates the opposition between Chaeremon and Severus. Martial goes on to tell Telesphorus that once he has satisfied his lust he will tell the slave to "go to hell" (12): the master's promise, extorted when he is vulnerable, means nothing, since he had no choice.[31] In this, it is like the Stoic's empty praise of death. But how does this emphasis on empty speech acts reflect on the praise of Severus? Again, if the fragility of the Stoic's high-mindedness is comparable to the fragility of the sway exerted over his master by the boy's attractions, what of Severus's status as poet? Severus is *doctus* largely because he is called *doctus* in a poem. The final word of 11.57.2, *vocem*, coming hard on the heels of *docte Severe*, reminds us, if only subliminally, that Martial *calls* Severus *doctus*. Does he inhabit this category as tenuously as Telesphorus does that of "master" and as temporarily as Martial does the role of "slave of love"? Are relations between patron and poet as fragile as those between slave and master, their fictions equally artificial?

Telesphorus complicates the opposition between powerful and powerless by his very presence, and, more generally, the peculiar form of the presence of slaves is very relevant to the issues of this chapter. Constantly next to the free, slaves fade in and out of visibility, a third presence ambiguously situated with respect to the commerce between the free. Whether the world of slaves, and of relations with slaves, is sealed off from relations between the free or not is a moot point.[32] There is reason to believe that Martial was aware of this ambiguity, which he dramatizes in the juxtaposition of two poems from his twelfth and last book (12.96 and 12.97), both of which take up the subject of the married man who has sex with his slave boys.

The first poem, addressed to a wife, tells her to stop worrying. Her husband's dalliances with slave boys are insignificant, and can be no threat to her. The second poem is addressed to a husband, who is roundly condemned for neglecting his lovely wife in favor of slave boys. Here is the first one:

> Cum tibi nota tui sit vita fidesque mariti
>     nec premet ulla tuos sollicitetve toros,
> quid quasi paelicibus torqueris inepta ministris,
>     in quibus et brevis est et fugitiva Venus?
> plus tibi quam domino pueros praestare probabo:
>     hi faciunt ut sis femina sola viro;
> hi dant quod non vis uxor dare. "do tamen," inquis,
>     "ne vagus a thalamis coniugis erret amor."
> non eadem res est: Chiam volo, nolo mariscam:
>     ne dubites quae sit Chia, marisca tua est.
> scire suos fines matrona et femina debet:
>     cede sua pueris, utere parte tua. (12.96)

Since the life and fidelity of your husband are known to you, and no woman crowds or troubles your bed, why are you foolishly tormented by slave boy "mistresses," with whom sex is a brief and fleeting pleasure? I'll prove that these boys give more to you than to your husband: they guarantee that you are the only woman for your husband; they give what you as a wife don't want to give. "But I do give it" you say, "so that the love of my husband shouldn't go straying from the bedchamber." It's not the same thing: I want a Chian fig, not a big one: in case you are in doubt as to which is the Chian, yours is the big one. A *matrona* and woman should know her limits: leave their part to the boys; use your own.

The slaves are doing the wife a favor by distracting her husband from infidelities with women, who might truly be rivals. Martial's reassurance is cast in terms of a familiar misogynistic theme, which serves to insulate the marriage from the husband's straying: the same body part is not in fact the same, and the wife could not offer her husband what the slave boys do (*non eadem res est*, 9).[33] Complementarity and boundaries are stressed and the wife is reassured that the joy of sex with slave boys is *fugitiva*, a word that turns the potential recalcitrance of slaves (*fugitivi* are runaways) into a figure for their harmlessness. Contrast that with the next poem:

> Uxor cum tibi sit puella qualem
> votis vix petat improbis maritus,
> dives, nobilis, erudita, casta,
> rumpis, Basse, latus, sed in comatis,
> uxoris tibi dote quos parasti.
> et sic ad dominam reversa languet
> multis mentula milibus redempta;
> ut nec vocibus excitata blandis
> molli pollice nec rogata surgat.
> sit tandem pudor aut eamus in ius.
> non est haec tua, Basse: vendidisti. (12.97)

> Although you have a young wife such as a husband would scarcely wish for in his wilder dreams—rich, noble, learned, chaste—you bust your loins, Bassus, but on long-haired boys, which you've acquired for yourself with your wife's dowry. And your dick, bought with all those thousands, comes back to its mistress flaccid. So it doesn't rise whether excited by coaxing words or at the request of a soft finger. Have some shame for once, or let us go to court. It's not yours, Bassus; you've sold it.

This poem flatly contradicts the previous one; not only is it no longer acceptable that the husband is amusing himself with slave boys, but relations between the free are now *permeated* by slavery rather than untouched by it. The last line has been variously translated as "She is not yours, Bassus, you've sold her" (Ker 1919 ) and "It (sc. *mentula*) is not yours, you've sold it" (Shackleton Bailey 1993). The second is likelier if one has to choose, but I think Martial encourages a double reading. Not only did Bassus sell his *mentula* when he married for money, but insofar as he uses his wife's dowry to buy boys who render him useless for her, he has, in a sense, sold *her*. Slavery proves that people can be bought and sold, and the consciousness of that fact contaminates relations between the free. The equivalent of the previous poem's *fugitiva* is *redempta*, another word that has special associations with slavery: on one reading of this word, Bassus's *mentula* has been "bought" (*redempta*, 7) by his wife's dowry, so it is not his to share with the boys. But *redimo* also means "release [buy back] from slavery," and Bassus's *mentula* might be said to have been bought back from "slavery" to his wife by the thousands that he has spent on boys; after all, she is referred to as *domina* (6). If the word *fugitiva* served to mark reassuringly the noncommunicating parallelism between wife and slaves (the husband's *fides* is not compromised by the fleeting pleasures of boys), *redempta* is the focal point of a crossing between marriage and slavery (the husband's penis, bought by his wife/mistress, is redeemed from slavery to her by intercourse with slaves).

Standing back a bit, one could posit a broad opposition between two ways that the relation between slaves and masters/mistresses might be imagined. In the first case, one might take slaves as a substitute humanity, facilitating for the free a set of relations that run parallel to those with their fellow free, and yet allow all manner of conveniences because this shadow humanity was not fully human. So, concubinage might substitute for marriage, *alumni* for children, *delicati* for lovers, and so on. Alternatively, one might look at this presence, and indeed some of the same aspects of it, as infiltrating the world of the free, complicating or contaminating it. This contradiction is central to Martial's treatment of slavery throughout his oeuvre. For instance, the indignities to which Martial is subjected in his persona of impoverished client struggling to survive are frequently characterized by metaphors from slavery.[34] But, if slavery provides the terms in which to cast everything that has gone wrong with relations between the free, slaves themselves often provide Martial with an arena of unsullied relations that are idealized as purely emotional, and of pleasures that are uncontaminated. In a long poem of mourning for the loss of his slave girl Erotion (5.37), for instance, Martial has a certain Paetus tell him that he should be ashamed of making such a fuss over a slave, given that Paetus himself has recently buried a wife who was noble, proud, and rich. What fortitude, Martial replies: "Paetus has inherited a million and he still lives on" (*quid esse nostro fortius potest Paeto? / ducenties accepit et tamen vivit*, 23–24; compare 12.75).

A particularly interesting case of a juxtaposition where relations with slaves inhabit a world set apart from the perversions of contemporary Rome is provided by 11.90 and 11.91. In the first of these Martial answers a critic, Chrestillus, who approves only of rough, archaic poems. Chrestillus cites approvingly Lucilius's epitaph for his slave Metrophanes, quoting a line which contains an archaic ("manly") elision of final *s* ("*Lucili columella hic situ' Metrophanes*," 4). Martial deftly confounds this ambitiously macho critic by concluding that he "certainly knows the flavor of cock." This move has very interesting implications for the positionality of the reader, but for our present purposes we should note that the *os impurum*, defiled by oral sex, hovers constantly over Martial's oeuvre.[35] An experienced reader of Martial will start to snigger at the mere mention of tongues, mouths, or lips. What, then, are we to make of the poem that follows, a very touching epitaph for a slave, Canace, who died of a wasting disease that attacked her face? In it, we find the following:[36]

> tristius est leto leti genus: horrida vultus
> abstulit et tenero sedit in ore lues,
> ipsaque crudeles ederunt oscula morbi
> nec data sunt nigris tota labella rogis.
> si tam praecipiti fuerant ventura volatu,
> debuerant alia fata venire via.
> sed mors vocis iter properavit cludere blandae,
> ne posset duras flectere lingua deas. (91.5–12)

Sadder than the death was the mode of death: a horrible wasting stole her face and settled on her tender mouth, and the cruel disease ate away her very kisses, preventing her lips from reaching the black pyre whole. If fate had to come in such hasty flight it should have come another way. But death hurried to close the passage of her sweet voice so that her tongue could not sway the hard goddesses.

One could almost say that Lucilius's "manly" elision of the *s* has materialized in the disease that elides Canace's face. Martial provides a more up-to-date version (not only metrically) of the genre represented by Lucilius's poem as a riposte to Chrestillus. But, astonishingly, the lavish description of Canace's defiled mouth follows hard on a poem that ends with a joke about oral sex. The final line of 11.91, with its collocation of "tongue" and "hard" (*ne posset duras flectere lingua deas*, 12), is particularly provocative in this context. Martial looks us in the face and dares us to snigger—and we don't. The idealized relationship between master and beloved slave inhabits a world that is free from the constant suspicion of double entendre haunting so much of Martial's poetry.[37] There is no more here than meets the eye, Martial tells us, nothing to unmask.[38] Martial's juxtapositions, as we have already seen, may demand a conscious and deliberate switch in attitudes. Here Martial pushes this to the limit, requiring of us the effort to put out of our mind what will inevitably intrude.

Relations with slaves are a crucial component of the network of power relations in Martial's world. Demeaning aspects of the client's relations with social superiors are frequently figured in terms of slavery, and this means that the domination of slaves may serve to balance the humiliations of client service.[39] This compensatory relation is common in Martial's juxtapositions. When Rusticus, whose name already marks him as a bumpkin, disapproves of Martial's beating of the cook, the poet responds with brutal wit (8.23):[40]

> Esse tibi videor saevus nimiumque gulosus,
>   qui propter cenam, Rustice, caedo cocum.
> si levis ista tibi flagrorum causa videtur,
>   ex qua vis causa vapulet ergo cocus?[41]

To you, Rusticus, I seem brutal and a bit of a glutton because I beat my chef when the meal is bad. If that seems to you a frivolous cause for whipping, then for what reason would you have me beat my chef?

The next poem (8.24) finds the poet in much less confident form, or so it seems at first:

Si quid forte petam timido gracilique libello,
  improba non fuerit si mea charta, dato.
et si non dederis, Caesar, permitte rogari:
  offendunt numquam tura precesque Iovem
qui fingit sacros auro vel marmore vultus,
  non facit ille deos: qui rogat, ille facit.

If I should happen to make a request in my timid, slim little
book, and if my page is not presumptuous, grant it. And if
you don't grant it, Caesar, allow yourself to be asked: incense
and prayer never offend Jupiter. The man who makes sacred
images from gold or marble, he's not the one who makes
gods. The one who petitions the gods, he makes them.

*Forte, timido,* and *gracili,* all in the first line, strike a very different note from the black humor of the previous poem. Martial has
slaves whom he is free to beat, but he also has "lords," the patrons
(*domini;* cf. 1.112, 2.68, 5.57) who expect slavish behavior of him, and
the "lord and master" (*dominus et deus*) of all, Domitian. In these
two poems Martial's sovereign and arbitrary power over the slave
compensates for the deference with which he addresses his petition
to the emperor.[42]

But there is more to it than that, for the contrast between these
poems is counterpointed by a surprising analogy. One could draw
this out by paraphrasing as follows: "If you think I'm greedy and
cruel because I beat the cook for a bad meal, then what would you
have me beat the cook for? After all, it's beatings that make a person
a slave, and beatings for bad cooking that identify a slave as a cook"
(23), and "Even if you don't grant my petition, Caesar, allow yourself to be asked. After all, it's being the object of prayer that makes
someone a god" (24). A slave is a human being who, by virtue of
how he or she is treated by "us," is less than a human being. An emperor is a human being who, by virtue of how we treat him, is more
than a human being (a god). Martial beats the slave *because* he's the
cook, and he petitions the emperor *so* he's a god. The phrase *permitte
rogari* (8.24.3) reminds us of what was said to the wealthy Severus: "If
you don't want what you already have, what then will you accept?"
(11.57.6, above). The social distance between speaker and addressee

obliges the superior as well as the inferior. If petitions, not statues, make a god, then this petition (*libellus*), which is circulated in a book (*libellus*), functions rather like a statue as well. A favorite pun on *libellus* (cf. 11.1.5) allows Martial to "epigrammatize" the topos that it is poets who ensure the reputation of the great. So the poem that at first seemed to present a stark contrast with the attitude of the previous poem turns out to be more equivocal, insofar as the poet can claim to have the whip hand when it comes to making the emperor what he is, as he did in the case of the slave. Martial draws the parallel between these two exceptional beings in each case through a point that revolves around a characteristically demystified view of the way things work. We will see that this is not the only occasion on which he will juxtapose emperor to slave.

## THE EMPEROR'S COUNTERPARTS

The emperor is human and more than human, the slave human and less than human. As *dominus* the emperor puts his subjects in the position of slaves, a position they can mitigate only by reminding themselves that they are masters of slaves themselves. But polarities attract, and between emperor and slave there are some striking similarities. As luxury items, slaves come wreathed in Greek mythology, which is so often the source of their names.[43] The emperor, too, is associated with the world of gods and goddesses. Rome's Joves and Ganymedes may be worlds apart, but they are similarly artificial creations, and both are subject to an admiring gaze, as our next pair of poems emphasizes. Poem 9.24 is the second of two consecutive poems addressed to a Carus, who has just won an olive wreath at Domitian's Alban games, held in honor of Minerva. Carus is displaying the wreath at his home on a bust of the emperor, to which, apparently, it flew of its own accord. Though the poem is addressed to Carus, there is, of course, a strong implication that Domitian is the "overreader."[44]

> Quis Palatinos imitatus imagine vultus
>     Phidiacum Latio marmore vicit ebur?
> haec mundi facies, haec sunt Iovis ora sereni:

> sic tonat ille deus cum sine nube tonat.
> non solam tribuit Pallas tibi, Care, coronam;
>   effigiem domini, quam colis, illa dedit. (9.24)

Who was it who produced a bust of the Palatine visage
which surpassed Phidian ivory with marble from Latium?
This is the face of heaven; this the expression of unclouded
Jupiter. This is how that god thunders when he thunders in a
cloudless sky. Pallas gave you not only a wreath, Carus; she
gave you an image of the Lord, which you worship.

In 9.25, the addressee, Afer, at first seems to be one of Martial's stingy
hosts, but since Martial is praising one of his prized possessions, the
poem may be panegyric and the complaint merely jocular.

> Dantem vina tuum quotiens aspeximus Hyllum,
>   lumine nos, Afer, turbidiore notas.
> quod, rogo, quod scelus est mollem spectare ministrum?
>   aspicimus solem, sidera, templa, deos. . . . (9.25.1–4)

Whenever we look at your Hyllus as he serves the wine, you
mark us, Afer, with a gloomier expression. What, I ask you,
is the crime in gazing at your pretty waiter? We look at the
sun, the stars, the temples, and the gods.

Both poems compliment their addressee on his possessions, but the
connections go deeper. The speaker of 9.24 is gazing at the bust of
the divine emperor; the speaker of 9.25, discouraged from gazing at
the slave boy, exclaims that he is free to gaze on the sun, the stars,
the temples, and the gods. Once the connection has been made between the gaze indulged and the gaze forbidden, we can contrast
the sunny countenance of the emperor (*sereni, sine nube*, 9.24.3–4)
with the cloudy (*turbidiore*, 9.25.2) expression of the grudging host,
and perhaps the emperor's divine aloofness with the slave's flirta-
tion.[45] Poem 9.24 ends with the word *dedit*, and an act of giving
that joins Minerva, emperor, Carus, and Martial;[46] 9.25 begins with
*dantem*, but it is a slave, not a god, who is giving, and the accusa-
tive prepares for him to become a bone of contention between host
and guest. So, in both poems, speaker and addressee meet over an

admired third party; in the one case they join in worship and in the other they clash over a jealously guarded possession.[47]

Once again, the human exceptions at either end of the social hierarchy prove to have something in common, for beautiful waiter and divine emperor, slave and master (*domini*, 9.24.6) alike are beings whose nature it is to be on display, and both should shine on all. One need only consider Statius's thank-you for an invitation to dinner at the palace (*Silvae* 4.2) to see that this is true for the emperor: "But not on the feast, not on Moorish wood propped on Indian supports, not on fleets of servants in serried ranks: on him, on him alone had I leisure avidly to gaze, tranquil in his expression, with serene majesty tempering his radiance and modestly dipping the standards of his eminence; yet the splendor that he tried to hide shone in his countenance . . . ," and so on, for nearly twenty lines. The emperor has become, in some respects, a magnificent object, like the slave boy. Accordingly, both emperor and slave are hedged around with mythological paraphernalia; if it is de rigueur to associate Domitian with Jove, Hyllus is just as predictably Ganymede (9.25.8), and of course his name is itself a mythological reference.[48] The crucial point about this pairing is that the status of the emperor as object of worship is paralleled with the objectification of the slave. Newlands (2001.274) comments on the Statian passage that "in *Silvae* 4.2 Statius does not perceive the emperor as a human being. Rather he views the emperor as a godlike statue, an object not of conversation but of the poet's gaze, and a figure whose face in its refulgent and ambiguous divinity ultimately excludes secure interpretation. But this is in itself unsettling." Martial follows his poem on Carus's statue of a godlike Domitian with one on a slave boy who *is* a topic of conversation and who serves to divert the unsettling quality of the emperor's presence into something more tractable.

As Statius's effusions attest, an invitation to dinner at the palace was not something to hide under a bushel, and a poem in the previous book suggests that Martial had enjoyed the Palatine visage at closer quarters. Celebrating the completion of the emperor's new palace in 8.39, Martial rejoices that the emperor is finally able to entertain in a space worthy of his hospitality:

> Qui Palatinae caperet convivia mensae
>    ambrosiasque dapes non erat ante locus:
> hic haurire decet sacrum, Germanice, nectar
>    et Ganymedea pocula mixta manu.
> esse velis oro serus conviva Tonantis:
>    at tu si properas, Iuppiter, ipse veni.

Before now there was no place that could hold the feasts and
the ambrosial fare of Palatine hospitality: here, Germanicus,
is a fit setting in which to quaff the sacred nectar and the
cups mixed by a Ganymede's hand. I beg you to choose to
be a late guest of the Thunderer, but if you, Jupiter, are in a
hurry, come yourself.

The following poem addresses a Priapus, warden of Martial's modest copse.

> Non horti neque palmitis beati
> sed rari nemoris, Priape, custos,
> ex quo natus es et potes renasci,
> furaces moneo manus repellas
> et silvam domini focis reserves:
> si defecerit haec, et ipse lignum es. (8.40)

Priapus, guardian of no garden or rich vineyard, but of a
sparse copse, from which you were born and can be reborn; I
ask you to ward off thieving hands and keep the wood for the
hearth of its master: if that gives out, you're wood yourself.

Once again, the dialogue between the two poems plays across a
comic contrast, between the two properties. Martial's own modest
circumstances are, absurdly, juxtaposed to the emperor's previous
lack of an appropriate banqueting hall. The climactic structure of
the poem of praise (*non erat ante . . . hic decet*, 8.39.2–3) is matched
by the bathetic gesture of the next (*non horti . . . sed rari nemoris*,
8.40.1–2). But Martial's final threat to his Priapus casts the poet
as lord of his domain and master of reality, all-powerful as the
emperor. A more explicit parallel is drawn between Jupiter and
Priapus by the *ipse* in the final line of both poems. The panegyrist's
breezy and irreverent exaggeration in 8.39 (*ipse veni*, 6) focuses on

that *ipse* which, in the following poem, reminds the Priapus that he is as good for burning as the wood he guards (*ipse lignum es*, 8.40.6). Priapus's divinity is of perishable material: promoted from wood destined for burning to become the tutelary divinity of the copse itself, he is a god to serve a purpose. Should he fail to fulfill that purpose he can be demoted again. Jupiter, too, becomes a god to serve a purpose, as he is brought down to earth in order to elevate Domitian.

Martial subjects the Olympian divinity to much the same instrumentalization as he does the rustic god. But what about the two main figures, emperor and Priapus? On the face of it, they are poles apart: while he threatens Priapus with a dissolution that would return him to mere material, Martial deprecates the death of Domitian, which will make *him* a god. And yet, the juxtaposition of these two poems reminds us that the divinity of the emperor is as factitious as that of "Priapus," composed as it is of the flattery of his subjects.[49] As Martial has put it earlier in this same book, in fact a mere fifteen poems earlier, "The one who petitions (the emperor) makes him a god." Furthermore, just as "Priapus" is a name that can be transferred to other instantiations, as Martial reminds his scarecrow, so is "Caesar" ("Caesar is dead; long live the Caesar").

In Martial's books, the emperor finds himself next to a range of figures who turn out to share some characteristic with this human exception. For the most part, these figures are themselves exceptional, the slave being a stark example. To the slave and the slave/god Priapus we can add other figures who are exceptional in quite different ways. The emperor is not only a god, he is also a reader, albeit a very special kind of reader. Martial's *lector* is also a special kind of reader, constituting a category as novel and unorthodox as that of emperor. We will see in the next chapter that emperor and *lector* occupy symmetrical and analogous positions in Martial's world and that each provides a means of understanding the other, a possibility that is realized by strategic juxtapositions. But within the world of poetry, whose studied artificiality is governed by the arbitrary fiat of the poet's word, it is not surprisingly the poet who comes closest to the power of the emperor, as we see in a group of three poems that closes Book 2. In the first, Martial asks the emperor to grant him the *ius trium liberorum*, which, he tells us in the following poem, was granted.[50]

> Rerum certa salus, terrarum gloria, Caesar,
>     sospite quo magnos credimus esse deos,
> si festinatis totiens tibi lecta libellis
>     detinuere oculos carmina nostra tuos,
> quod fortuna vetat fieri, permitte videri,
>     natorum genitor credar ut esse trium.
> haec, si displicui, fuerint solacia nobis;
>     haec fuerint nobis praemia, si placui. (2.91)

Caesar, guarantor of the world's salvation, glory of the earth, whose safety confirms our belief in the gods, if my poems collected so often in hurried books have detained your glance, permit that what fortune forbids to happen should seem to be, namely that I should be believed to be the father of three children. Let this be my consolation if I have displeased and this my prize if I have pleased.

---

> Natorum mihi ius trium roganti
> Musarum pretium dedit mearum
> solus qui poterat. valebis, uxor.
> non debet domini perire munus. (2.92)

He who alone had the power gave me the right of three children when I asked for it, as a reward for my poetry. Goodbye, wife. The lord's gift should not be wasted.

It can hardly be a coincidence that Martial is asking for the "right of *three* children" at the end of the *second* book, especially since he is making this request on the basis of his poetry (*si . . . detinuere oculos carmina nostra tuos*); the next book will be his third "child."[51] The two poems on the *ius* requested and granted are followed by the closing poem of the book:

> "Primus ubi est," inquis, "cum sit liber iste secundus?'
>     quid faciam si plus ille pudoris habet?

tu tamen hunc fieri si mavis, Regule, primum,
  unum de titulo tollere iota potes. (2.93)

"Where is the first book," you say, "if this is the second?"
What am I to do if the other is more shy? But, Regulus, if
you prefer this to be the first, you can take one iota from
the title.

The emperor can make three from none (if this is the third child,
where is the second?) and Regulus, little king that he is, can turn
second into first, exercising, with Martial's permission, the same
power over appearance that is credited to the emperor (*quod fortuna vetat fieri, permitte videri*, 2.91.5). The first poem of this group
(2.91) draws a characteristic analogy between the flattery Martial
bestows on the emperor and the honor the emperor is to bestow on
him. In the first pentameter, Caesar is the world's sure salvation and
if he is safe we *believe* there are gods (*sospite quo magnos* credimus
*esse deos*, 2);[52] the third pentameter requests of the emperor that
Martial should be *believed* to be the father of three (*natorum geni-
tor credar ut esse trium*, 6). Are these two beliefs equally arbitrary,
equally disingenuous? Poem 2.92 proceeds to make brilliant play
with the artificiality of the situation, and, characteristically, social
subordination is compensated by gender domination as Martial
cracks one of his cleverest "take my wife" jokes.[53] If the right of
*three* is to be granted by the only *one* who can, then there mustn't
be *two*, so "goodbye wife, the emperor's gift must not be wasted."[54]
The book's final poem is also about a gift. Regulus receives the second book, but asks why he didn't get the first. In a sense, the gift
of the second book only reminds him of what he did not receive
before.[55] So Martial needs to come up with the first if his gift of the
second is not to go to waste (*non debet . . . perire munus*, 2.92.4), and
he does so not by adding but by subtracting, just as he did in the
previous poem: iota must go the way of wife.

In this terminal sequence to Book 2 (91, 92, and 93), Martial plays
with the numbers 1, 2, and 3, linking the emperor's power over appearance to his own. The *ius trium liberorum* is drawn into Martial's
construction of his own oeuvre, which is entirely appropriate given

that the request is made on the basis of his poetry. This juxtaposition takes us back to the drunken Myrtale and Martial's assimilation of panegyric to insult as forms of the "you may say." Here Martial implicitly assimilates to each other various forms of power over seeming: what his subjects believe of the emperor (*credimus*, 91.2), what the emperor makes others believe of Martial (*credar*, 91.6); what the emperor allows to seem to be the case (*quod fortuna vetat fieri, permitte videri*, 91.5) and what Martial empowers the reader to make of his oeuvre (*tu tamen hunc fieri si mavis, Regule, primum*, 93.3). Add to this the almost metaphysical conceit of the two gifts preserved by subtraction (92 and 93) and we are left with the impression of a poet drawing attention to the arbitrary power of speech to create new realities. The emperor and the poet are not only analogs in this respect, they mutually support each other.

# CHAPTER·FIVE

# THE·SOCIETY·OF·THE·BOOK

This necessity of self-prostitution on the market before an anonymous public induced the author to have intensive contact with the recipient of the work, and vice versa, leading to a spiritual community created by the book.   R. WITTMANN, *on the eighteenth-century reading revolution*

If I prefer to write what pleases, though I could write serious poetry, you are the cause of that, my friend, the reader (*Seria cum possim, quod delectantia malo / scribere tu causa es, lector amice, mihi*).   MARTIAL 5.16.1–2

It is a long way from Martial in the first century AD to what has been described as the reading revolution of the eighteenth century, but in any history of the notion of a reading public, particularly as it concerns the "community created by the book," Martial would play a prominent role. Ovid may have been the first ancient poet to address himself to the reader, but it was Martial who made the anonymous reader integral to his work.[1] In this chapter I will look at the book of epigrams not from the perspective of its internal relations but from that of its consumption. I will argue that the consumption of the book creates its own virtual society and that the peculiar status of the anonymous reader prompts Martial to imagine a particularly complex "society of the book" composed of multiple interlocking relationships.

The idea of an unknown public is taken for granted by us moderns, for whom the relation between author and reader is mediated by publishers, bookshops, newspapers, schools, and universities. But this was only vestigially the case in ancient Rome. Texts circulated among the elite for the most part through private contacts and ties of *amicitia*.[2] Copies were made by private (slave) copyists for individuals, and publication, which was preceded by sending the work to friends for corrections and suggestions, consisted simply in the understanding that the text had now reached a definitive state and copies could be made without the permission of the author.[3] Private circulation, however, was not the only means by which books could be acquired. When Catullus (c. 14) threatened Calvus with revenge for the latter's ghastly Saturnalian gift of an anthology of bad poets, he promised to rummage through the stalls of the booksellers for the complete Caesius, Aquinius, Suffenus, and all the other "poison." A book trade clearly existed in the time of Cicero and Catullus, and yet the impression of his readership that Catullus is at pains to give us is one of a close-knit coterie of the like-minded. Horace, too, mentions bookshops and booksellers, but tends to regard the general public, beyond the elite to which he addresses himself, with disdain.[4] It is only with Ovid that the author addresses himself primarily to a general public enthusiastically committed to the poet.[5] In the *Amores*, as Citroni points out, there is a striking lack of dedications and addresses to distinguished *amici*, and the general audience does not have to measure itself against a circle of patrons from which it is excluded.[6] But it is in the exile poetry that Ovid most frequently addresses himself to a *lector,* though this reader shares the stage with a number of influential addressees, paraded before the *princeps* as character witnesses.[7] Ovid's very separation from the literary center seems to conjure up for him the image of an anonymous public.[8]

The Ovid of the exile poetry influences Martial's conception of a public that is not constructed of a circle of people connected by personal ties, directly or indirectly, but which is sufficiently variegated to represent a reality foreign to him, a reality with which he enters into contact only through the medium of his book.[9] This public has brought Martial fame, if not fortune, because it has a taste for his work, whose progress it follows.[10] It is prepared to pay money for his work, available at all the better bookstores, and it has made him a celebrity. It is a public that may not be proud to put their Martial on the coffee table, but loves to read him all the same.[11] Martial and his reader enter an implied contract in which each party gets what it wants, sometimes against its better judgment.[12] Martial's "Lucan" (14.194) answers those who think he is not a poet with the reply that the bookseller thinks he is.[13] Is Martial a poet? He is if readers "buy" him. As we shall see, this is not unlike the relation between emperor and subjects, as Martial describes it. The connection between the emperor's subjects and the author's readership constitutes one important way in which Martial can be considered an imperial author. Not for nothing does the third poem in modern editions of Martial's oeuvre identify the subjects of the emperor as an audience. When this audience at the games hails the emperor as *pater patriae*, its diversity becomes a unity (*Spec.* 3.11–12). We find a similar mutual relation between Martial and his audience in the first poem of Book 1, where the diverse readership is compressed into the *lector studiosus* who asks for his (or indeed her) Martial: Martial's *lector* is the other side of the *lector*'s Martial. A further imperial connection is provided by the centurion who reads Martial in the Getic snows (11.3) and so makes the reach of Martial's poetry coextensive with that of the emperor's armies. Later in this chapter we will see more of what Martial makes of the analogies between emperor and poet, and indeed between *lector* and emperor.

Though Martial's conception of his readership was something new, relations between author and reader were still far removed from those with which we are now so familiar. It is true that Martial makes much of the fact that his books are available to all at a price, but his references to booksellers have more to do with circulation than with profits, for a Roman author earned no royalties and made little from the sale of his book to a bookseller; copyright was unknown.[14] When Martial addresses himself to a *lector* he is stressing that his book does not circulate exclusively through the mechanisms of elite social exchange. But neither does it dispense with these mechanisms entirely, for there is much to remind us that the anonymous *lector* shares the stage with a host of named individuals whom we may call, with all appropriate caution, patrons. These are often described as having special access to Martial's poems and as sharing personal relations with the author which involve responsibilities that are broadly and vaguely defined. The *lector*, by contrast, gets exactly what he wants qua *lector* and no more.

If we consider the individuals named in Martial's poetry we get a quite different picture than in the case of Catullus and Horace, for instance. By comparison, Martial's named addressees are a very numerous and heterogeneous group, ranging from the emperor himself to a centurion.[15] Many of these named individuals are known to us from other sources, but others are either of disputed identity or impossible to distinguish from the generic or speaking names to which a significant portion of Martial's poems are addressed.[16] Another difference from the poetry of Catullus and Horace is that there is no suggestion that Martial's addressees, or a significant subset of them, belong to a coterie with its own distinctive values, common enemies, and language. They are, for the most part, individuals, although some exception has to be made for those connected with the court.

Martial describes two kinds of relations with his readers: on the one hand, the long-term social relations of patronage, with their undefined reciprocities and their disguised asymmetries; on the other, the commercial transaction that required no personal contact between author and reader. I see no reason to doubt that some of the epigrams in the books Martial published were originally presented to specific dedicatees, individually or in little collections (*libelli*); that some were improvised at dinners or other social occasions; that others were composed for inscriptions or other particular purposes. Some material of this sort has probably been integrated into the books we read, and possibly modified in the process. But we cannot with any confidence tell which poems belong to this category and which were in fact composed for the book but pose as having other contexts originally. The important point is that the book as it is published presents the fiction (which may sometimes coincide with the reality) of different contexts of production, so that the *lector* is confronted with the possibility that other readers have come across particular epigrams in different, indeed more privileged, contexts.[17] Items of gossip or scandal are usually addressed to particular individuals, exchanged, it is to be hoped, for a more material return.[18] The *lector* who enjoys these squibs may imagine that they have been communicated directly to the addressees, perhaps at a dinner, and his secondary access enhances the status of the principals. So the *lector* is made aware of other readers who have had privileged access to the poems, or some of them, while the named dedicatees share their relationship to the author with an anonymous, far-flung and heterogeneous readership (*lectores*). Cavallo has observed, of the Roman reading public, that "cultural divisions among readers did not always imply different reading choices. Different groups might read the same texts; what differed were the ways in which they read, comprehended and appropriated a given text."[19] Martial makes this part of the fiction of his text.

## HOW DID YOU GET YOUR COPY (AND WHEN DO YOU READ IT)?

When Martial sends Marcus Antonius a copy of his book, he makes it clear that it matters how you acquire the book:

> Vilis eras, fateor, si te [sc. librum] nunc mitteret emptor;
>     grande tui pretium muneris auctor erit.
> multum, crede mihi, refert a fonte bibatur
>     quae fluit an pigro quae stupet unda lacu. (9.99.7–10)

> You (sc. the book) would be cheap, I admit, if a buyer were sending you now; the author will be a large part of the value of the gift. Believe me, it makes a great difference whether one drinks from the living spring or from the water that sits in the sluggish lake.

The contrast between the living spring and the sluggish lake must be an allusion to Callimachus's famous distinction between the Assyrian river, carrying dirt and refuse, and the undefiled spring of a holy fountain (*Hymn to Apollo* 108–12). Characteristically, Martial has shifted the focus from the poet's production to the reader's consumption, and in this he is probably following Ovid, who applies the figure to the experience of reading a friend's speeches in far-off Tomi, rather than hearing them as they were delivered in the forum (*Ex Pont.* 3.5.17ff.). But Martial takes the revision one step further by applying the Callimachean contrast to the *acquisition* of the book. It is a paradox to say that the book would be cheap if it were the gift of one who had bought it. But Martial is contrasting one kind of value with another, and commercial value itself is thereby marked as cheap.[20] The epigram is in fact not addressed to Marcus Antonius, but to an Atticus, who, though he receives the *poem* straight from the author, is not receiving the same *book* that is going to Antonius (*Marcus amat nostras Antonius, Attice, Musas*, 9.99.1). So there are three layers of readers, with the *lector* at the furthest remove. How did we acquire *our* copy?

The book that may be acquired in different ways may be consumed differently, too. Typically the named individuals are represented as having no time to read the book that the leisured, unnamed reader is now devouring; that reader is purely a consumer, whereas the patron might well be hailed as a writer himself. Parthenius, the dedicatee of Book 11, for instance, will have no time for the book. He writes his own poetry and reads petitions, not literature (*libros non legit ille, sed libellos*, 11.1.5). However, if the book is content to be handled by lesser hands, it should make for the porticoes where an idle crowd hangs out (7–16). The busy Parthenius, who has no time to read, is complemented by the fanatical *lector* who, in the final poem of Book 11, still wants a few more couplets (11.108). So, the anonymous and leisured *lector* reads, but does not support the poet, while the busy patron supports him, but has no time, or inclination, to read him.[21] Which would you rather be?

*Lector* and patron may diverge not only in how they read (or not) but in what they read, if we are to believe White's theory that the published books themselves bear traces of prior collections tailormade for individual patrons.[22] A significant part of White's evidence for these *libelli* is the presence of poems that seem ill-suited to their position as they stand. If indeed there are poems that make sense only in a context to which the *lector* has no access, this would produce a radical splitting of the readership. White's arguments came under fire from Fowler, and one of the poems at the center of this controversy concerning the *libellus* theory is 11.106:[23]

> Vibi Maxime, si vacas havere,
> hoc tantum lege: namque et occupatus
> et non es nimium laboriosus.
> transis hos quoque quattuor? sapisti.

> Vibius Maximus, if you're free to say hello, read only this;
> for you're a busy man and not one to make work for yourself.
> You're passing by these four as well? You're wise.

White argues that the poem could not originally have come at this point in a book, as "Maximus would have had to unroll to the third last poem in the book before he discovered the one item of which Martial begs him to take notice" (1974.47). Fowler rightly points out that it is absurd to make absurdity a problem, since, even on White's reading, Vibius is complimented in a poem he is represented as passing over. We should rather embrace the absurdity, Fowler argues, and note further that Martial is playing with the distinction between *sermo* (speech) and text: "On one level Martial depicts himself as stopping Vibius in the street and pressing on him his latest production . . . while on the other the poem moves within a wholly textual world, and Vibius snubs (*transis*) not Martial, but 'these four verses'" (1995.47). If White has missed the joke, Fowler, here and elsewhere in his article, is a little too ready to leave it at that. Fowler is right that "in trying to take this poem seriously, to think when and where one could possibly utter these words, White is in a sense being the exactly the reader Martial wants." But let us linger with the fiction a little longer; if we recognize that Vibius is hailed not only as though by a petitioner with a *libellus* (think of Augustus and the *graeculus*) but also as a passerby is hailed by an epitaph, then Fowler's sharp distinction between text and *sermo* is blunted. It is a convention of the epitaph that the addressee needs to be urged to read as he passes by.[24] If the poem speaks as an epitaph, then it doesn't presuppose a reader who has unrolled the book to this point. The book is represented as a series of epitaphs along a road, each soliciting the reader's attention (*siste, viator . . .*), sometimes by name. What is absurd about the poem as epitaph is that a passerby is hailed *by name*. Usually, an anonymous *viator* is asked to stop and read the *name* of the person who is commemorated by the epitaph. Though Vibius passes the epitaph by, someone must be reading it. It is the *lector* who plays the traditional role of the anonymous passerby, but the inscription he reads names not the speaker but the person whose attention it would solicit, and that person is not the *lector*. I suggest that instead of elaborating the paradoxes of this poem's mode of utterance, its play between textuality and orality, we consider its fictions in terms of the relations between different readers of the same book. As we (*lectores*) read this poem, we are made to look over our shoulders at Vibius, hurrying by. Once again, the reader feels diminished, just as when she is informed that it makes a difference whether you have been sent the book by the author or, having bought it from a shop, are drinking from a stagnant pool. But it is not always the named addressee who lords it over the anonymous *lector*, as we shall see later in this chapter.

## WHO ELSE IS READING?

Class is only one of the factors that differentiates Martial's readers. Gender, too, raises its head, and here Cavallo's observation about the different ways that particular constituencies of the readership consume the text is again relevant.[25] Martial's imagined female readers probably tell us little, if anything, about how a female readership actually read Martial, but they do illustrate the fact that Martial self-consciously presents us with different categories of readers consuming the text in different ways.

Not surprisingly, the gender of the reader is usually raised in the context of obscenity. Some of Martial's books, or portions of them, are appropriate for Cato's wife and Sabine matrons (11.15.1–2, 5.2.1–2), but others are not. The situation becomes more interesting when the question of suitability is raised in the context of a mixed audience. The fifth book is dedicated to Domitian and eschews obscenity; it is the kind of book the emperor can read without blushing in the presence of his beloved Minerva (*coram Cecropia legat puella*, 5.2.8). In Vienne, Martial is read by young and old, male and female alike—even by the virtuous wife in the presence of her forbidding husband (*et coram tetrico casta puella viro*, 7.88.4). But not all of the books are quite so suitable for mixed company. The eleventh book is free with its language and stimulating enough to excite a Curius, a Fabricius, or even a girl from Patavium, that bastion of respectability (*uda, puella leges, sis Patavina licet*, 11.16.8). "On this, Lucretia blushed, and put the book aside; but only in the presence of Brutus: once he's gone she'll read it" (*sed coram Bruto; Brute, recede, leget*, 11.16.10). Lucretia may not be reading in Brutus's presence, but she is reading with *us*, and the secret reading of women communicates with the privacy of the anonymous *lector*, reading, perhaps, with one hand (11.16.5–6, 12.95.6–7, 1.2.4: *me manus una capit*). The combination is not altogether respectable, and when Martial shuts the door on the woman reader a little over halfway into Book 3, he identifies the rest of the book as the place where men strip off, as they do at the baths or the gymnasium (*exuimur: nudos parce videre viros*, 3.68.4). But his warning only serves as a come-on:

> Si bene te novi, longum iam lassa libellum
> ponebas, totum nunc studiosa leges. (11–12)

> If I know you right, you were already putting aside the long book with a yawn. Now you will read the whole thing, and keenly.

Taking the long book—all of it—the female reader surely grabs something else, identified at the beginning of the next poem by name (*Omnia quod scribis castis epigrammata verbis / inque tuis nulla est* mentula *carminibus*, 3.69.1–2). Not even the distinguished Polla, widow of Lucan, is spared this insinuation when Martial asks her not to be censorious if she handles (*contigeris*, 10.64.1) his books. Again, the last line of the previous poem contains the word *mentula* (10.63.8), both potential cause of her disapproval and object of her handling.

That a book can have, or be, a *mentula* is made explicit in some of Martial's programmatic statements, but the presence of the female reader inspires more subtle references to the book's private parts.[26] The female reader whom Martial earlier suspected would take his warning as a come-on is still there in 3.86: "I told you and warned you before, virtuous lady, not to read *part* of my naughty book, but here you are, reading it" (*ne legeres* partem *lascivi, casta, libelli, / praedixi et monui: tu tamen, ecce, legis*, 3.86.1–2). This "part" is anything but innocent if we consider the poems that flank it. The previous poem mocks a cuckold who has cut off the nose of the adulterer concerned: "That's not the *part* which offended you" (*non hac peccatum est* parte, *marite, tibi*, 3.85.2). In the poem which follows 3.86, Chione, rumored to have never been fucked, is told that she covers the wrong *part* when she bathes (*tecta tamen non hac, qua debes*, parte, *lavaris*, 3.87.3); her panties should cover her *face*. Is the female reader of 3.86 chaste in the same way that Chione is pure (*nihil cunno purius esse tuo*, 3.87.2)? The reference to bathing takes us back to 3.68, where the environment into which the female reader has strayed is one where men strip off, as in the gymnasium, the baths, or the stadium (3–4). But the baths are counterbalanced by a different figure for the scene of reading at the end of 3.87: "If you watch Panniculus and Latinus, chaste lady, this is no more disrespectable than the mime. Read on!" (3–4). The mixed audience of the mime enjoys erotic performance publicly and innocently, whereas the baths are the place where private secrets are both hidden and exposed; somewhere between the baths and the theater we must locate the virtual mixing of Martial's mixed readership.

Just as Martial makes us notice Vibius, hurrying by as we read, so he opens the door on the female reader with whom the predominately male readership is enjoying a titillating proximity. Vibius is not reading, though we are, in his stead; the female reader is still reading, and we know what her husband does not. Obviously, the *lector* is situated quite differently in relation to these two figures who share the world of the book with him, but in both cases some aspect of his situation as reader is particularized by the relation. Certainly there is a transgressive thrill for the male reader in imagining that he shares the female reader's secret pleasures, and this female reader serves to put at issue the potential privacy of the act of reading. Is reading the book like attending the mime along with a mixed audience, or is it a secret activity that takes advantage of (for instance) a husband's absence? Do other kinds of readers constitute a presence that changes the reading experience, or are the varied constituencies of this readership subsumed into a homogeneous audience? By raising these questions Martial makes the consumption of the book into the focal point of a complex virtual society.

## YOUR AD HERE

One of the most basic stratifications of Martial's readership is that between named addressees and anonymous mass. Martial's book is a place where patrons like to find their names, and it is also a place from which the anonymous readership can look in on the lives of their social superiors. We readers are delivered to the houses of the high and mighty, even the highest and mightiest, both as voyeuristic tourists and as respectful *salutatores*. Martial's fame among the anonymous masses supports the fame of his honored addressees, for his circulation is ultimately theirs. This point is clearly made by the juxtaposition of 7.88 and 7.89. In the first of these Martial expresses satisfaction that his books are popular in Vienne (*non nihil ergo sumus*, 9). This poem, which primarily concerns Martial's own fame and the circulation of his books, is also a puff for Vienne, whose taste for Martial means more to him than being read in Egypt (5–6). In the following poem (7.89) Martial sends a rose to Apollinaris:

> I, felix rosa, mollibusque sertis
> nostri cinge comas Apollinaris;
> quas tu nectere candidas, sed olim,
> sic te semper amet Venus, memento.

> Go, lucky rose, and with your soft garlands circle the hair of my friend Apollinaris. And, so may Venus always love you, remember to bind them when they're white, but in the distant future.

The poem is a beautiful example of Martial's epigrammatic art. Complicating the direct simplicity of the first two lines' envoi, the relative clause that completes the poem accumulates a wealth of temporal indicators (*candidas, olim, semper, memento*). The single arc of the poem's first half contrasts with the qualifications of the second half (*sed, sic*), broken into four sections and coming together only with the final word. The epigram's two halves carefully add the future to the present, the memory of posterity to the immediate gesture. Because the poem is bare of all context, the utterance suggests that rose and poem are coextensive, a connection strengthened by metaphors such as the *Garland* of Meleager. Only the rose as poem or book could continue to grace Apollinaris in the future when his hair is white. The previous poem reminds Apollinaris that the poem which is coming to him is contained in a book which is read even in Vienne, and the juxtaposition of the poems enhances the attractions for the addressee of this "rose," which will do honor to Apollinaris wherever Martial is read.

Patron and client can also mutually enhance each other's status. Iulius Martialis is going to display his namesake's books in his library (7.17), and when Martial sends him seven books, he echoes the phrase he had used of his own fame in 1.1 (*toto notus in orbe Martialis*, 2) but applies it to the library that is to preserve his books (*quae cantaberis orbe nota toto*, 7.17.10). Because Martial is known throughout the world, the same will be true for Martialis's library.[27] But the library has its part to play in the history of the book, for this copy is corrected by the author's own hand, and available to other readers in Martialis's library. It is an authorized edition from which copies can be made and against which other copies can be checked.[28] Book and library, then, mutually protect each other's survival. Though we ourselves are not reading this *book* in Martialis's library, the future of the *work* we are reading may depend upon it.

In the preface to Book 9, it is not a book but a bust of Martial that is destined for a patron's library, and Martial sends an epigram to stand under it. The occasion is the opportunity for an extraordinary reflection on the mutual support of various audiences and relations:

Have, mi Torani, frater carissime. epigramma, quod extra ordinem paginarum est, ad Stertinium clarissimum virum scripsimus, qui imaginem meam ponere in bibliotheca sua voluit. de quo scribendum tibi putavi, ne ignorares Avitus iste quis vocaretur. Vale et para hospitium.

> Note, licet nolis, sublimi pectore vates
>     cui referet serus praemia digna cinis,
> hoc tibi sub nostra beve carmen imagine vivat,
>     quam non obscuris iungis, Avite, viris:
> "ille ego sum nulli nugarum laude secundus,
>     quem non miraris sed, puto, lector, amas.
> maiores maiora sonent: mihi parva locuto
>     sufficit in vestras saepe redire manus."

Greetings, my Toranius, dearest brother. I wrote the epigram that stands outside the sequence of pages to the most illustrious Stertinius, who wanted to put my bust in his library. I thought I should write to you about him so that you know who this person called Avitus is. Farewell and prepare a welcome.

Illustrious poet (though you would not have it so), poet of lofty inspiration, whose ashes will receive their late reward, may this short poem live for you beneath my bust, which you are joining to men of no small repute: "I am the poet whose reputation for trifles is second to none, whom you do not revere but I suspect, reader, you love. Let greater poets make a greater sound: for me, who speaks of small matters, it is enough to return often to your hands."

Unlike the other prose prefaces (books 1, 2, 8, and 12), which clearly address the book to an individual, this preface presents a very complicated situation, with three separate addressees: the consular Avitus Stertinius (*clarissimum virum*), Toranius (*frater carissime*) and the *lector*. The combination produces a hall of mirrors in which relations between the four principles reflect each other in various modes.[29] Martial identifies Avitus to Toranius and then identifies himself to his reader in the inscription for Avitus's library, which also serves to introduce the present book. He asks Toranius to prepare a welcome, apparently for himself, but also (metaphorically) for Avitus, whom Toranius the reader is to welcome into the book.[30] Possibly, Avitus is identified to Toranius in order to distinguish him from others in the collection with the same name, and he here makes his debut.[31] Less metaphorically, Avitus is also preparing a welcome for Martial, a virtual hospitality extended to the poet in the form of his statue; Martial reciprocates by putting Avitus in the place of honor in his book (*in bibliotheca sua*; cf. *extra ordinem paginarum*). The epigram addressed to him is placed both in the book and outside the *ordo* of its pages, at its head, just as the consular Avitus stands at the head of his *ordo* (rank).[32] Here Avitus finds himself next to the emperor, addressed in the first poem of the book proper (9.1), just as Martial will be placed next to distinguished individuals in Avitus's library (*quam non obscuris iungis,*

*Avite, viris*, 4), and as Toranius is associated in this preface with the distinguished Avitus.

Poet and addressee mutually promote each other's status. From Avitus's library Martial speaks to identify himself, modestly, to the reader as a writer of *nugae*, and so the object of the reader's affection rather than admiration. But first he greets Avitus as "poet of lofty inspiration" (*sublimi pectore vates*), erecting, as it were, a statue of Avitus in his own virtual library. Indeed the line "may this short poem live for you beneath my bust" (*hoc tibi sub nostra breve carmen imagine vivat*) could as well apply to the whole epigram as to the inscription that follows: this short poem will *live* for Avitus (*tibi vivat*), whose own poetry will bring him merely posthumous fame.[33] The effect of the ambiguous deictic (hoc . . . *breve carmen*) is to make us wonder where we are—in Martial's book or in Avitus's library.

Does the inscription with which the poem ends really speak from Avitus's library? Yes and no. The disjunction between the singular in the first two lines of the inscription (*lector, amas*, 6) and the plural with which it concludes (*vestras . . . manus*, 8) might distinguish two separate audiences—the visitor in Avitus's library and the book's public. In the line that is the last of Avitus's inscription, as well as of the honorific epigram and of the book's preface, Martial is speaking from two different places, and if the library honors him, the book honors Avitus. The *lector*, too, is flattered, because, for all the welcoming that is going on between Martial and his illustrious friends, it is the hands of the *lector* that are the ultimate, and most desirable, resting place. So the poem presents a spectrum of receptions, capped by the final word of the epigram: the hands of the *lector* are the place in which the poet is content to rest (*in vestras saepe redire manus*), and that is because Toranius and Avitus are, finally, readers, absorbed into the readership of Martial's book. Is this then the final act of homage that is served by all the others?

In a very particular way, Toranius and Avitus as a pair are subsumed by the *lector*, for the contrast between Toranius, *frater carissime*, and Avitus, clar*issimum virum*, between dearness and distinction, is echoed in the words *quem non* miraris *sed, puto, lector*, amas. The *lector* relates to the poet (not so much admirable as lovable) in terms that replicate Martial's different relations to his two friends. But in the burlesque of personal relations provided by Martial and his *lector* the most immediate responses (*amas*) rule at the expense of a higher judgment (*miraris*). From one angle, the relation between the *lector* and author seems more abstract, less real, than that between author and patrons, but from another angle it is more intimate because of the paradoxical emotions and preferences that it provokes. This is Martial's version of Catullus's *odi et amo*!

Before we leave this preface we should note the striking analogy provided by Pliny's famous letter on Martial's death, the closing letter of Book 3 of Pliny's *Epistles* (3.21).[34] Here we find a situation comparable to the mutual honoring of Martial by Avitus (in his library) and Avitus by Martial (in his book). In 3.21 Pliny announces the death of Martial to his addressee, Cornelius Priscus, who is also told that Pliny had given Martial his travel expenses when he left Rome for Spain, a munificent return for Martial's poem on Pliny (10.19). Perhaps Priscus would like to know what verses these were? "I would refer you to the volume itself, if I didn't have some by memory. If you like these, you can look up the rest in the book" (*Remitterem te ad ispum volumen, nisi quosdam tenerem; tu, si placuerint hi, ceteros in libro requires*, 3.21.4). Pliny then quotes a cropped version of Martial's poem (10.20.12–21). The quotation betrays Pliny's anxiety that Martial's poetry might not make it to posterity (*at non erunt aeterna quae scripsit*, 3.21.6), and so Pliny preserves the honorific portion of the poem in his letter which, we are to assume, is destined to last.[35] In Martial's poem the poet sends his Muse on a visit to Pliny's house; Pliny cuts the description of the itinerary (10.20.1–11) and makes sure that the Muse stays there (*remitterem te ad ipsum volumen, nisi quosdam tenerem*, 4), displaying the poem in a letter which preserves Martial for posterity so that he can continue to pay homage to Pliny, whom future generations will compare to Cicero (*dum centum studet auribus virorum / hoc quod saecula posterique possint / Arpinis quoque comparare chartis*, 15–18). As in the preface to Martial's Book 9, we have to ask who is displayed in whose gallery.[36]

In the trio author-patron-*lector*, the *lector* is the odd man out, representing a level at which the text circulates that is separate from, but related to, the exchange between patron and poet. As we turn to the trio author-emperor-*lector* we find that two of the men are odd, though not necessarily out. *Lector* and emperor are both distant from the author, though in quite different ways. The very abstraction of the *lector*, a figure who is more than a person, and whose judgment is definitive, makes him comparable to the emperor, even though he stands at the opposite end of the social hierarchy of Martial's readership.

## EMPEROR AND ANONYMOUS PUBLIC

It is appropriate that the first of Martial's published books that survives is the *Liber spectaculorum*, for here the subjects of the emperor are constituted as an audience. Conversely, the polyglot spectatorship of the games is transformed into an audience when it acknowledges the emperor (*tum tamen una est / cum verus patriae diceris esse pater, Spec.* 3.11–12). One might compare Martial's list of the miscellaneous types who read him (11.24) to the beginning of *Spec.* 1, where some of the exotic foreigners attending Caesar's games are identified. When they read Martial, these various readers are absorbed into the *studiosus lector* (1.1.1) just as the variegated audience at the arena becomes one in its greeting of the emperor. There are other ways we might pursue this analogy. For instance, when Martial's "Lucan" says (14.194), "Some think I am not a poet, but the bookseller who sells me thinks I am," he is making a point not so far removed from what Martial says about the emperor's divinity: it is not statues that make a god, but the one who prays to him (*Qui rogat ille facit*, 8.24.6). Similarly, it is not the critic who makes a poet, but the reader who pays for him.

Not only are emperor and author analogous in their common relation to an audience, it is also the case that the emperor and the anonymous *lector* are analogous in their relation to the author Martial. We have already seen that in the opening sequence of the first book Martial replaces the reading public of Rome (*dominae . . . Romae*, 1.3.3) with the emperor himself (*terrarum dominum*, 1.4.2) as the ultimate arbiter of his book's fate. Martial's anonymous *lector* and his divine emperor, disposed on either side of his named patrons as higher and lower respectively, are the final arbiters of his success in their different ways. Both could be said to measure the *reach* of Martial's poetry, which aspires to find its way to the emperor and at the same time diffuses itself to a varied, widespread, and unknown public that is the medium of Martial's fame. As *censor perpetuus*, Domitian can condemn Martial's poems for the very same traits that might make them popular among the true agents of his *fama*, his anonymous readership.[37] If Martial's habit of addressing his *lector* is inspired by Ovid's exile poetry, where Ovid plays the affectionate *lector* off against the recalcitrant emperor, it also follows Ovid in making the *lector* on occasion a substitute for the emperor.[38] Each might be considered a court of last appeal, a final refuge, one from the other.

We find a particularly stark confrontation between these two courts of last appeal in 7.12, where Martial protests that his poems harm no one, in spite of a poet who tries to pass off vitriolic poems under his name. Though the bulk of the poem is addressed to Faustinus, it begins by gesturing, over his shoulder, to the emperor himself (compare 7.80):

> Sic me fronte legat dominus, Faustine, serena
> excipiatque meos qua solet aure iocos,
> ut mea nec iuste quos odit pagina laesit
> et mea de nullo fama rubore placet.
> quid prodest, cupiant cum quidam nostra videri
> si qua Lycambeo sanguine tela madent,
> vipereumque vomat nostro sub nomine virus
> qui Phoebi radios ferre diemque negat?
> ludimus innocui: scis hoc bene; iuro potentis
> per genium Famae Castaliumque gregem,
> perque tuas aures, magni mihi numinis instar,
> lector inhumana liber ab invidia. (7.12)

So may the master read me with unruffled brow, Faustinus, and receive my jokes with his usual ear; I swear that no page of mind has harmed even those it hates with justice, and that no reputation pleases me that is won from another's shame. But what good is that if there are some who would brand as mine any missiles that drip with Lycambean [i.e.,

> Archilochian] gore; if someone who cannot bear the light
> of day spews his viper's poison under my name? My play
> is harmless, you know that well; I swear it by Reputation's
> head and by the Castalian flock, and by your ears, you who
> are to me like a mighty god, reader free of malignant envy.

At the end of the poem the emperor by whom the poet initially swears that he is innocent has been replaced by the anonymous reader, whose ears guarantee the poet's good intentions.[39] In the process, the meaning of "ear" has shifted from the "reception" appropriate to a superior (*qua solet aure*, 2) to something like "discernment" (*perque tuas aures*, 11). The *lector* Martial invokes is generic, an implied reader, whose freedom from *invidia* is surely related to his lack of a name (he is "out of play"; see below). This facelessness makes him the opposite of the emperor, an individual whose personal reactions might have dire consequences for the poet. The *lector* also acts as an antidote to the malicious audience (*quidam*, 5) that supports the forger, an audience that will make Martial a brand name like Archilochus (*Lycambeo*, 6). The *lector*, then, is located by significant analogies and oppositions in relation to the emperor and to the malicious *quidam*. He will become the court of last appeal in the final lines, where not only have the emperor's ears been replaced by those of the *lector*, but the addressee shifts from Faustinus, to whom Martial addresses his protestation of innocence (*ludimus innocui: scis hoc bene*, 9), to the generous reader. Both emperor and patron are displaced as the poem broadens out into its resonant finale.[40]

Poem 7.12 is a particularly vivid demonstration of the complex relations between different readerships, not only between emperor and *lector*, but also between emperor and addressee (Faustinus). By fusing the address to Faustinus with an oath by the emperor's continuing favor in the opening couplet, Martial honors Faustinus as the addressee of an author who has the emperor's "ear." Faustinus's name is juxtaposed to the emperor's title (*dominus*), and sandwiched between *fronte* and *serena*, a phrase whose implications of divine favor pun on the name Faustinus (Fortunate) itself. As Bowditch has observed of Horace, the symbolic capital of the poet's lofty connections is passed on to his addressees.[41] But in this case that symbolic capital is in danger of devaluation at the hands of forgers. Faustinus may be in a position to scotch these nuisances, and certainly Martial gives him a motive to do so. Furthermore, publishing this protestation/request to an important patron, while mentioning an even more important one, Martial warns away with a show of force those who would blacken his name: "These are my allies," Martial warns them. Before the emperor, Faustinus is paraded as guarantor that Martial doesn't write invective against individuals.[42] No doubt the question of whether a poet had contravened the emperor's edict against defamation was decided as much by what people thought, and which people thought it, as by investigation into authorship.[43] It makes a difference who will stand up for Martial, and it matters whether Martial's regular readers take up these forgeries as his. With his final appeal to the unbiased ear of the *lector*, Martial is appealing also to posterity, in the hope that it may proleptically influence the emperor in his favor.[44]

I turn now to another awkward moment that is negotiated by playing off reader and emperor, namely the transition of rule from Domitian to Nerva. Book 10 is "dedicated" not to an emperor, but to the *lector.*[45] The first poem has no addressee, but invites us to make the book as short as we wish by reading selections, or even individual pages. The second poem introduces us to this, the second edition of the tenth book, and asks the reader, addressed honorifically as "my wealth" (*opes nostrae*, 5), to favor both. This is the place where we would expect a dedication to the emperor, as in the previous two books and, almost certainly, as in the first edition of Book 10. But that dedication, and any other traces of Martial's cultivation of Domitian, have disappeared from this edition, published after Domitian's assassination. If the first epigram suggests how we might shorten the book, the second is very careful not to talk about excisions: in this new edition the reader will find some old favorites, polished up, but the greater part is new (10.2.3–4). What has dropped out from the previous edition, of course, is the imperial dedicatee whom the *lector* replaces. The unorthodoxy of dedicating the book to the *lector* is marked by a paradox: it is only metaphorically that the reader could be called *opes nostrae*, and the very unconventionality of the idea reminds us that this book lacks a patron. The "wealth" that the reader represents for the poet is the survival of his name.[46]

Pace Pliny, Martial's name *will* survive, and this prospect is elaborated with the *topos* comparing monuments to books:

> marmora Messallae findit caprificus et audax
> > dimidios Cripsi mulio ridet equos:
> at chartis nec furta nocent et saecula prosunt,
> > solaque non norunt haec monumenta mori. (10.2.9–12)

> The fig tree splits Messalla's marble and the brazen mule-teer laughs at the halved horse of Crispus. But paper is not harmed by theft and only helped by the ages, and these monuments alone know nothing of death.

Surely here the decay of monuments would remind a contemporary reader of the *damnatio memoriae* that the senate inflicted on the dead Domitian, whose statues and honorific shields were torn down and destroyed, and whose name was erased from inscriptions.[47] This is precisely what has happened to Domitian in the second edition of Book 10. Having hitched his name to a fallen star, Martial will survive through his readers, rather than by virtue of the association with Domitian which he vaunts elsewhere.[48] The various substitutions, elisions, and reversals of this poem point to the disruption that has promoted the *lector* to dedicatee. But it also reminds us that emperor and *lector* are both potential guarantors of Martial's fame, and that in many ways they function as alternatives.

In 10.2, the *lector* replaces the dead and disgraced emperor; in 12.4 the new emperor displaces the *lector*.[49] Martial had apparently given Trajan a condensed version of Books 10 and 11. In 12.4 we seem to be reading over the shoulders of the emperor:

> Longior undecimi nobis decimique libelli
> artatus labor est et breve rasit opus.
> plura legant vacui, quibus otia tuta dedisti:
> haec lege tu, Caesar; forsan et illa leges.

The longer labor of my eleventh and tenth books has been compressed and filed down to a short work. Let idlers, to whom you have given leisure and security, read more: you read these, Caesar; perhaps you'll read those also.

When we get to the word *haec* it is quite clear that what the addressee has in front of him is not the book that the *lector* is reading. But if that is the case, why is the poem in Book 12? This is one of the poems cited by White (1974) as evidence that private brochures (*libelli*) were the primary means of presenting poems to patrons. There are many poems in the published books, White argues, that betray signs of having been extracted from different collections and are ill-suited to their present context. Poem 12.4 would be an egregious example of this inasmuch as *haec* refers to an epitome of books 10 and 11 that is most emphatically not "this." But, as Fowler points out (1995.41), whether or not this poem originally appeared in a different context, it plays a distinctive role within Book 12. The implied reader is not necessarily the same as the addressee, and though the reader of Book 12 is not addressed, he is referred to in the phrase *plura legant vacui*. So the *lector* of Book 12 is being sighted from somewhere else. As readers of Book 12, some of whom have read through books 10 and 11, we are made aware of a privileged reader of the same material proceeding on a separate, swifter, track. We have a walk-on part in his reading as the *vacui* to whom he has awarded the necessary *otium* to read the uncut Martial. Those who have been following Martial's books as they come out will have read Book 10 in its original version, rather than the revision published after Book 11 (in 98); that original version, now lost, was published before Domitian's assassination, and it would have included flattery of the subsequently disgraced emperor. Books 10 (first edition) and 11 between them span the change of regimes, and the anthology alluded to here has elided (*rasit*, 12.5.2!) that awkward shift in Martial's allegiance.[50] Those who have read the original sequence are not only leisured but compromised; it is reassuring to them, as it is flattering to Nerva, that their leisure has been made safe by the new emperor (*otia tuta dedisti*, 3). In this context, *forsan et illa* [sc. the complete 10 and 11] *leges* (4) is a breezily optimistic way of referring to the awkward fact that the original tenth book is still in circulation. Martial has very skillfully papered over the problem of how all the agents—the author himself, Nerva, and the general reader—were to negotiate the sudden change of allegiances by casting this problem in terms of a recurring motif in his work: the distinction between the busy patron, who has no time to read Martial, and the general reader, who has time and inclination to spare. The busy emperor guarantees the safety of the *lector* who has followed the whole sordid story, but he is too busy to concern himself with it. Here, too, as in the preface to Book 9, we are left with the question of which site of reading is primary and which secondary. Is this place where we are reading sighted from a more special place where the emperor is reading, or is the emperor's particular reading included in the more capacious space of Martial's total oeuvre? Inside and outside are unstable categories that shift depending on relations between the various components of the book's readership. Martial's *haec* makes of the book a notional entity that is the meeting place of his various readers.

As we have seen, at the beginning of Book 10 (second edition) the *lector* is substituted for the now dead, and disgraced, Domitian. If one guarantor of Martial's fame has failed him, the other can step into the breach. Emperor and *lector* are both alternatives and analogs, and one of the factors that makes them analogous is their distance from the author. Distinct from the ordinary patrons to whom Martial addresses his epigrams, they may claim to be out of play with respect to the game of patronage. In poems 15 and 16 of Book 5, they take a detached view of what they are reading—curious or approving, they are merely readers. In 5.15 Domitian listens to Martial's protestations that no one has been harmed by his poetry (and indeed many a reader has been pleased to have his name celebrated) and then proceeds to ask him what he has got from all this praising (*quid tamen haec prosunt quamvis venerantia multos?* 6). "Perhaps I haven't made any profit," Martial replies, "but I like it" (*sed tamen ista iuvant*, 6). The emperor takes the realistic position usually voiced by Martial, and Martial seems to take the mystified position on patronage.[51]

But his reply is surely ironic, especially given the fact that Martial elsewhere plays on the double sense of *iuvat*, both "it pleases" and "it profits" (cf. 3.37.2). In the next poem, Martial identifies the favorable reader (*lector amice*, 5.16.2) as the cause of his poverty. If the reader had not made him famous as a poet he would have pursued a more lucrative calling, as lawyer. His poetry pleases only if it is free, and his book is treated as a dinner guest—pleasant company, but not requiring remuneration (9–10). Poets weren't always content with praise, and there was a time when the minimum gift to a poet was an Alexis (11–12). "Well spoken," replies the reader. "We like what you say [*iuvat*, 13] and we'll keep praising you." To which the poet comes back with "You pretend not to understand? Reader, you'll make me take up law [*dissimulas? facies me, puto, causidicum*, 14]." Though the second of the poems is more than twice as long as the first, the reader, like the emperor, speaks in the penultimate line, and to very similar effect. The echo of *iuvant*, the last word of 5.15 in the reader's exclamation (*iuvat et laudabimus usque*, 5.16.13), casts an ironic light back onto Martial's reply to the emperor, and it is surely part of the role of the *lector* to allow Martial indirectly to say to the emperor what couldn't be said directly. But the flow goes both ways, and we can apply to 5.16 the previous poem's protestation that "many a reader" (*multus lector*, 5.15.3) rejoices to have his name honored in Martial's books: the friendly reader (*lector amice*) of 5.16 could *become* one of the readers whose names are honored, if only he were to take the hint.[52] What is said to each of the addressees of these two poems has implications for the other. Naturally, the emperor is in a better position to provide Martial with the necessary support, and to some extent the *lector* serves as an alibi for what Martial wants to say to him.[53]

In these two poems, the disembedded, commodified, or aestheticized relation between poet and reader interferes with the reciprocal model of relations between patron and client. Both emperor and *lector* stand aloof from the mutual responsibilities of *amicitia*. The disinterested "pleasure" expressed, however disingenuously, by both Martial and the *lector* (*iuvant*, 5.15.6; *iuvat*, 5.16.13) is appropriate to the book as an object that is available, for those who want it, at bookstores, and from which the author receives no profit. But although the reader has established no relationship with the author, the *lector*'s favor has had material consequences for Martial, who could have been a lawyer and made a good living (5.16.5–8). Whether he recognizes it or not, the *lector* might be expected to reciprocate. The hint to the reader is a joke, but a revealing joke: it tells us that there is something anomalous about the society of this book, where poet and *lector* are related neither in purely commercial terms nor through the operations of patronage.

## IN AND OUT OF PLAY (". . . THE PEW CHARITABLE TRUST, AND VIEWERS LIKE YOU")

A recent *New Yorker* cartoon provides a useful analogy to Martial's jokes about the *lector*'s responsibilities. In the cartoon, an alien watching television on a spaceship turns to another alien behind him and reports, "It says this program is made possible by viewers like us." As usual, we feel that the *New Yorker* has put a deft finger on it. But what, exactly, is "it"? Perhaps it is PBS's attempt to create a homogeneous public out of those who tune in to this program simply by assuming it. The aliens are a *reductio ad absurdum* of what we all know about the arbitrary and shifting constitution of any particular program's audience at any moment: viewers surf the waves and one never knows who is watching, or why. But to laugh at the illusion of *an* audience is also a vindication of privacy for those who might fear that focus groups and market research have made this Olympian pronouncement ("like you") all too feasible; perhaps they do know us (their target audience), even though we don't know each other; or at least they know what we are "like" even if they don't know who we are (so does it matter who we are?). The cartoon reassures us that, in fact, they don't know about "us"; there is no us.[54] Another approach is suggested by the pleasure, and self-satisfaction, on the alien's face. The effectiveness of the words he quotes depends on a kind of *hysteron proteron*. The aliens have completely missed the rhetoric of the statement, which does not so much report a fact as try to bring one about ("once you support this program you will join a group of people like you"). Here again, it is a pleasant fantasy that not everybody is already attuned to the implications and rhetoric of such a message. It is also satisfying to see the aliens innocently fail to assume the guilt that is being laid on them. What the message tells us is that we are, or *should be*, involved; that it's not just other people, rich people like the Pews and the MacArthurs, who are responsible for these programs; as viewers, we are not out of play, however private an act we may think it is to tune in to this channel.

When Martial waylays the onlooker he can make us feel uncomfortably that we are not as safely out of play as we think. Epigram 5.25 is one of a sequence of poems in Book 5 on Domitian's enforcement of the *Lex Roscia theatralis*. This law, dating from 67 BC, assigned the fourteen rows of seats at the theater immediately behind the senators to the knights, a privilege that had been usurped over the years. Up to this point in the book we have been enjoying the discomfiture of nonequestrian poseurs at the hands of the bouncers Leitus and Oceanus (5.8, 5.14, 5.23). The poem starts in familiar fashion. "You don't have the necessary 400,000, Chaerestratus, so get up; Leitus is coming: stand, flee, run or hide" (5.25.1–2). So far, so good. But the poet now turns on the bystanders to ask if no one will call him back and make him a knight with the gift of an equestrian fortune. Is there no generous patron who wants his name to live forever (5–6)? The poem concludes, "Rich to no purpose, you denier of your friend (client), do you read this and praise it? What a reputation passes you by" (*o frustra locuples, o dissimulator amici, / haec legis et laudas? quae tibi fama perit*, 11–12). So it is not only Chaerestratus who is pointed out, but also nameless readers, dragged from the comfort of the aesthetic relation and branded as dissimulators, like Chaerestratus himself. Of course, most anonymous *lectores* are in no position to make gifts of 400,000 sesterces, and so one level of the readership enjoys the discomfiture of the other in Martial's "theater" (1 praef.): the Pew Charitable Trust, but not viewers like me.

In 5.16, discussed above, the reader is pretending not to understand Martial's not so subtle appeal for support. "Well said, we approve the sentiment and will always praise it" (*belle . . . dixti: iuvat et laudabimus usque*, 13). On the face of it, this looks like a pitch of the kind that is ridiculed in the *New Yorker* cartoon, but in fact it is probably more like the cartoon itself—an absurdity. In ancient Rome support of poets was the business of individual patrons, the Pews and the MacArthurs, but not of readers like us. So what claim can Martial have on the "dissimulating" reader? At the beginning of the same poem he maintains that the reason he writes entertaining poetry (*delectantia*, 1), rather than the serious stuff of which he is capable (*seria*, 1) is that he is compelled by the fame that the reader has forced on him. It's nice to be famous, but in this case there's a price to pay. Martial could have been a lawyer, and rich (5–8). As it is, his book's a "dinner companion and a reveler, and only finds favor when free of charge" (*at nunc conviva est comissatorque libellus / et tantum gratis pagina nostra placet*, 9–10). It was different in Vergil's time, when the minimum gift to a poet was an Alexis (11–12). This praise of times past elicits the reader's approval and the poet's closing comeback that the reader will make a barrister of him yet (*facies me, puto, causidicum*, 14).[55] It may seem to the reader that he is simply buying a book, which leaves him with no obligation to the author, but in fact this choice of the reader's has had repercussions on the poet's life (*nescis quanti stet mihi talis amor*, 4). The reader is an *amicus* (*lector* amice, 2), whether he likes it or not. So Martial is casting this virtual relation with the reader in terms of the familiar relations of *amicitia* celebrated (or deplored) elsewhere in his book, and the imperfect fit is both witty and analytically astute.

When Martial complains that the book is "a dinner companion and a reveler" he is alluding to the fact that the book will be read at dinners.[56] It is a welcome companion only when "free of charge" (*gratis*, 10) in the sense that its author need not be invited, for access to the book can bypass the author, and the fact that it is the book, not Martial, who is the *conviva* stresses the virtual nature of the relation between poet and reader.[57] However, Martial's inability to refuse the fame offered by the reader, at whatever cost, mirrors the parasite's inability to dine at home, which the poet attributes to himself more than once (11.24, 2.18). Reader and poet are related through an inability to resist their baser natures: the reader loves Martial not for serious poetry but for pleasant stuff (*delectantia*); the poet can't resist fame, even if it costs him dearly. Such is the virtual exchange between them.

In 5.16 Martial has used the dinner to figure an opportunism that bypasses the relations of reciprocity between client and patron, relations that were epitomized by the hospitality of the patron's dinner.[58] Something similar happens in 5.15, where Martial refers to the advocacy from which he could have made a better living as "selling" words (*sollicitisque velim* vendere *verba reis*, 6). The word *vendere* reminds us that advocates could now charge fees for their services, though this had been forbidden before the time of Claudius. A relation falling under the category of *officium* or *beneficium* was now a financial transaction in which a particular service was remunerated directly.[59] Martial's own profession shows a more radical development. Writing partially for an unknown public which buys his books and gives him fame but does not remunerate him, Martial fits into neither category of relations. He marks the unorthodoxy of this situation by demanding of the unnamed *lector* that he step in and pay up, rather than just appreciate.

The same demand brings the eleventh book to a close.

> Quamvis tam longo possis satur esses libello,
>     lector, adhuc a me disticha pauca petis.
> sed Lupus usuram puerique diaria poscunt.
>     lector, solve. taces dissimulasque? vale. (11.108)

Although you could well be sated with a book this long, reader, you still ask for a few more couplets. But Lupus wants his interest and the slaves their daily rations. Reader, pay up [or, possibly, "solve this riddle"]. You say nothing and pretend not to understand? Farewell.

White (1974.60) comments on this poem: "The poet dispenses his apostrophes and accolades on credit, as it were, and awaits recompense from the beneficiary. But in 11.108 . . . that convention is transferred to the relationship between author and reader, which it does not fit. Only in jest could Martial have claimed from unknown readers the due to which he felt entitled from individuals honoured by his poems." Not only is there no mechanism by which a reader, qua reader, could support a poet, but the only way that a poet could lay the reader under obligation would be by complimenting him by name. But Martial makes the unorthodox demand that if the reader wants more, he must pay for it. Since this poem is the last in the book, it makes a nice closural effect that the reader's silence in response to this implausible demand results in the poet's. As Nauta (2002.118–20) points out, this poem belongs to a closural group that situates the *lector* in relation to other kinds of readers. In 11.106 Vibius Maximus is hailed and asked to read only this poem, but he's busy and doesn't like to give himself trouble: "You pass by these four lines too? You're wise." In 11.107 Septicianus, a poet, has returned Martial's book to him unrolled, as though to say that he has read it to the end. "I believe you," Martial replies. "I've read several of *your* books to the end in just the same way." So, in 11.108, we are left with the *lector*, neither patron nor fellow poet, but at least enthusiastic. The book's closing address to the *lector* makes an effective ring with the first poem, in which the book is eager to be off to Parthenius. "You'll return untouched" (*inevolutus*, 11.1.4; contrast *explicitum*, 11.107.1), comments the author, and then proceeds to suggest that the book betake itself to the temple of Quirinus, where it will find a lazy crowd that might be interested once the charioteer chitchat has dried up. The opening poem's contrast between busy patron and leisured, anonymous reader returns in the final sequence, with the added irony that the eager *lector* who wants to read more can do nothing to prolong the book.

It is a long way from Martial's "dissimulating" *lector* to the *New Yorker*'s alien "viewer," but both jokes depend on the ambiguous status of the audience in relation to a medium that is creating new and puzzling kinds of community. The reader who pretends not to understand (and what else could she do in his position? ) represents a readership that is ambiguously situated in relation to the society of the work: the circle of reciprocity can't quite close and the *lector* is neither in nor out of it. Martial's *lector* is certainly a precursor of the eighteenth century's "community of the book," but the imagined community I have been describing in this chapter is neither homogeneous nor stable. Indeed, the book itself is not a single space where diversity is absorbed into unity, as in the emperor's arena. Instead, different categories of readers and readings form shifting configurations in a virtual space which is one important dimension of the *world* of Martial's books.

# BANALIZATION·AND·REDEMPTION: MARTIAL'S·CATULLUS·AND·OVID; BURMEISTER'S·MARTIAL

The final chapter will take us from Martial's great Republican forbear, Catullus, to a surprising descendent in the Renaissance, the neo-Latin poet Johannes Burmeister. Poetic worlds collide as later poets misread, reread, and rewrite their forbears from the perspective of their own very different worlds. At the revisionary extreme is Johannes Burmeister, whose 1612 parody of Martial's complete oeuvre recasts it as a monument of Christian piety; at the other end of the spectrum, Martial adapts the exile poetry of Ovid to his own different, and yet continuous, political context. Somewhere in the middle come Martial's misreadings and rereadings of the aristocratic Catullus in the light of his own situation as a client poet, urban rather than urbane. The chapter moves from Martial's banalizations of Catullus to Burmeister's redemption of Martial, via Martial's repatriation of the exiled Ovid.

The history of reception has a way of reversing chronology. By a now familiar trope we might study the influence of Joyce on Homer or Dante on Vergil.[1] The paradox serves to remind us that we can never entirely dismiss our experience of what comes after from our reading of what comes first. With some poets, it is more literally true that the earlier is read through the later. The Renaissance did not rediscover or imitate the ancient writers in chronological order; in the case of Martial and Catullus, as Julia Gaisser has shown, Martial was known before Catullus, who learned to speak in the accents of the later poet.[2] Pontano, and more famously Politian, read

Catullus's *passer* poems though Martial's imitations and sparked a controversy that has lasted to this day.[3] Having read Martial's smirking offer (threat?) to give his boy "all of Catullus's *passer*," how can we not smirk when we read Catullus? But can Martial 11.6 be taken, as it sometimes is, as evidence that Martial read double entendre in Catullus's *passer* (and he should know)?[4] Harold Bloom has taught us that reading, or misreading, is one of the forms that writing takes in the case of epigonic poets,[5] and Martial may be deliberately misreading the earlier poet in order to bring about the very state of affairs he is taken to reflect.[6]

Though Martial could never have known that his poetry would become the stage on which Catullus would enter his modern reception, he was not ignorant of the possibility that time might be reversed. Toward the end of his twelfth, and final, book he inserts the name Catullus into one of his poems on legacy. This Catullus has been tantalizing, and probably exploiting, the speaker with the promise of inheritance.[7]

> Heredem tibi me, Catulle, dicis.
> non credo nisi legero, Catulle. (12.73)

> You tell me that I am your heir, Catullus. I won't believe you until I've read it!

The fact that Martial so frequently cites Catullus as model and authority for his epigrams must surely give the name Catullus here a double referent, both to some (real or imaginary) contemporary and to the Republican poet.[8] Behind the squib about legacies lies a statement about Martial's relation to the poet Catullus. Furthermore, Catullus the contemporary legator becomes an ineffectual version of the Martial who, in 1.1, boasts that he has not had to die in order to achieve fame: this Catullus is trying to cash in on the prospect of his death *before* he has died, but Martial is not taking the bait. So Martial reading his contemporary Catullus is on top, but what about Martial reading Catullus the dead poet? To be read after death is usually considered the highest honor to which a poet may aspire, a form of continued life. Are we not reminded that, as a poet, Martial is forced to acknowledge that he stands in Catullus's shade as well as his debt? Yes, and no. Perhaps the poet Catullus can be neutralized as effectively as the author of the putative will, since the later poet is at liberty to read into the predecessor's poetry whatever he wants; he has the advantage of being alive to (mis)read and to write. Martial engineers a brilliant interaction between levels of meaning as relations between epigone and forbear are read in terms of one of the predominant types of Martial's social satire, a context in which this poet will always come out on top. Furthermore, the epigram's point is a Bloomian reminder that for the precursor poet to be read is as dangerous as it is flattering.

Martial finds another way of saying "Catullus is dead" in 3.12, and this time he plays off a poem by Catullus himself (c. 13):

> Unguentum, fateor, bonum dedisti
> convivis here, sed nihil scidisti.
> res salsa est bene olere et esurire.
> qui non cenat et unguitur, Fabulle,
> hic vere mihi mortuus videtur.

The perfume you gave your guests yesterday was, I admit, a good one, but you carved nothing. It's amusing to smell nice and go hungry. He who doesn't dine but is anointed, Fabullus, really seems to me a corpse.

Catullus's urbane little invitation, featuring the elegant poverty that was to become such an important component of the Augustan poet's persona, is now seen from the perspective of the invitee. In Martial's poem, Fabullus strikes back, answering Catullus's boast with a concession (*unguentum,* fateor, *bonum dedisti,* 1) and then proceeding to a devastating comeback.[9] But though Martial's poem is spoken from the point of view of Catullus's Fabullus, the name of the addressee (here, the stingy host) remains Fabullus. Why? Surely because "Fabullus" is the name of the butt: for Catullus, the straight man who serves as foil to the poet's wit and sophistication; for Martial, the stingy host/patron who is the antagonist of his persona as poet-parasite.

Reading the invitation poem of Catullus through the agenda of the professional poet, Martial does to his precursor poet what Catullus did to his invitee.[10] Lured onto the poet's home turf, the

Fabullus of c. 13 finds himself willingly assimilating to Catullus's system of values, or so the poet boasts; but, seen from the perspective of the client-poet Martial, Catullus finds himself taking the position of his own Fabullus, a straight man who facilitates the poem's parting shot. Even more radically than his Fabullus, Catullus can't talk back—he's dead. The word *vere* clinches the poem: *of course* Catullus is dead, but now the evidence of one of his own poems convicts him of having been dead all along.[11] If it seems a cheap shot to make poetic capital out of the fact that Catullus is dead, it is nevertheless one of Martial's proudest boasts that he has not had to die in order to become famous (1.1.4–6, 5.13.4). That claim is aggressively banal, a refusal of the lofty ambitions which even Catullus can't resist in his coyly self-deprecating dedication poem (*quod, o patrona virgo, plus uno maneat perenne saeclo,* c. 1.9–10). Similarly, Martial's take on Catullus's teasing and sophisticated invitation is blatantly materialistic—Catullus is simply trying to get away with a cheap dinner.

So, according to the metapoetic conceit of 12.73 ("I won't believe that I'm your heir unless I read it"), Martial reads in Catullus c. 13 that its author is already dead. But where in Catullus's oeuvre does Martial read of himself? For this we must turn to one of his attempts on Catullus's kisses (cc. 5 and 7).[12]

> Tantum dat tibi Roma basiorum
> post annos modo quindecim reverso
> quantum Lesbia non dedit Catullo.
> te vicinia tota, te pilosus
> hircoso premit osculo colonus;
> hic instat tibi textor, inde fullo,
> hinc sutor modo pelle basiata,
> hinc menti dominus periculosi,
> +hinc+dexiocholus, inde lippus
> fellatorque recensque cunnilingus.
> iam tanti tibi non fuit redire. (12.59)

On your return after fifteen years, Rome gives you as many kisses as Lesbia never gave Catullus. The whole neighborhood, along with a hairy farmer with the smell of a goat, presses kisses on you. Here the weaver advances on you, and

there the fuller, and here comes the cobbler who has just
kissed his leather, and the owner of a dangerous chin, and
the man who limps with his right foot, and the one with the
bleary eye, and the cocksucker, and the cunnilinctor, fresh
from his ministrations. It really wasn't worth your while to
come home.

Though the poem alludes to the famous kiss poems of Catullus (cc. 5
and 7), c. 9 is an equally important intertext. There Catullus raptur-
ously greets Veranius, who has returned home from abroad to his *pe-
nates*, brothers and mother, replaced here by the smelly tradesmen.[13]
But prominent among Veranius's welcoming party is Catullus himself, who will put his arm round his friend's neck and kiss his eyes
and mouth (*applicansque collum / iucundum os oculosque suavia-
bor*, c. 9.8–9)—altogether a more pleasant homecoming than what
awaits Martial's unfortunate addressee.[14] Catullus looks forward to
hearing about the "places, events, and peoples" (*loca, facta, nationes*,
c. 9) that his talkative friend has encountered, whereas Martial is the
loquacious one in his poem, and he's also chattering about "places"
(*vicinia tota*, 4) and "peoples." It is Martial who is the anthropologist here, and Rome provides an inexhaustible stock of remarkable
*facta* to the inquisitive poet. This is a typically Martialian revision,
roughly equivalent to his programmatic claim that life is here, not
in the monsters of myth and epic poetry (cf. 10.4). What clinches the
connection between Catullus c. 9 and Martial 12.59 is the fact that
Catullus's Veranius is returning from Spain (*Hiberum*, 6), the home
of Martial himself. The Spanish poet in Rome (and now, at the end
of his career, returned to Spain) reverses the anthropologist's gaze
and delivers the account that Catullus anticipates from his Veranius, only it is an account of Roman districts and peoples. Rome is
the exotic place for this Iberian, and he translates Catullus's list of
topics (*loca, facta, nationes*) into a more explicit list of individual
types. Martial's poem delivers on what is only anticipated by Catullus, and no one is more qualified to deliver this account than the
Spanish Martial, a native of the very place from which Veranius has
returned. Martial has "read" himself into Catullus's writing, but not
before he has established that Catullus is dead.

On one of the relatively rare occasions when Martial expresses an ambition to take his place in the canon, it is Catullus to whom he refers by name.[15] Poem 10.78 concludes "but rank me only behind Catullus" (*uno sed tibi sim minor Catullo*, 16). Here, then, we would seem to have a more appropriate acknowledgment of secondary status on the part of the epigone. But the acknowledgment arrives by way of a compliment to the addressee, Macer, which cannot but remind us of certain poems of Catullus. Macer is about to take up the post of propraetor of Dalmatia. Martial, too, is leaving the capital, but his destination, far from being a career move, is tantamount to retirement: he is leaving for his native Spain, from which he will not return. Perhaps this is what gives him uncharacteristic thoughts of immortality. The poem ends with an ambitious hope for Martial's survival into posterity, phrased as an act of deference to Catullus. But this closing gesture of deference ends a poem whose attitude to imperial government is totally opposed to the urbane sense of entitlement flaunted in Catullus cc. 10 and 28. In these poems Catullus complains, on behalf of himself and his friends, of governors who have not enriched their accompanying entourage (*comites*). But the world has changed. Provincial governors must now reflect the virtues of the emperor in whose name they govern, and poets name names only in praise. The upright Macer (cf. 5.28.5) will return poorer than he has set out, and this is cause for praise, for Macer's *comes* is *pudor*, not a grasping poet like Catullus:

> ibit rara fides amorque recti
> et quae, cum comitem trahit pudorem
> semper pauperior redit postestas.

> With you will go a rare good faith and love of what is right
> and a power that, when it takes along restraint in its retinue,
> always returns the poorer.

Nothing here verbally recalls Catullus cc. 10 or 28, but any reader of those poems will remember the poet's disappointment that he had not brought back from Bithynia a "sleeker head" (*caput unctius*, c. 10.11). Martial's proud secondariness is parallel to Macer's virtuous impoverishment, which flies in the face of the attitudes reflected in Catullus's poems on governors and their entourages. To be less, in this case, may be more.

Whether in the scoptic or the panegyrical mode, then, Martial reads Catullus from the perspective of his own very different world, and this brings Catullus's casual assumptions into question. In some cases, however, Martial is in a position to return Catullan genres and language to contexts from which they have been diverted, and so to go behind Catullus's back. This is the case in 11.52, another take on Catullus's famous invitation poem (c. 13), whose prototype is Philodemus's epigram addressed to his patron Piso (*AP* 11.44).[16] Martial's opening, "You will dine well, Iulius Cerealis, at my place" (*Cenabis belle, Iuli Cerealis, apud me*), maintains the vocabulary of Catullus c. 13 (*Cenabis bene apud me, mi Fabulle*), but turns the first line into a hexameter, which diverts us into the meter of Greek epigram. Ironically, it is the substitution of the word *belle*, a quintessentially Catullan word, for Catullus's *bene*, that first steers us out of Catullus's hendecasyllables into the elegiacs of Philodemus and the Greek epigram. From there the poem veers sharply from Catullus.[17] After specifying the arrangements for meeting and bathing, Martial describes the simple menu in loving detail and contrasts it with the luxuries that Martial is unable to provide. It is at the end that Martial returns to engage Catullus and to mark the generic difference between the two poets. Catullus concludes by boasting of the perfume that he will provide Fabullus, a perfume given to him by his girl, which will leave Fabullus wishing himself "all nose." Martial's parting gesture and climactic hyperbole, far from being an overwhelming apotheosis of his own poetic creation, is an act of deference to Cerealis, patron and poet. For his own part, Martial promises to recite nothing, a promise worth more than any amount of delicacies.[18] Instead, Cerealis can recite his "Battle of the Giants" right to the end (*usque*, 11.52.17), and throw in his *Georgics* too, worthy of Vergil himself (*rura vel aeterno proxima Vergilio*, 18). Cerealis is both flattered and teased: the word *usque* (right to the end) assimilates him to the presumptuous Giants of his own poem; if he comes close to the divine Vergil, it is by piling verse upon verse. The gigantism of Catullus's man-become-nose is transferred to Cerealis's poem, and Martial retains the upper hand in his deferential gesture by the very excess of his flattery. Where Catullus imposes his own world on his guest and thereby transforms him, Martial ribs his invitee for transgressing a poetics of slightness.[19] Again, the poem implies that less is more, a principle which can be applied to the relation of the latecomer to his great forbear, who is outflanked with the help of his own aesthetic principles.

Martial's diversion of Catullus's invitation (c. 13) into the context of patronage appeals to the parallel tradition of Greek epigram at Rome represented by Catullus's contemporary, Philodemus. Something analogous happens when Martial alludes to the poems in which Catullus himself adapted the language of social relationships for his own amatory agenda. As David Ross (1969) pointed out, the vocabulary of the elegiac section of Catullus's oeuvre draws on the language of aristocratic social relations to characterize his affair with Lesbia. It is appropriate, then, for Martial to return those poems to the sphere of *amicitia* in a move that parallels his diversion of Catullus's invitation poem back into the world of Greek epigram. Martial 1.112 recalls the elegiac poems of Catullus's disillusioned love, but the addressee is now not a beloved but a certain Priscus:

> Cum te non nossem, dominum regemque vocabam:
> nunc bene te novi: iam mihi Priscus eris.

> When I didn't know you I called you lord and king: now I
> know you well: in future you'll be Priscus (Ancient).

Martial's Priscus has a speaking name: he *will be* (*eris*), as far as Martial is concerned, a "has been." In this poem we are reminded of Catullus c. 72, which expresses a rather different consequence of the disillusionment that has come from knowing Lesbia: "You used to say that you knew only Catullus, Lesbia, . . . and I loved you . . . but now I know you, and so I burn more deeply" (*Dicebas quondam solum te nosse Catullum, / Lesbia, . . . dilexi tum te . . . nunc te cognovi: quare etsi impensius uror,* c. 72.1–5). Is the relation between patron and client in Martial invested with the intensity of Catullus's love affair by the allusion? Or are we to welcome this pattern of experience back to its rightful sphere? Surely the latter. Martial's brilliantly dismissive use of his addressee's name is about as far as we can imagine from Catullus's tortured inability to stop loving Lesbia and break with her. In fact, Catullus's perverse use of the language of patron-client relations (*benefacta, officium, fides*, etc.) is a large part of what gives the elegiac love poetry its peculiar intensity, and Martial here turns down the heat by returning this language to its rightful context while alluding to Catullus's appropriations.

Catullus c. 72 ends with his familiar distinction between *bene velle* and *amare*: "because such an injury compels a lover to love (*amare*) more, but to like (*bene velle*) less" (c. 72.7–8). Martial makes a similar distinction in 2.54, another complaint of a disillusioned client:

> Vis te Sexte coli, volebam amare.
> parendum est tibi: quod iubes, coleris.
> sed si te colo, Sexte, non amabo.

> Sextus, you want me to pay court to you; I wanted to love you. I must obey you: as you ordain, I'll pay you court. But if I pay you court, Sextus, I won't love you.

The psychological compulsion under which the Catullan lover suffers (*cogit*, c. 72.8) becomes a matter of the patron's will (*vis, iubes*, 2.54.1, 2), to which the client accedes, but with a warning. Catullus's pained paradoxes are transformed by Martial into an exchange, a trade-off. The emotional heat of Catullus's world is turned down a notch or two, but that, in its modest way, is the point of Martial's address to Sextus.[20] In these panegyrical poems (10.78, 11.52, 1.112), the relation between client and patron is overlaid by, or onto, that of poet and precursor, and the two agendas mutually support each other.

Another case of Catullan love poetry resurrected in the very different world of patron and client is the poem in which Martial regrets that he and his namesake cannot share the life of heedless abandon to which Catullus invites his Lesbia in c. 5:

> Si tecum mihi, care Martialis,
> securis liceat frui diebus,
> si disponere tempus otiosum

> et verae pariter vacare vitae.
> nec nos atria nec domos potentum
> nec litis tetricas forumque triste
> nossemus nec imagines superbas;
> sed gestatio, fabulae, libelli,
> campus, porticus, umbra, Virgo, thermae,
> haec essent loca semper, hi labores.
> nunc vivit necuter sibi, bonosque
> soles effugere atque abire sentit,
> qui nobis pereunt et imputantur.
> quisquam, vivere cum sciat, moratur? (5.20)

If, my dear Martialis, I could enjoy with you untroubled days; if I could dispose of time at leisure and we could both be free for real living, we would know nothing of the reception halls or houses of the powerful, nor of bitter lawsuits or the gloomy forum or proud family trees. Instead there'd be litters, conversation, books, the Field, the colonnade, the shade, the Virgin [an aqueduct], the baths—these would be our habitual places, these our labors. As it is, neither of us lives for himself, but feels the good days ["suns"] escape and disappear, days which are lost to us but charged to our account. Does anyone who knows how to live delay?

Martial speaks to his friend in counterfactuals, rather than in Catullus's rousing iussives (*Vivamus, mea Lesbia, atque amemus*, c. 5.1). The "bitter lawsuits and the gloomy forum" (*litis tetricas forumque triste*, 5.20.6) may be the equivalent of Catullus's "grumblings of old men" (*rumores senum severiorum*, c. 5.2), but they are the daily bread and butter of both Martials. Catullus's invitation to Lesbia to live it up in the face of death surfaces as a question at the end of the poem, with a pun on *moritur/moratur* (dies/delays); the mood is regretful rather than anticipatory.[21] When Catullus demands his kisses of Lesbia his wording suggests that an account is being kept (*da mi basia mille, deinde centum*, c. 5.4); in the end, however, the poet resolves to declare bankruptcy in order to avert the evil eye (*conturbabimus illa*, c. 5.11). Martial echoes the financial metaphor with his *imputantur* (are charged to our account, 13), which has a meaning exactly the opposite of Catullus's *conturbabimus*: the two

Martials cannot evade the accounts that are kept of their time, however little use they have of it. This time is represented by the suns that will be put down to their account, and those suns are on a one-way journey (*effugere et abire*, 12) not a round trip, as in Catullus (*occidere et redire*, c. 5.4). The lovers, who unlike the sun cannot return, are spurred on to amass their hoard of kisses and then confuse the accounts (*soles occidere et redire possunt / nobis cum semel occidit brevis lux / nox est perpetua una dormienda*, 4–6). Catullus's polar *occidere et redire* is matched by Martial's cruelly paradoxical *pereunt et imputantur*. Typically, Martial has transformed Catullus's ecstatic accumulation of the same (*basia mille, deinde centum*), in the enclosed world of the reckless twosome, into an expansive, if wistful, catalog of urban places. There may be no impressive numbers in Martial, but the specificity of the list ensures that less, once again, is more.

## URBANE AND URBAN

As we have seen in the case of 12.55 and 5.20, Martial likes to inject the sprawl of urban life into the tight little world of Catullan urbanity. Nowhere is this more in evidence than in his version of Catullus c. 12, the elegant put-down of the would-be urbane Asinius Marrucinus, who thinks it is witty to steal napkins. Martial puts his cards on the table right from the start:

> Urbanus tibi, Caecili, videris.
> non es, crede mihi. quid ergo? verna es. (1.41.1–2)

> You like to think of yourself as urbane, Caecilius. You aren't,
> believe you me. What are you then? You're local.[22]

The first two lines are an epigram in themselves, with the closing *verna es* echoing and revising *urbanus* to devastating effect. There follows one of Martial's most vivid urban lists, a lovingly observed ten-line (3–13) catalog of street hawkers who have more wit than the unfortunate Caecilius. In place of Catullus's stolen napkin, treasured gift of Veranius and Fabullus, Martial brings on sulfur matches, broken glass, pease puddings, vipers, dancing girls, and sausages—cheap wares for the urban mob. Martial has exchanged Catullus's exotic Spain, origin of the treasured napkin (*sudaria Saetaba ex Hiberis*, c. 12.14), for the everyday world of commercial Rome, where everybody has something to hawk.[23] Caecilius is as urbane as the people who hawk these urban wares, or as the lousy town poet (*urbicus poeta*, 1.41.11); the precise nuance of *urbicus*, an extremely rare word, is not known, but it is likely that this poet presents a burlesque version of the urbane Catullus. Catullus's purpose in attacking Asinius is as much to turn an elegant compliment to Veranius and Fabullus as it is to put down Asinius, whose punishment is to be excluded from the circle that the poem constitutes. For Catullus there is an in and an out, and it is the careful shutting out of Marrucinus that creates the charm of the inner circle; outside it, there is only weeping and gnashing of teeth.[24] By contrast, Martial's Caecilius serves to provide a window onto the expansive world of Martial's poetry, urban rather than urbane. Where Catullus pits urbanity against its opposites (*sordida, invenusta* c. 12.5), Martial expands into synonyms and analogs (*verna*, 2; *urbicus*, 11). *Verna* is another form of the local, like *urbanus*, and the home-born slave (*verna*), licensed to exercise a cheeky wit, is also a cut-price version of the *urbanus*. *Urbicus* is equivalent to *urbanus*, but with the metaphor leached out. And it is not only Caecilius who is deprived of his metaphor in the shift from *urbanus* to *urbicus*, for Catullus's *salsum*, the quintessence of urbanity (*hoc salsum esse putas?* c. 12.4), is materialized in Martial's *salarii* (salt merchants, 1.41.8).[25] Similarly, Martial's list of hawkers is derived from the Catullan metaphor by which Marrucinus's brother Pollio would have his brother's thefts *changed* "for as much as a talent" (*vel talento* / mutari *vellet*, c. 12.7–8). Typically, in Martial's version, the exchange is between two similarly banal kinds of object, and it takes us as far away from the Catullan figurative as we could imagine (*qui pallentia sulphurata fractis* / permutat *vitreis*, 1.41.4–5).

The poems come together (and then diverge) in their endings, both of which revolve around the names of people to whom the target is contrasted. In Catullus, it is his friends Veranius and Fabullus, donors of the napkin, whose names are fetishized in the final lines:

> nam sudaria Saetaba ex Hiberis
> miserunt mihi muneri Fabullus
> et Veranius; haec amem necesse est
> ut Veraniolum meum et Fabullum. (c. 12.14–17)

> For Fabullus and Veranius sent me as a gift from Spain nap-
> kins from Saetabis; these I must love as my own little Vera-
> nius and Fabullus.

The diminutive *Veraniolum* suggests that Fabullus is itself a diminutive (of *faba*, bean). Martial's final line also conjures an object out
of a name. Caecilius thinks he is as witty as Tettius Caballus, but
Martial knows otherwise:

> ludit qui stolida procacitate,
> non est Tettius ille, sed caballus. (1.41.19–20)

> Anyone who fools around with blockheaded cheek is not a
> Tettius but a nag.

There is no mention, in Martial's imitation, of the napkin theft that
is the ostensible occasion for Catullus's attack on Marrucinus. But
this aspect of Catullus's original receives ample attention in 12.28,
where the napkin thefts of Hermogenes are described at length.
Again, Catullus's intimate social world is expanded in Martial's
version, this time to take in the public celebrations of imperial
Rome. Hermogenes steals napkins waved in the amphitheater for
the discharge of a gladiator (7–8) and then proceeds to steal the
whitened napkin used by the praetor to start a race (9–10); such
is his reputation that when he appears at the games the canopy is
withdrawn as a precaution against theft, even if the sun is beating
down (15–16).

### KISSES

The emperor's spectacles intrude again on the intimate world of
Catullus in 6.34, another of Martial's assaults on Catullus's kisses.

> Basia da nobis, Diadumene, pressa "quot" inquis?
>> Oceani fluctus me numerare iubes
> et maris Aegaei sparsas per litora conchas
>> et quae Cecropio monte vagantur apes
> quaeque sonant pleno vocesque manusque theatro
>> cum populus subiti Caesaris ora videt.
> nolo quot arguto dedit exorata Catullo
>> Lesbia: pauca cupit qui numerare potest.

> Give me kisses, thick and fast, Diadumenos. "How many?"
> You say. You ask me to number the waves of the ocean, and
> the shells scattered along the shores of the Aegean sea, and
> the bees that drift over the Cecropian mount, and the hands
> and mouths that sound in the packed theater when the peo-
> ple suddenly sees the face of Caesar. I don't want as many as
> the tuneful Catullus begged from Lesbia: he who can keep
> the count wants little.

Turning from various literary topoi of uncountability to his own world, Martial conjures up the roaring, clapping crowd that greets Caesar when he appears in the amphitheater.[26] In the sudden appearance of Caesar's face at the games we have Martial's version of the innumerable stars that watch the secret love affairs of men on earth in Catullus c. 5 (*aut quam sidera multa cum tacet nox / furtivos hominum vident amores*, 8–9). It is in every way the opposite of Catullus's image: noise for silence, day for night, suddenness for permanence, public for private and, above all, particularized realism for literary topos.[27] If Catullus makes himself and his beloved the envied objects of the gazing stars, Martial is aligned, less gloriously, with the cheering multitude at the games. The couple isolated under the night sky is replaced by Martial's emperor, a single figure who appears in the firmament, like the sun, to dispel Catullus's constellations, and with them much of the anxiety of Catullus's poem. Catullus's star-studded, silent sky foreshadows or images the *curiosi* whose envy the poet is at pains to foil with the sheer quantity of his kisses. Transferring Catullus's precarious and threatened love scene to the arena, where the emperor is unstintingly acclaimed, Martial has drained the envy out of Catullus's world; similarly he replaces Catullus's anxious *contrast* between nature's self-renewing cycles and human mortality with the people's *equation* of the emperor's appearance with the break of day. Martial's poem is turned outward, not inward; acclamation, rather than spying, characterizes its social world, and the emphasis is throughout on sound: the waves of the ocean and the bees on Hymettus are outdone by the roar of the crowd in the packed amphitheater, against which "tuneful [clear-voiced, witty] Catullus" sounds rather puny (*arguto . . . Catullo*, 7; contrast Catullus's *vesano Catullo*, 7.10). Martial's closural point (*pauca cupit . . . qui numerare potest*) has been described as a misunderstanding of Catullus's counting, which is emphatically not an enumeration.[28] But surely this is a deliberate misreading which makes the aggressively banal point that more is, indeed, more.

Martial's tendency to situate the self-enclosed poems of Catullus's amatory and social world in the larger frame of city life is well exemplified by 11.6, which brings together those two emblems of Catullan poetry, the kisses and the sparrow. In c. 5 Catullus invited Lesbia to an abandoned life of love heedless of the "murmurs of censorious old men" (*rumores senum severiorum*, c. 5.2). Martial situates his request for Catullan kisses at the *Saturnalia* (*falciferi . . . senis*) and prefaces his sympotic poem with a request to "liberated Rome" (*pilleata Roma*) for permission to speak freely. Far from being an act of Catullan defiance, his invitation to love is set within the communal celebration of the whole city, to which he defers:

> Unctis falciferi senis diebus,
> regnator quibus imperat fritillus,
> versu ludere non laborioso
> permittis, puto, pilleata Roma. (11.6.1–4)

During the greasy days of the sickle-wielding god [Saturn], over which the sovereign dice-box rules, you permit me, I think, liberated Rome, to play with a verse that does not labor.

But invitation is perhaps not the right word, since here, as in 6.34, the beloved who stands in Lesbia's place is a slave.

> misce dimidios, puer, trientes,
> quales Pythagoras dabat Neroni,
> misce, Dindyme, sed frequentiores:
> possum nil ego sobrius; bibenti
> succurrent mihi quindecim poetae.
> da nunc basia, sed Catulliana:
> quae si tot fuerint quot ille dixit,
> donabo tibi passerem Catulli. (11.6.5–12)

Boy, mix me cups of half and half, like the ones Pythagoras would give to Nero, mix them, Dindymus, but keep them coming: I can't do anything when I'm sober; when I drink, fifteen poets will come to my aid. Give me kisses, but Catullan ones, and if you give me as many as he told, I'll present you with Catullus's "sparrow."

Does the Catullan lover torment himself with "servitude" to a "divine" *domina*? In Martial it is the beloved who is, quite literally, a slave. The names Diadumenos (6.34) and Dindymus (11.6) connote the culture of classical Greece as surely as does "Lesbia," but they are a mark of the master's right over his beloved, not a glorification. This change is not only a matter of turning down the emotional heat in a banalization of Catullan passion, but also of appealing to commonly understood social realities in place of literary metaphors.[29] As so often in Martial, it is slaves and slavery that are emblematic of his genre.

The final line of this poem is sometimes taken as evidence that Catullus's *passer* of cc. 2 and 3 is more than it seems. But it would be more accurate to say that Martial, in a characteristically banalizing move, makes the Catullan *passer* into a phallic symbol, so that we cannot read Catullus's ambiguities without a dirty joke intruding on our minds. We have already seen how, in 1.7, the phallic *passer* gives a crude turn to Martial's compliment to Stella and to Catullus's suspiciously bare compliment to Cicero, on which it is modeled. Here Catullus's ambiguous and teasing suggestiveness is turned into a terminal point: the final line (as Kay 1985 has pointed out) is a *para prosdokian*, for if it ended at *passerem* we would have a conventional transaction between lover and boy: the boy is given a traditional lover's gift in return for his kisses. The modifying *Catulli* both changes the "gift" and implies that Catullus meant more than just "sparrow," and it's not hard to imagine what.[30] Far from being satisfied with kisses, as Catullus seems to have been on the evidence of cc. 5 and 7, Martial will take things to the next level—the giving of the *passer* becomes a form of taking, an assertion of ownership. But perhaps there is a further joke: Dindymus is the mountain sacred to Cybele, and it features in Catullus's lament of the self-castrated Attis (c. 63.91). The *passerem Catulli* is what anyone called Dindymus might be expected, on the evidence of Catullus 63, to lack (and therefore need?).[31]

Not only is Catullus's Lesbia replaced in Martial by a slave, but so is her *passer*. The genre of poems on the death of pets, common in the Hellenistic epigram, was adapted by Greek epigrammatists at Rome to celebrate the death of their patrons' favorite slaves.[32] The *deliciae* of Lesbia and her forbears became the *delicati* of Roman aristocrats, celebrated by Martial to endow their owners with an aura of culture, luxury, or refinement.[33] Transforming Lesbia's pet into a slave, Martial is shadowing a development within the history of Greek epigram. But Martial is not above spoofing his own epitaphs on slaves, and in 7.14 he does so while alluding to Catullus's *passer* poems, and in the process complimenting two of his patrons:[34]

> Accidit infandum nostrae scelus, Aule, puellae;
>   amisit lusus deliciaeque suas:
> non quales teneri ploravit amica Catulli
>   Lesbia, nequitiis passeris orba sui,
> vel Stellae cantata meo quas flevit Ianthis,
>   cuius in Elysio nigra columba volat:
> lux mea non capitur nugis nec amoribus istis,
>   nec dominae pectus talia damna movent:
> bis senos puerum numerantem perdidit annos,
>   mentula cui nondum sesquipedalis erat

A monstrous crime has been committed on my girl, Aulus: she has lost her plaything and her darling. Not the kind that Lesbia the tender girlfriend of Catullus bewailed, bereft of her sparrow's naughty tricks, nor the kind of darling

> mourned by Ianthis, subject of my Stella's verse (her black
> dove flies in Elysium). My beloved is not attracted by such
> trifles or affections, nor do those losses move my mistress's
> heart. She lost a slave of twelve years old, whose cock was not
> yet eighteen inches long.

Catullus and Stella have been compared in terms of the size of their
respective birds in 1.7, but size is not initially the issue here. The
priamel (*non quales . . . vel . . .* ) is silent about the respect in which
these birds are to be compared, and allows Stella, patron and poet,
to be endowed with the elegant aura of Catullus's *passer*.[35] Stella
is flattered and Aulus, the addressee, who is not a poet (cf. 8.63),
receives the dirty joke.[36] As for Martial's "mistress," she remains
nameless, but the sense in which she is a mistress is the crux of
the joke. In line 8 *dominae* is naturally taken to be equivalent to
*nostrae puella* (1) and *lux mea* (7), but the appearance of *puerum*
in the following line changes the scenario. Once again, Martial
marks the divergence of his own genre from his models by bringing a slave onto the scene. If his mistress's darling is taken to be
something in the nature of Catullus's *passer*, then the final joke is
another of Martial's literalizations of Catullus's teasingly ambiguous bird. What is distinctive about this one is that the size of the
prodigious slave's *mentula* is indicated by a word that refers us to
another poem of Catullus. The extremely rare *sesquipedalis* occurs
in c. 97, a prime example of Catullan *Vetulaskoptik* (mockery of old
women); the urbane eroticism of Catullus 2 has been diverted into a
branch of Catullus's poetry that is more to Martial's taste.

We return to a more direct application of Catullus's lament to
the world of patronage in 1.109, a poem on Publius's pet dog, Issa,
whose death Publius has forestalled by having her portrait painted
(*hanc ne lux rapiat suprema totam, / picta Publius exprimit tabella*,
17–18). The intertextual relation with Catullus 2 and 3, announced
in the first line (*Issa est passere nequior Catulli*, 1), is itself reflected
in the final lines, where model and portrait are declared to be in-
distinguishable (*Issam denique pone cum tabella: / aut utramque
putabis esse veram, / aut utramque putabis esse pictam*, 21–23). But
Martial's poem, while modeled on Catullus's, is quite different. Issa

is altogether more decorous than Lesbia's provocative *passer,* and the erotic playfulness of Catullus's poems has been replaced by an accommodating obedience. Catullus's *desiderium* ("beloved," c. 2.5), who solaces her pain by playing with the sparrow, is recalled here by the *desiderium* ("need," 1.109.10) that compels the well-trained dog to ask to be put down before she soils the coverlet (*et desiderio coacta ventris / gutta pallia non fefellit una,* 10–11). The complicated, fluid relations between the desire of Catullus for Lesbia, the desire of Lesbia for Catullus, and the sparrow through which they both play with that desire, all focused in Catullus's *cum desiderio meo nitenti / carum nescioquid lubet iocari* (c. 2.5–6), have been reduced to the simple urge to pee, managed by good housetraining. Where Catullus's *passer* had pecked its mistress's provoking finger, Publius's dog uses her paw to signal that she needs to be put down from the couch (12–13). Catullan ambiguity and suggestiveness are controlled as efficiently as the dog controls its bladder. Coming, as it does, toward the end of Martial's first book, this poem forms a ring with 1.7, in which Stella's *columba* is said to have outdone Catullus's by as much as a dove is bigger than a sparrow. The two poems span this book so as to make the book itself programmatic for Martial's oeuvre. In both cases, Martial conflates the contest with his precursor with an elegant compliment to a patron, and in the process he drains the teasing ambiguity from Catullus's *passer* to replace it with something much more obviously tongue-in-cheek.

By way of transition to our next author, we can note another category of Martial's revisionary relation to his forerunner, namely his promotion of a poetic type that is marginal in Catullus's oeuvre to a more prominent position in his own. A Catullan rarity that will become a staple in Martial is the urban itinerary, exemplified in cc. 55.3–6 and 58b, where Catullus tries to track down the elusive Camerius. The list of landmarks in c. 55 culminates in the colonnade of Pompey's recently dedicated theater (*Magni . . . ambulatione,* 55.6). We can compare Martial 2.14, in which Selius's search for a dinner invitation takes him all over the Campus Martius, so that in the course of his peregrinations he replicates the world-mastering journeys represented by the monuments there.[37] Urban itineraries are an important component of Martial's oeuvre, and many contain references to imperial monuments, but in this the influence of Catullus will be mediated by another body of work that is of fundamental importance to Martial, Ovid's exile poetry.[38]

## MARTIAL REPATRIATES OVID

As in the case of Catullus's love poetry, Ovid's exile poetry is subjected to banalizing transformations as it is accommodated to Martial's poetic agenda, but that, as we shall see, is by no means the whole story.[39] Luke Roman encapsulates one aspect of this relationship well when he observes that "in general, Martial adapts motifs formed in the context of 'poetry in exile,' and rewrites them in terms of 'poetry as usual.'"[40] This rewriting can produce a striking dissonance with the painful circumstances of Ovid's exile. For instance, Martial insists that if there are lapses of Latinity in his poetry, that is the fault of the copyist trying to keep up with the demands of an insatiable public (2.8.1–4), and not (we are reminded) the result of relegation to a barbarian land (*Tristia* 3.1.17–18).

Ovid's dispatching of his books from Tomi to Rome is a theme that can be conveniently recycled, in less dramatic terms, by the client-poet ensconced in the capital. In *Tristia* 1.1 and 3.1 the exiled Ovid dispatches his book, which he cannot accompany, to Rome; in 1.70 Martial sends his book off to Proculus's *salutatio* in his stead, for if he is to be a *salutator* he cannot be a writer.[41] Ovid in Tomi has stronger reasons for sending the book to act on his behalf, as the distinction between Martial's *pro me* (1.70.1) and Ovid's *sine me* (*Tr.* 1.1.1) suggests, but the circumstances of the two poets are not in all respects as different as in the case of diminished Latinity. As John Geyssen points out, the monuments which Martial enumerates in the itinerary he gives his book all have associations with Domitian, who is the imagined overreader of Martial's poem to Proculus.[42] For Martial to allude to Ovid's exile poetry is to remind us both of the differences and of the similarities of their condition. Both poets must approach an emperor who may be, and in Ovid's case has been, censorious of his poetry, an emperor on whose favor they both depend. But Martial is in Rome;

unlike Ovid, he has found imperial favor in spite of the content of his poetry.[43] When he boasts that Domitian praises his poetry, the title by which he addresses the emperor is carefully chosen to remind us of Ovid (*Saepe meos laudare soles, Auguste, libellos*, 4.27.1).[44] Similarly, Martial's own "exiles," to Forum Iulii in Book 3 and to his homeland Spain in Book 12, are voluntary.[45] Echoes of Ovid in these cases (e.g., *Romam vade liber . . .* , 3.4.1) certainly remind us that Martial's condition is more fortunate, but though the allusions to Ovid's exile poetry have a self-congratulatory air, they are much less revisionary and polemical than his allusions to Catullus. Roger Pitcher is surely right when he suggests that Ovid's geographical distance from Rome, and the emperor whose forgiveness he seeks, is recycled by Martial as a different kind of distance, one that separates the ordinary citizen from the divine emperor; it acquires a panegyrical edge.[46]

When Martial celebrates the emperor's arena and its spectacles, he is writing a poetry whose effectiveness depends on the poet's presence at Rome, but here too Martial is taking up from where Ovid left off. This is brilliantly argued by Mario Labate, who speculates, with Ovid's own authority, on the poetry Ovid would have written had he been returned to Rome.[47] His very absence from Rome prompts Ovid to outline a poetry of presence that, should the emperor allow him, would celebrate the rituals and social events of the court. This he adumbrates in a negative image by complaining that his own accounts of recent triumphs must suffer from the fact that he wasn't present, and that by the time they reach Rome they will be old news.[48] Labate argues that this imagined poetry of presence includes a model of reception, instructing its public how to enjoy the events it celebrates.[49] The relevance of Labate's description to Martial's *Liber spectaculorum* is obvious, but it is not restricted to that book. With Martial, the exiled Ovid comes home and writes the poetry conceived in, but prevented by, his exile.[50]

Ovid, then, ushered in a new kind of imperial poetry in the very particular circumstances of his exile, and Martial adapted Ovidian motifs to his own happier condition. But he did so under a political system continuous with that which relegated Ovid to Tomi, and there are occasions in Martial where he too senses the precariousness of the poet's condition. Martial's books approach their dedicatees with trepidation or confidence, but always deferentially, waiting for the right moment. The prototype for this motif is *Tristia* 1.1.93–98, where Ovid gives his book advice about approaching the emperor who has the power to bring him home. In Martial's case it is always possible that the patrons approached by his book won't have time for such frivolity—they have better things to do.[51] If they do take up the book, it will only be in a vacant hour, and until then the book must bide its time. Meanwhile, there are other, lesser readers, whose interest can be guaranteed. In the first poem of Book 11 the author addresses the book, all dressed up to visit Parthenius (*cultus Sidone non cotidiana*, 2). Possibly it will return unrolled, for Parthenius reads more serious stuff (*libros non legit ille sed libellos*, 5). In that case the book should make for the colonnade of the temple of Quirinus, where there is always an idle crowd of people who will read the book once the betting and talk about horses has played itself out. "Do you consider yourself happy enough if lesser hands take you up?" Martial asks his book (*ecquid te satis aestimas beatum, / contingunt tibi si manus minores*? 7–8), echoing the end of *Tristia* 3.1, where the book comes to Rome, only to find itself barred from the public libraries. "If a public location is denied me," says Ovid's book, "then in the meantime I can lie low in a private place." It concludes:

> Vos quoque, si fas est, confusa pudore repulsae
>   sumite plebeiae carmina nostra manus. (*Tristia* 3.1.81–82)

> You too, plebeian hands, if I may say so, take up my songs
>   dismayed by the shame of their rejection.

The circumstances of these two poems may not be as different as they seem. Book 11, written after the assassination of Domitian, addresses itself to the new regime of Nerva. The addressee of 11.1 is Parthenius, Domitian's freedman *a cubiculo*, who played a leading role in the assassination of Domitian and had, temporarily at least, successfully weathered the transition from one regime to another, as Martial himself hoped to do. This poem, then, may have almost as much at stake as Ovid's. In both poems two different readerships are situated in relation to each other, and this complementarity between the court and the general public becomes, as we have seen, a significant structure in Martial's imagining of his readership.[52]

As a writer of risqué verse, which may fall foul of the emperor, Martial must hope that he does not go the way of Ovid. In the meantime he can flatter the emperor who has exercised in his case a *clementia* which Ovid sought, without success, from *his* emperor. But the age of Augustus also provides Martial with a model of imperial patronage from which the present age, as he frequently points out, has sadly declined.[53] He is, then, both more and less fortunate than Ovid. This ambivalence is well brought out by 11.3, in which Martial boasts that his poetry is read by the stiff centurion in the Getic frosts (*sed meus in Geticis ad Martia signa pruinis / a rigido teritur centurione liber*, 3–4). That centurion, rigid not only from the cold but from Martial's stimulating poetry, is located where Ovid spent his years of exile, a place that now marks the extent of the poet's fame rather than his removal from the center of literary activity. Martial's books reverse the direction of Ovid's exile poetry, which makes hopefully for the imperial city from the margins of the empire where Ovid languishes among the Getae. Now it is the emperor's army that is reassuringly located on the margins of the empire. But what good is it to Martial that a centurion posted among the Getae reads his poetry? Like Catullus, he has an empty wallet (*nescit sacculus ista meus*, 11.3.5; cf. Catullus, c. 13.8). Augustus has been returned to earth, but where is Maecenas (*at quam victuras poteramus pangere chartas . . . cum pia reddiderint Augustum numina terris, / et Maecenatem si tibi, Roma, darent!* 11.3.7–11)? The emperor is both flattered as an Augustus *renatus*, and urged to follow the example of the first *princeps* in the matter of patronage; conveniently, the figure of Maecenas allows Martial to detach this complaint from the emperor himself. The present emperor is Nerva, and Martial is approaching the new regime hopefully.[54] In the previous poem he quotes Ovid to make an optimistic contrast not only between Augustus and Nerva but between Nerva and Domitian: now that political freedom has been restored, his book cries *io Saturnalia* and returns to its wonted freedom of speech where sexual material is concerned. As for "austere readers" (*lectores tetrici*, 11.2.7), "I have no business with you" (*nil mihi vobiscum est*, 8), Martial exclaims, echoing Ovid, who asks of his poetry, *quid mihi vobiscum est?* (*Tristia* 2.1.1). When he asks this question, Ovid is beginning a new book, fully aware that his poetry may dig him deeper into the hole with Augustus, whereas Martial, at the beginning of his eleventh book, is celebrating a new regime which, he claims, will afford him a poetic freedom he has lacked under Domitian. Martial's poem concludes, "I have no business with you [sc. *lectores tetrici*]. This book is mine" (*nil mihi vobiscum est: iste liber meus est*, 8), virtually the opposite of the opening line of *Tristia* 2 (*Quid mihi vobiscum est, infelix cura, libelli?*).[55] If Martial's approach to the new emperor alludes hopefully to the situation of Ovid, later in the same book Martial will reclaim Augustus as a champion of obscene poetry, quoting a scurrilous poem by the first *princeps* as an authority for his own obscenity, or *Romana simplicitas*, as he coyly puts it (*absolvis lepidos nimirum, Auguste, libellos, / qui scis Romana simplicitate loqui*, 11.20.9–10). With Martial playing Ovid in a more hopeful context, Augustus finds himself in the unaccustomed position of "acquitting" books (*absolvis . . . libellos*)!

## BURMEISTER REDEEMS MARTIAL

Martial's "repatriation" of Ovid's exile poetry is nothing to the redemption inflicted on Martial's poetry by Johannes Burmeister, and I turn now to what must appear to be one of the most perverse of all literary endeavors. In 1612 Johannes Burmeister published his *Martialis renatus*, a sacred parody of the entire oeuvre of Martial, in which each poem of Martial is faced on the opposite page by a parody that finds a Christian equivalent of the original. This feat was accomplished at the same time that Ben Jonson was busy de-expurgating his text of Martial, not only copying in the excised naughty bits but explicating the sexual jokes.[56] Burmeister could hardly have chosen a less likely author for this kind of exercise; even Plautus's *Amphitryo*, another text he parodied, seems more promising.[57] But Burmeister censors nothing, and does not even shy away from the unpromising books 13 (*Xenia*) and 14 (*Apophoreta*), which, admittedly, present a challenge to which even he is not equal. Not surprisingly, it is Martial's book of wonders, the *Liber spectaculorum*, which works best of all.

If nothing else, Burmeister's feat is a prodigy of industry, and he begins his preface by quoting Scaliger to the effect that laziness is the greatest threat to a learned mind. So Martial's idle books for an idle hour (*liber otiose*, 11.1.1) have become a weapon in the war against idleness, and Burmeister's parody of Martial cures the very sins that the original provokes. This relation between original and parody manifests itself also on the level of content. As a byword for obscenity and irreverence, Martial is not an author to be read, let alone duplicated, without explanation. Burmeister's apologia has two parts, not exactly compatible with each other. The first denies the charge against Martial: his obscenity was simply an appropriate response to his times, a satiric device in what is essentially a moral oeuvre. But Burmeister's description of his own project takes a different tack:

> Trium equidem criminum insimulor, reus non deprehendor. Levitatem in Martiale agnosco; sed gravitate obvelo. Vanitatem in illo video; sed veritate immuto. Profanitatem denique in eodem non abnego. Sed pietate absorbeo. (Preface to First Part)

> So, I am charged with three crimes, but cannot be apprehended as a culprit. I recognize the frivolity of Martial but veil it in seriousness. I see the falsity in him, but I transform it into truth. Finally I do not refuse his profanity, but wash it down with piety.

Burmeister's poems "cover" Martial, protecting the reader from the corruption of the original. But this protection will work only if there is some equivalence between original and parody, some reason why we should accept the parody as a substitute for the original. Parodies of the kind with which we are more familiar, parodies *downward*, could also be thought of as a form of protection, from the pretensions of the author parodied: if the parody is successful we can no longer read the original without the parody obtruding itself. Martial achieves something of this kind with his banalizations of Catullus. Parody *upward*, so to speak, cannot quite perform the same feat, but it too must engage something in the original which points, or can be made to point, toward the redeemed version, rather as the Old Testament is taken to point to the New. Burmeister's parallel text, with Martial before and after rebirth on either side of the page, is not unlike the Christian Bible itself.[58] In fact, the project is not as improbable as it seems at first. The perversity of the flesh; the ironies and reversals of a religion whose God has been crucified; the apothegms that should guide the Christian life—all these are suitable for epigrammatization. Furthermore, the Old Testament conveniently supplies Burmeister with plenty of wrongdoers to match Martial's rogues' gallery; when that fails, the Lutheran Burmeister can always turn to pope-bashing for an equivalent of Martial's scoptic epigrams.

The sheer variety of Martial's books may itself be seen as a provocation to the idea of a Christian literature with a single message, as Burmeister indicates in his parody of 1.16. Martial's original is

> Sunt bona, sunt quaedam mediocria, sunt mala plura
> quae legis hic: aliter non fit, Avite, liber.

> There are some good things, some indifferent, and more bad to be read here: a book, Avitus, can't be made in any other way.

Burmeister replies with

> Sunt sacra, sunt flatus oracula vera sacrati,
> quae legis heic, aliud nil sacra biblia habent.

> They are sacred things, the true declarations of the Holy Ghost, which you read here; the Holy Bible has nothing else.

The miscellany of Martial's world is matched by Burmeister's inclusive parody, which finds a Christian equivalent for everything, and yet this everything is in fact one, the true word of the Holy Ghost. The good book absorbs Martial's oeuvre, and heterogeneity is transformed into unity. Burmeister might reply to Martial that a book *can* be made differently (*aliter*), but not by a human.

Appropriately, Burmeister's single most successful parody is Martial 1.1, where the stately progress of Martial's self-confident thanks to his reader is matched to Burmeister's solemn enjoining of the reader to fear God:

> Hic est, quem colis ille, quem vereris,
> Toto solus in orbe Rex Deorum,
> Crucifixus ob omnium salutem,
> Quem, lector studiose, si timebis
> Fatenti ore, fideque cordis,
> Caeli, post cineres, habebis aulam.

This is the one you worship, whom you reverence, the only king of Gods in the world, crucified for the good of all, and, dedicated reader, if you fear and acknowledge him with tongue and heart, you will possess the court of heaven when you're dead.

Burmeister convinces us that the dignified movement of Martial's epigram, whose structure he follows carefully, is worthy of greater things: *Rex Deorum* seems more adequate to the tone than the author's name. The third line matches the crux of one world with that of another. If Martial regards it a matter of wonder that little books of epigrams should make a man famous the world over, Burmeister trumps this with a God crucified, one man sacrificing himself for all in order to ensure life after death, rather than fame before it. In the final lines Burmeister reverses Martial's own reversal of the usual relation between death and reward. This "Martial" will aspire higher than the emperor's court (*aula*), which is the limit of the Roman poet's ambition, and he will reach his "court" after death. But the special relation between *lector* and book can also be cast in a Christian mold. If Martial is a poet known the world over through his books (1.1.3), the Christian God is a god of the book, worshiped by those who know him from his book. The *lector studiosus* here (4, echoing Martial 1.1.4) is the diligent reader of the Bible, directed throughout by Burmeister's marginal notes to the appropriate passages in the scriptures.

Taking the generic self-deprecation of the epigrammatist into the territory of Christian humility, Burmeister transforms the coy advertisement of 1.113 into the fervent prayer of a sinner, creating a more complex, but remarkably parallel, utterance. Martial has

> Quaecumque feci iuvenis et puer quondam
> apinasque nostras, quas nec ipse iam novi,
> male collocare si bonas voles horas
> et invidebis otio tuo, lector,
> a Valeriano Pollio petes Quinto,
> per quem perire non licet meis nugis.

> Whatever I produced as a young man and as a boy once upon
> a time and all my rubbish, which I myself don't know, you
> can get from Quintus Pollius Valerianus, reader. If, that is,
> you want to make ill use of good time and begrudge yourself
> your leisure. Valerianus won't let my trifles perish.

Burmeister begins with exactly the same line, makes literal the
phrase *quas nec ipse iam novi* (original sin?) and substitutes the
hope of resurrection for the faux complaint of *per quem perire non
licet meis nugis*:

> Quaecumque feci iuvenis et puer quondam,
> Scelerisque labem, quam nec ipse iam novi,
> Punire iusta si in tua voles ira,
> Solutionem eorum, age O Pater Caeli,
> A filio tuo unico petas Christo
> Per quem perire non licet meae vitae.

> Whatever I did as a young man and a boy once upon a time,
> and the stain of sin, which I myself don't know, if you want
> to punish that in your just anger, father of heaven, may you
> seek payment from your only son, Christ, through whom
> my life is not allowed to waste away.

With a play on names worthy of Martial himself, Burmeister turn
Quintus into *unico . . . Christo* and so paves the way for the substitution of *meae vitae* for *meis nugis*, singular for plural. Martial's final
line must itself be an allusion to the girlfriend of Varus in Catullus
c. 10, whose last line rounds on her as the sort of person before whom
one can't make a careless remark (*per quem non licet esse negle-
gentem*, c. 10.34). Martial's juvenilia were not meant to survive, and
the bookseller is embarrassing the author. But the insertion of the

word *perire* hints at the ambition of the self-deprecating poet, and perhaps what makes Burmeister's parody so successful is the pride that is being so conspicuously held in check by Martial. Something is bursting to break out, and Burmeister has his own ideas about what it is.

We have seen how Martial returns Catullus's language of *amicitia* to the social world from which it came before Catullus adapted it to speak of his love. What Martial retains in these echoes of Catullus is the protest of the cheated. The world of patronage in which the mask of *amicitia* covers a different reality leads to Catullan contrasts of emotion if not to the same agonized paradox:

> Vis te, Sexte, coli: volebam amare
> parendum est tibi: quod iubes, coleris.
> sed si te colo, Sexte, non amabo. (2.55)

Burmeister's version retains the second line intact and finds a different relation between paying court and loving:

> Vis te Christe coli, ante qui me amasti.
> Parendum est tibi: quod iubes coleris.
> Nam si te colo Christe, tunc amabor.

You want to be worshiped, Christ, who loved me first. I must obey you: as you demand, you will be worshiped. For if I worship you, then I'll love you.

The Christian context leads us back to a paradox which uses Martial's terms to produce something of Catullus's emotional intensity.

Does Burmeister pull off his extraordinary stunt, or does Martial prove too much for him? J. P. Sullivan argues that, by publishing his parodies opposite Martial's originals, Burmeister sets up an unstable juxtaposition, for what is to stop us from reading right to left, finding an irreverent parody of the Christian message in each of Martial's originals?[59] Here we may think of Martial's strategy of banalizing Catullus, a strategy which makes it difficult for us to register the earlier poet's subtleties under the noise of Martial's broader humor. The cruder joke subsumes the subtler, the earlier is read through the later, and Martial achieves something like the reversal of history implied in the words "I won't believe it, Catullus, until I read it." Once Sullivan's suggestion occurs to the reader, is it any more impossible to resist than Martial's "readings" of Catullus's *passer*? The evidence of the copy of Burmeister in the British Library, underlined only on the Martial side, reminds us that it is the reader who decides how to use this book. And yet, I think that Sullivan's suggestion, which is very much a trope of our times, should not be accepted too readily. Let us take one of Martial's raunchier poems and its parody:

> Nulli Thai negas. sed si te non pudet istud,
>   hoc saltem pudeat, Thai, negare nihil. (4.12)

> You refuse no one, Thais. But if you're not ashamed of that, let
> it at least shame you, Thais, that you refuse them nothing.

---

> Nulli, Christe negas. Et te non paenitet istud.
>   Nos pudeat fidei pectore habere nihil.

> You refuse no one, Christ. And you do not regret it. Let it
> shame *us* to have no faith in our breast.

The juxtaposition is shocking, but not inappropriate. Thais' degradation might be a moving image of Christ's voluntary self-diminution, of the humiliation undertaken by a god. And hasn't Burmeister included a response to the reader's potential reaction in *fidei pectore habere nihil*? Isn't the very point of this epigram that all (everything) can be redeemed if we have the courage of faith? Burmeister here plays Jesus to Thais' (and Martial's) Mary Magdalen. Burmeister's parody, then, doesn't simply cover Martial, but rather uses the energy of Martial's epigrams to move beyond them. Sullivan's response suggests that Burmeister's parody "upward" is, for all our modern reverence of instability, the one form of instability we cannot countenance.

Burmeister's parody bring us back full circle to the arena of the *Liber spectaculorum*, in which all that happens is referred to a single divinity. Like the unscheduled or misfired event in the arena, the unlikeliest epigram of Martial can be made to speak of the one true God, and in many respects Burmeister makes his own book of wonders out of the raw material of Martial's epigrams. Martial's *Liber spectaculorum* has proven to be both a valuable introduction to his oeuvre and an anomaly. Far from being the presence that presides over the wonders of the arena, the emperor will, in the "Dodecalogue," become a figure who must find his place by analogy in the shifting world of Martial's "theater." The people of the world, assembled in the circle of the arena to hail the *pater patriae*, certainly present a useful model of Martial's far-flung and anonymous readership, but the model will give way to more complex and variable layerings in the imagined readership of the later books. If the arena is the low-tech version of the Parisian editor's "sublime communication of souls" who read a common newspaper to become one nation, Martial's later books take us closer to this modern conception of readership as audience and at the same time move us further away from it. Although Martial will take a decisive step toward the idea of a virtual society, related through the reading of the book, though not physically present to each other, that society will be anything but homogeneous. In fact, Martial will deliberately address the diversification of use and interest that we sometimes glimpse beneath the posturings of unity in our own media ("and viewers like you").

The subject matter of the numbered books that follow the *Liber spectaculorum* will also be quite different in character. The reader will be confronted with a succession of epigrams diverse in topic, attitude, and tone. John Henderson has compared the *Letters* of Pliny, a roughly contemporaneous oeuvre also made up of a varied, and ostensibly random collection of smaller items, to a kaleidoscope.[1] He prefers this comparison to the more usual figure of the mosaic, which implies a fixed pattern and a calculated effect, leaving nothing to the shakings and reshakings of the reader.[2] There is certainly more of the mosaic in Pliny's books than in Martial's, for it is surely part of Pliny's intention that if we see the individual letters from an appropriate distance, they coalesce into a single picture, that of the ideal senator under the ideal emperor. Martial, opportunistic rather than anxious, has no interest in maintaining a persona. His books might be more appropriately thought of as kaleidoscopic because his world has no center; it is a world of opportunities and exchanges.

As I suggested in chapter 1, Martial's epigram books might appeal to our postmodern sensibilities for their nonorganic form; the ideal of organicism, as Terdiman puts it, "registered the necessity, first, of representing the world as conflicted, and second, of mastering the contradictions within it which were thereby highlighted."[3] Martial relishes, rather than masters, the contradictions. His method is juxtaposition rather than subsumption and his books are impossible wholes. My initial question, "How does one *read* a book of epigrams?" might be answered quite simply by replying that one can't. Only the heterogeneous society of the book can be adequate to that paradoxical entity, a book of epigrams, which cannot be taken in by a reading. Those insatiable consumers who are still calling for more at the end of the book are addicts, not readers, like the compulsive televiewer who cannot tear himself away until sleep intervenes. The book requires us to imagine other readers, with different interests, occupations, and access to author and book, and it also invites us to try out new groupings and associations as we move from epigram to epigram. It does not add up, requiring us in some respects to be "witty in another's book"' (*ingeniosus in alieno libro*, 1 praef.).

At the extreme of nonorganic structures, we find the newspaper, and Terdiman describes the consequence of its way of representing the world as follows: "If every element of the social totality, through the operation of the market, may at any moment be randomly connected with any other element, then the notions of connection and . . . of contradiction are drained of much of their explanatory and much of their critical force."[4] We may recognize in this diagnosis one of the most common forms of postmodern intellectual anxiety, and no doubt my readings will have awakened such concerns to a greater or lesser extent in many of my readers. I would not want to dispel this anxiety entirely since it is, I believe, intrinsic to the environment of Martial's books. But, of course, the variety of these books is not infinite, and I hope to have shown that recurring themes and generic types fall into some characteristic configurations which are, if not explanatory or critical, at least analytically witty. Furthermore, the various paradoxes of the form itself serve to provide a particular angle on Martial's world. For instance, epigrams, embedded in the reciprocal world of patron and client, are at the same time ripe for commodification, and Martial loves to play off a monetaristic conception of exchange against one centered on the gift. Similarly, the fact that in Book 1 Martial juxtaposes commemorative epigrams featuring *exempla virtutis* of the past with occasional epigrams on dinners and dining reflects not only his imperial context but also the polar associations of the form. Occasional, improvised, and alienable (like a joke), the epigram is also lapidary and definitive. It is both inflationary and deflationary, and sometimes both at the same time. These and other tensions in the form itself help to give the epigram book a distinctive orientation on its world, while posing the question, increasingly relevant to our experience, of what an epigrammatic world might be.

NOTES

1. Pliny makes a very similar point about his speeches in 9.4: "You can read each section as a whole and judge me lengthy in totality, but very brief in my parts (*meque in universitate longissimum, brevissimum in partibus iudicare*). Martial applies this idea to his oeuvre as a whole in 4.29 (*tu quoque de nostris releges quemcumque libellis, / esse puta solum; sic tibi pluris erit*, 9–10).

2. Martial 13.17–18, 14.1.9–12, 5.30.5–8.

3. Martial 6.15, 6.64.26, 12.61.10.

4. Manley (1985.274–75) observes that the epigram's definitive closure, which makes it the appropriate inscriptional (and epitaphic) form, is the very quality that renders it ephemeral. Once its trick has been mastered, the epigram has been consumed and used up; it becomes stale.

5. Gowers 1993.245–49.

6. Manley 1985.259.

7. On opening sequences, see Merli 1993. For a closural sequence, see 2.91–93. On women readers, see Larash 2004.172–230.

8. Maltby, unpublished ms deals with this phenomenon.

9. As Pailler points out (1981.87, n. 30), *vicinus* is used by Martial some thirty times, and words like *prope, propius* and *proximus* are common. Pailler comments on the use of these words in lieu of an address in a city without road numbers.

10. Compare 1.28. Later, we will come across another woman with drink on her breath, again in a sequence that foregrounds proximity (5.3).

11. Just as, for instance, 1.16 and 1.18 both thematize and invite mixing.

12. Joyce's *Ulysses* turns this aspect of the modern city to good account. As Lehan (1998.109) describes it, "The contrast between commercial and human ends creates coincidences on which Joyce builds, often leading to an ironic juxtaposition of the sacred and the profane."

13. Terdiman 1985.125.

14. Organicism, according to Terdiman (1985.125) "registered the necessity, first, of representing the world as conflicted, and second, of mastering the contradictions within it which were thereby highlighted."

15. Schwartz (1998.9) identifies *flânerie* as "the mode of urban spectatorship that emphasizes mobility and fluid subjectivity."

16. Schwartz 1998.10.

17. Gutzwiller (1998.11) observes that "the authorial disengagement later associated with epigrammatic style is, then, an inheritance from the traditional objectivity of earlier inscribed verse," though she notes that recitation at the symposium may encourage the creation of persona.

18. See Lorenz 2002.4–42 and Damon 1997.158–71 on persona.

19. Martial's influence on Juvenal is studied by Colton 1991. Spisak (1997) argues that satire influences the way Martial represents his relation with the reader, and Sullivan (1991.104–5) points to some of the other satiric influences on Martial.

20. A similar approach is taken by Malnati (1988), who argues that where Juvenal expresses outrage at social mobility per se, Martial is not concerned about birth (though he makes an important exception in the case of those born into slavery). Rather, Martial's mockery is directed against pretence.

21. Nauta 2002.178. More on Martial and the *scurra* in Damon 1997 and Saggesse 1994.

22. On Martial and the *Saturnalia*, see Citroni 1989 and Nauta 2002.166–89.

23. Nauta 2002.188–89 (see n. 140 on the possibility that criticism undermines praise). Compare Damon 1997.165.

24. Spisak 1998.

25. The figure of the book as *verna* (home-born slave) is one aspect of Martial's programmatic association of his poetry with slavery, a topic that I will pursue throughout the book. For this particular figure, compare 3.1.5–6 (*plus sane placeat domina qui natus in urbe est; / debet enim Gallum vincere verna liber*).

26. For legacy hunters and hooks, cf. 4.56.5 and 6.63.5–6.

27. Compare 5.59, *fictilibus nostris exoneratus eris*.

28. On the etiquette of gift-giving, see Dixon 1993.

29. Contrast, for instance, the two very different attitudes to the expectation of reciprocity in 7.86.9 (*non est sportula quae negotiatur*) and 5.42.8 (*extra fortunam est quidquid donatur amicis*).

30. Terdiman 1985.122.

31. "In speaking of an utterance, poem, or couplet as 'epigrammatic,' we refer not only to a kind of verbal structure but to an attitude toward experience, a kind of moral temper suggested by that very structure. The

epigram seems to offer itself as the last word, an ultimately appropriate comment, a definitive statement" (Smith 1968.207).

32. Manley 1985.256, n. 28. Manley observes that the epigram helped to make the confusion and variety of London manageable by creating a catalog of easily recognizable types.

33. Hennig ends his section on Martial's Rome (significantly headed "*Flâneries*") with the words *Ne jamais être dupe. Jamais.* (Hennig 2003.67.)

34. See Reinhold 1971. Saller (2000.821–22) emphasizes the importance of the right to wear certain insignia as a badge of rank.

35. See 2.91, 2.92 and 2.93; also 8.31.

36. Saller 2000.821: "Special permission to wealthy freedmen to claim fictitious free birth in order to qualify for the equestrian *ordo* was expressed as the 'right of the golden ring' (*ius anuli aurei*)"; see also Reinhold 1971:285–89. Compare Martial 4.67.8, 5.23.8 (where Bassus tries to get around Domitian's edict on seating in the theater by wearing purple, and so claiming equestrian status), and 5.38.4.

37. On the gradual transformation of *Caesar* from name to title, see Jones 1996 on Suetonius *Dom.* 16 ad loc. (*Caesar consalutatus*). Compare Tacitus *Hist.* 3.86 and Dio 66.1.1.

38. For *dominum regemque* as a fixed formula of patrons, see parallels in Citroni 1975.344 at 1.112.

39. On *dominus* as a form of address, see Dickey 2002.77–109.

40. Martial 3.95, 5.8, 5.23, 6.9.

41. Attalus a freedman: Citroni 1975.255.

42. *innocuos permitte sales* (3) and *cur ludere nobis / non liceat* (3–4). Compare 1.4.7–8 (*innocuous censura potet permittere lusus: / lasciva est nobis pagina, vita proba*) and 7.12.9 (*ludimus innocui*).

43. Roman (2001.135) on the *Apophoreta*: "Martial's Saturnalian *libellus*, if we take this fiction literally, is itself just one more concrete gift-item like those represented in his poetry; conversely, if we view this fiction skeptically (as, to a certain extent we must), Martial's 'book' becomes the materially indeterminate, mimetic space within which such gift-items are playfully evoked."

44. Roman 2001.137.

45. Epigram 10.70, for instance, answers the accusations of Potitus that Martial is lazy and scarcely finishes a book a year. Martial replies that it's a marvel he does even that, giving an account of his round, which includes daylong recitations of poetry (*auditur toto saepe poeta die*, 10).

46. Fitzgerald 1995.38–42.
47. Nauta 202.122–4. The dedication is the sending of a copy, which the dedicatee can pass on, and so the work is published.
48. Watson and Watson 2003 ad loc.
49. Quoted by Terdiman 1985.131.
50. Notice the programmatic role of slaves in 11.104.13–14, which has been brilliantly analyzed by Hinds 1998.130–35. Compare the closural 9.103, where a polemical relation to epic is adopted by comparing two contemporary slaves to Castor and Pollux. If they had lived in mythical times, Paris wouldn't have bothered with Helen.

EXCURSUS

1. See Sullivan 1991.270–79 on Martial and later European theories of the epigram.
2. Martial uses the word thirty-one times, as compared with fifteen occurrences of *nugae* and six of *lusus*; *hendecasyllabi* is never used (Roller 1998.272). On the term *epigramma*, see Lausberg 1982, Puelma 1995 and 1996, and Grewing 1997.429. The Latin transliteration is attested before Martial only in prose, and when it refers to poetry it is used of short poems, sometimes invective or convivial, often in elegiacs (Roller 1998.301–2, with references). Pliny (4.14.8–9) announces that his *nugae* can be called *hendecasyllabi, sive epigrammata, sive idyllia sive eclogas sive, ut multi, poematia.*
3. On *argutus*, see Citroni 1975 ad loc., citing Pliny 4.3.4, where Antoninus's Greek epigrams and *mimiambi* are described as *arguta.*
4. Puelma 1996.137. On Catullus and Greek epigram, see Hutchinson 2003.
5. Tacitus *Dialogus* 10.4 for a list of genres, with *epigrammatum lusus* last and least (cf. Martial 12.94). Martial argues with addressees that the possibility of longer *epigrammata* should be allowed, which indicates that some concept of the epigram as a genre existed (1.110, 6.65, 3.83). Greek epigrammatists discuss the question of length at least as early as the first century BC (Parmenion *AP* 9.342; see Puelma 1996.138, n. 59; and Grewing 1997.424–28). On ancient epigram theory, see Lausberg 1982.
6. His only allusion to contemporary Greek rivals is 9.11. Bruttianus is praised in 4.23 as a Greek epigrammatist, but this is a courtly compliment, not a statement of indebtedness. In the same poem it is Callimachus who is named as the master of Greek epigram (4). On the influence of Greek epigram on Martial, see Sullivan 1991.78–93, 322–27; Szelest

1960; Burnikel 1980; Laurens 1965. Even Martial's epigrams on the games may have been inspired by Lucillius, as an intriguing epigram on the punishment of a certain Meniscus suggests (11.184, on which, see Nisbet 2003.123ff.; and Robert 1968).

7. On the history of the Greek epigram, see Gutzwiller 1998 and Laurens 1989.

8. The "bookishness' of the Hellenistic epigram has perhaps been exaggerated. Cameron (1993.70–103) argues that the symposium was the place for epigrams, and Nauta (2002.96–105) has made a good case that this was true for Martial's epigrams.

9. Epitaphic formulas: Gamberale 1993 and Veyne 1964. Stigma: 6.64.26; with Grewing 1997 ad loc. (and note particularly Suetonius *Jul.* 73 on the *perpetua stigmata* inflicted by Catullus on Caesar). Also 12.61.11, 2.29, and 3.21. For graffiti, see 12.61.10.

10. On the complicated history of the *Greek Anthology*, see Cameron 1993. On the possibility of Hellenistic books of epigrams, put together by the authors, see Gutzwiller 1998.

11. Gutzwiller (1998.227) speculates that "the flowering of the art of variation in the second century BC was connected with anxiety about the endangered status of Greek culture in the face of increasing Roman hegemony. One response to this perceived threat was preservation through repetition, the remaking of the past for present consumption." She also makes an interesting association between epigrammatic variation and the replica series of artworks (such as Myron's cow) for the Roman market (245–46).

12. Edited, with commentary, by Austin and Bastianini 2002.

13. Gutzwiller 1998.189.

14. Nisbet (2003.35) argues for organization by theme.

15. Dedicated to Nero. Nauta (2002.91, n. 2) points out that Leonidas of Alexandria dedicated his third book to *Kaisar*, probably Nero or Vespasian (*AP* 6.328).

16. Some of these will be described below. It is worth noting that the literary influence was not all one-way, and Williams (1978.124–34) points out that Greek epigrammatists occasionally show the influence of Latin poetry.

17. On this poem, see Nisbet 2003.37–47.

18. On all of these, see Nisbet 2003.113–33.

19. Gutzwiller (1998.238–9) on Antipater's attitude to Rome (citing *AP* 7.493, 9.151, 9.567): "As a native of a Greek colony in a period when Greece itself was being colonized by Rome, Antipater carved an intellectual niche

for himself with his Roman patrons through his facility in reproducing, without substantial change but with novelty of expression, various textual topoi of Greek culture" (236).

20. Cicero (*Pro Archia* 18) describes Archias improvising poems on the events of the day and then producing alternative versions; see also *de Oratore* 3.194, on Antipater. Gutzwiller 1998.231–34 (on improvisation) stresses the art of variation and compares the practice of declamation. Martial 9.89 provides evidence that he might be called upon to improvise epigrams at dinner (Nauta 2002.99–100). Epigrams 3.67 and 78, which both feature Greek puns, have the look of improvisations composed on a boating trip and demonstrating that Martial can beat the Greeks at their own game.

21. On Greek epigram under Augustus, see Williams 1978.122–38. Hardie (1983.44) comments, "It is significant that, when Ovid fell from favour, no other Roman poet emerged at Augustus's court. The patronage of Roman poets, and their emergence to real distinction, was a rarer phenomenon than the evidence sometimes suggests. It was essentially secondary to the far more systematic business of promoting Greeks." See Coppola 1999 for epigrammatists at court, from Tiberius to Trajan.

22. "At last it has found the right hand that it was owed by fate," *AP* 9.552 (cf. *AP* 6.241 and 6.335; and Coppola 1999.447–48). One might compare the first two poems of Martial, Book 7, in which a cuirass is presented to Domitian.

23. Laurens 1989.122f.

24. Antipater, for instance, prays that Augustus will be favorable both to Piso and to himself (*AP* 10.25).

25. In *AP* 9.545, for instance, Crinagoras presents M. Claudius Marcellus (son of Augustus's sister, Octavia) with a copy of Callimachus's *Hecale* ("and may you have a fame equivalent to Theseus"); Sullivan 1991.84–85.

26. See 9.40 for mockery of Greek professional poets.

27. "It is in [Domitian's] games policy that one can see most clearly one of the central features of the age: the placing of literary innovations, often based on Greek or eastern models, in a Roman setting. In these circumstances, Latin experiments in departments of literature hitherto dominated by Greek exponents was bound to win approbation. It is no coincidence that the Greek epigrammatists writing at Rome do not win prominence at this time, although they too were writing for the court" (Hardie 1983.46–47).

28. Quoted by Gellius 19.9.10. For commentary, see Courtney 1993.70 and 74ff.

29. On this, see White 1993.3–34, especially 27. In *AP* 9.93, Crinagoras sends Proclus a pen, a small but heartfelt gift, consonant with Proclus's newly acquired readiness in learning, and M. Claudius Marcellus receives from him a copy of Callimachus's *Hecale* (*AP* 9.545).

30. Contrast Cicero *Pro Archia* 25, where Sulla gives a gift to a poet who had handed him a bad epigram on condition that he never write anything again.

31. Compare the story of Augustus writing a Greek epigram for the painting of Aphrodite Anadyomene by Apelles, which he received from Cos as an offset against taxes (Pliny *NH* 35.81; Williams 1978.137–38). Suetonius *Aug.* 85.2 for Augustus's epigrams (*quae fere tempore balinei meditabatur*).

32. On the *Perusinae glandes*, see Hallett 1977.

33. Compare *Spec.* 2.4: *unaque iam tota stabat in urbe domus.*

34. Other references to anonymous epigrams directed against emperors: Suetonius *Dom.* 23.2; *Aug.* 55; *Tib.* 28, 59, 66; *Otho* 3.2; *Vit.* 14.4; Tacitus *Ann.* 1.72.4, 4.31.1, 14.48.1; and Dio 66.11.1

35. On Martial and the pasquinade, see Spaeth 1939.

36. Martial 7.12, 7.72, 10.3, 10.5, 10.33.

CHAPTER 2

1. Labate 1987.103–12.

2. Compare Statius 1.6 and 2.5, with Statius's remarks, in the preface to Book 2, on the importance of improvisation and immediate presentation to the emperor. Another early book of Martial's is called *Apophoreta* ("the takeaways"), and consists in tags to accompany gifts taken away from dinners and public celebrations. Tacitus's *Dialogus* provides evidence that contemporary audiences prized the portable and excisable in rhetoric: *iuvenes . . . non solum audire sed etiam* referre domum *aliquid illustre et dignum memoria volunt, traduntque in vicem ac saepe in colonias ac provincias suas scribunt, sive sensus aliquis arguta et brevi sententia effulsit sive locus exquisito et poetico cultu enituit* (*Dialogus* 20.4). Compare 22.3 (on Cicero): *pauci sensus apte et cum quodam lumine terminantur. Nihil excerpere, nihil referre possis.* The taste for *sententiae* and pointed endings in contemporary rhetoric is illustrated by Barwick 1959.11–26.

3. "Elles ne s'entendent pas sub specie aeternitatis, mais encore une fois, hic et nunc. C'est un lieu privilégié, le Colisée, à un moment privilégié, celui des jeux, grace à un interprète privilégié, le poète, que ce numen [the emperor] s'affirme . . . L'arène y est le point de convergence des regards de tout l'empire . . . Ces regards à leur tour sont créateurs de merveilles" (Pailler 1990.182).

4. Complementary to my account of imperial spectacles are Gunderson 1996 and 2003.

5. I follow the text and numbering of Shackleton Bailey 1993.

6. Brantlinger 1983. Veyne 1976 considers the Roman spectacles in the light of ancient euergetism.

7. Dupont 1985.19–42 and Nicolet 1980.343–382 are both good descriptions of the spectacular character of Roman public life. Feldherr 1998.4–19 also discusses the political function of spectacle.

8. Debord 1983, para. 1.

9. Bartsch 1994.189 and Leigh 1997.

10. Crary 1988.98–100.

11. See Sauter 1934 on the emperor's divinity in Martial.

12. A succinct account of the simulacrum can be found in Camille 1996.33–44.

13. This is the subject of Leigh 1997.

14. Carratello (1965b.303–4) compares Antipater *AP* 9.58 (ending "apart from Olympus the sun never saw anything so grand"); see also Weinreich 1928.1–20. At 8.36.1 Martial compares the emperor's new palace to the pyramids of Memphis.

15. Compare the ending of *Spec.* 34: *Fucinus et +tigri+ taceantur stagna Neronis / hanc norint unam saecula naumachiam.* Weinreich (1928.26) cites this ring composition as evidence that 34 is the last poem of the original book. It is a further argument for terminal position that the poem neatly brackets the Julio-Claudian dynasty which the Flavians have superseded, since its opening couplet refers to a *naumachia* of Augustus and its last to the lakes of Nero.

16. Debord 1983, para. 23.

17. Carratello 1965b.306–7.

18. Coleman (1993.68) points out that Martial's reference to the *stagna Neronis* (6) reminds us that the amphitheater now holds aquatic displays for the benefit of all.

19. On the arena as an image of Rome and Roman order, see Gunderson 1996 and Edmondson 1996.

20. For *spectator* as tourist (*OLD* 1b) Coleman (1998a.16) cites Ovid *Heroides* 16.3 3. Compare *Spec.* 27.1: *Si quis ades longis serus spectator ab oris.*

21. See Moretti 1992.56 on the public as spectacle to itself (citing Ovid *Ars* 1.173–4 and 1.213–28).

22. Examples in Apuleius *Metamorphoses* 10.30; Strabo 6.273; Calpurnius *Ecl.* 7.69–72.

23. Potter (1996.132–41) speculates that the practice of public acclamation in the theater and arena, as these institutions spread across the empire, "may have helped to spread phrases in Greek and Latin among people to whom these were not the languages of ordinary discourse" (135).

24. The barbarians who are silenced in *Spec.* 1 are allowed to speak (Latin) in *Spec.* 3, in which the amphitheater is speaking *for* the wonders of barbarian lands.

25. Compare Suetonius *Titus* 8.5; and see Coleman 1999 on the parade and punishment of informers.

26. Gunderson 1996.133.

27. Various forms of *Ausonia* or *Ausonius* occur thirty-nine times in the *Aeneid*. For Aeneas as *exul* (cf. *exulat*, 1), see *Aeneid* 3.11 and 7.359.

28. See the uses of *defero* cited in *OLD* 1, "to carry (a person etc. to a destination)." For a similar pun, compare Suetonius *Nero* 39: *Quis negat Aeneae magna de stirpe Neronem? / Sustulit hic matrem, sustulit ille patrem.* Kellum (1997.173–81) has interesting things to say about burlesque parodies of the *Aeneid* in public places.

29. Coleman 1998a.

30. So Coleman. Weinreich (1928.1–73) is particularly useful on Martial and Greek epigram.

31. Newlands 2001.45. When things go wrong during the games, Martial can turn it to positive account with the same exclamatory swiftness he exhibits in the case of the successful displays (cf. *Spec.* 12).

32. See Coleman (1998a), who compares the "Magerius mosaic" from Smirat and speculates that the emperor himself circulated this book. She points out that these representations may stress the relationship of patronage between sponsor and beneficiaries of his *liberalitas*, as does Martial in *Spec.* 23 and 31.

33. Sontag 1977.20.

34. "Dans cette série d'instantanées visuels, bien spécifiques du monde de l'arène, la realité sacrale des scènes et des objets representées n'est si obstinement revendiquée, aux depens même du mythe qui leur sert de

prétexte, que par ce qu'elle exalte le souvenir d'un instant éphémère"
(Pailler 1990.182).

35. Moretti (1992.62–63) contrasts the writers who celebrated the *inter-
medi* of Renaissance Italy.

36. Pailler 1990.182.

37. Martial is imitating Philippus of Thessalonica (*AP* 9.311), though
Philippus does not feature the duality of Diana.

38. Perhaps we should translate *ingenium*, with Weinreich 1928.67, as
"instinct."

39. *Ingenium* also alludes to the talent of the poet, who has written these
poems extempore (*Spec.* 35: *da veniam subitis: non displicuisse mer-
etur, / festinat, Caesar, qui placuisse tibi*). Compare *subitis . . . casibus*
here.

40. Weinreich 1928.32–33. Compare *Spec.* 19.1–2, 17.1–2, 32.

41. The verb *praesto* recurs in this connection: *Spec.* 6.4, 11.1–2, 34.9–10;
also 24.1–2 (*exhibuit*). Coleman (1990.51) understands these passages as
depicting the arena's spontaneous tribute to the emperor. My emphasis
is slightly different.

42. Pailler 1990.180–81.

43. Cf. *Aen* 9.79: *prisca fides facto, sed fama perennis.* The transformation
of the Trojan ships into nymphs is precisely the kind of event the arena
might have reenacted.

44. The injunction to believe is common in the *Spec.* (6.1, 14.8, 20.4, 27.5,
33.8, 30.4). For a modern parallel to this conflict between seeing and
believing, though inflected quite differently, see Gunning 1994 on the
films of Méliès, one of the founders of cinema: "Méliès's theater is in-
conceivable without a widespread decline in the marvelous, providing a fundamental rationalist context. The magic theater labored to
make visible that which it was impossible to believe. Its visual power
consisted of a *trompe l'oeil* play of give and take, an obsessive desire to
test the limits of an intellectual disavowal—I know, but yet I see" (117).
The closest Martial gets to this is in *Spec.* 30, where, à propos a display
of synchronized swimming in which "Nereids" outline a ship in the
water, he exclaims "credidimus remum, credidimusque ratem" (4).

45. Weinreich (1928.34) cites as a model for *Spec.* 6 an epigram by Philippus
of Thessalonica (*AP* 9.88), spoken by a (the) nightingale (Philomela).
The nightingale tells how, troubled by Boreas (another man from
Thrace) she settled on the back of a dolphin and so charmed it with
her song that it served as her oarsman. She concludes, "The story of

Arion is no lie." Here, one fantastic occurrence confirms another and the parallel only serves to emphasize the hint of disenchantment that Martial has introduced.

46. Wyke 1997.123–24.
47. Sobchak 1990.231.
48. Benjamin 1970.219–53; and Baudrillard 1994.
49. Benjamin 1970.224–25.
50. Fitzgerald 1995.140–68.
51. Hardie 2002.154–55, citing also *Pont.* 2.8.1 and 37–38.
52. Ahl 1989.78: "For Caesar's name now became, ironically, the official title assumed by someone who accomplished a successful *coup d'état*, rather than an adoptive or inherited name which implied that its owner had, if only by family prerogative, some right to be ruler of the Roman world."
53. Listed by Bartsch 1994.224–25, n. 6.
54. Waters 1963, especially 212–13.
55. Coleman (1986.3099) remarks on the Flavian policy of promoting contemporary literary celebration of their exploits to compensate for their lack of historical tradition. The words of Debord (1998.15–16) are relevant: "The precious advantage which the spectacle has acquired through the *outlawing* of history, from having driven the recent past into hiding, and from having made everyone forget the spirit of history within society, is above all the ability to cover its own tracks–to conceal the very progress of its recent conquest. Its power already seems familiar, as if it had always been there. All usurpers have shared this aim: to make us forget that *they have only just arrived.*"
56. On "fatal charades," see Coleman 1990, Bartsch 1994.50–62, and Wiedemann 1992.83–90. Coleman (1990.64) suggests that "Pasiphae" might have been tied to the bull, in which case *iunctam* is a pun. Hopkins and Beard (2005.47) go further: "Martial's contribution to the celebration, in other words, might have been to take a piece of play-acting in the Colosseum and to *make it real.*"
57. Coleman, 1990.46.
58. Foucault 1979.56.
59. I would also similarly modify Bartsch (1993.50ff.), who rightly notes the element of violation in these charades: "It is this violation of the theatrical by the actual, or rather this conflation of the two, that seems to have leant their attraction to these displays, adding a certain frisson to the experience of the spectators" (51).

60. Housman 1901. Compare *AP* 11.254.

61. Carratello 1965a.138.

62. Moretti, 1992.59.

63. Pailler (1990.180) sees a distinction between *theatro* and *arena* in which the theater, where the memory of the myths is rehearsed and transmitted, is replaced by the arena, which makes the myths live.

64. Gellius 5.14.24 recounts how the story of Androclus and the lion was conveyed to the audience in the arena via a placard (*tabula*); Livy 28.46.16 uses *titulus* of a placard carried in a triumph. More on *tabulae* and *tituli* in Wiedemann 1992.

65. Weinreich 1928.74–160; cf. *Spec.* 20 and 33.

66. In fact, he suggests in the next poem (*Spec.* 25) a quite different connection with the orthodox story of Orpheus, though the text is very shaky. See Carratello 1965a.138–44.

67. Compare the poem of Lucillius (*AP* 11.184), in which a certain Meniscus steals apples from Zeus's (Nero's?) garden, becoming a latter-day Heracles. When he was caught he was burnt alive like Heracles, a "great wonder/spectacle" (*mega theama*). See Coleman 1990.60–61.

68. Ahl 1984a.107: "Martial's poor substitute Laureolus, whatever he did, earns the status of Prometheus, which, in this incident, gives him more claim to divinity than any imperial Jupiter. Even in the pagan Martial, the stage is set for the suffering Christ."

69. Bartsch 1994.52–53 (with bibliography on p. 228, nn. 26 and 27).

70. *Esse quandam illi beluae cum genere humano societatem*; cf. Dio Cassius 39.38.1–4. Compare the reaction of the audience to Nero's savage execution of Christians after the fire of 64 (Tacitus *Annals* 15.44).

71. For a similar dramatization of an artistic *figure*, see Fitzgerald 1995.154–55, on Catullus's Ariadne (c. 64).

72. Crary 1988.100.

73. There is at least one other occasion where Martial alludes to a poem in another book: at 5.23.8 he alludes to 2.57.4 (reprised at 5.26).

74. Scaevola was a much cited *exemplum* of *patientia*. See the passages collected by Citroni 1975.76–7, and note Martial 6.19.7. For Republican exempla in the imperial period, see Gowing 2005, and especially 102–31, on the Flavians.

75. Wiedemann 1992.138–39.

76. Quoted by Gunderson 1996.148. For more on this event, see Wiedemann 1992.42 and 53, n. 126.

77. There is a valuable treatment of these poems in Carlin Barton's discussion of the redemption of honor in Roman culture (Barton 1994.41–6).

She argues that Mucius redeems his honor by appropriating the enemy's savagery against himself.

78. Feldherr 1998.17 and passim. Surprisingly, he doesn't discuss this passage.

79. It is probable that the burning of Mucius's right hand was originally a punishment for perjury, which would explain the language of crime that hovers over Livy's account of Mucius's exploit. Ogilvie 1965.262–23.

80. This is the very utterance that normally invoked the Roman citizen's immunity from corporal punishment (Gellius 10.3.12; compare St. Paul in Acts 22). Mucius, by contrast, will prove that he is a Roman citizen by *taking* his punishment.

81. *"Tu abi," inquit "in te magis quam in me hostilia ausus. Iuberem macte virtute esse, si pro mea patria ista virtus staret."* (2.12.14).

82. Compare the use of *Caesar* in 1.78, where the suicide of Festus is preferred to the suicide of Cato because *huius* (sc. Festus) *Caesar* (sc. Domitian) *amicus erat* (10).

83. Something similar happens in 1.89 where the names of Cinna and Caesar are juxtaposed, though the Caesar is, again, the current emperor: *adeoque penitus sedit hic tibi morbus / ut saepe in aurem, Cinna, Caesarem laudas*, 1.89.5. The postponement of the verb until the final word allows Martial to stray into dangerous territory and then veer off at the last moment. Juxtaposed to Caesar, the addressee's name conjures up the primal scene of the principate, Caesar's murder, immediately after which another Cinna (Lucius Cornelius) delivered, all too publicly, a speech against Caesar. So is this Cinna a conspirator? No, that was another time, another place. Now Caesar (no relation) and Cinna (no threat) can safely cohabit in the world of Rome's second dynasty.

84. Jameson 1991.18–21.

85. Leigh 1997.279–81.

86. Barton's different approach to these poems is encapsulated in what she says about this one: "When Martial ascribed free will to the man in the arena, he created a series of transparencies in his mind: between himself and the actor; between the actor and the legendary Mucius Scaevola; and amongst himself, the actor, the hero and the audience. When he perceived the actor as a man compelled into the arena, he no longer sympathized with him, and a whole series of alienations and diminutions were effected. . . . And when the value of life goes up, the sense of community, of social connectedness, necessarily goes down" (Barton 1994.55).

CHAPTER 3

1. On prose prefaces, which first appeared in books of poetry during Martial's time, see Janson 1964.

2. *Si quis tamen tam ambitiose tristis est ut apud illum in nulla pagina latine loqui fas sit, potest epistula vel potius titulo contentus esse.* Compare the play with the notion of beginning in the final sentence of the preface to Book 2. Martial's *ambitiose tristis* is an anticipation of Tacitus's striking put-down of the imperial martyrs who died *ambitiosa morte* (*Agricola* 42); as we shall see, in this book Martial will give short shrift to the heroic suicides of the past.

3. See Howell 1980.95 and Citroni 1975.4.

4. *Hos [sc libellos] eme, quos artat brevibus membrana tabellis: / scrinia da magnis, me manus una capit,* 2.3–4. Martial's are the earliest references to codex editions of literary works (besides 1.2, see 14.184, 188, 190, 192). On the codex, see Roberts and Skeat 1983; and, for a provocative literary study of "Martial and the Book," see Fowler (1995), who describes the play between first-time reader of the *volumen* and the rereader of the codex in this book. This and the previous epigram are omitted in the B family of manuscripts. In the C family they appear just before the poem at the end of the epistle. Lindsay (1903.18) suggests that the cause of confusion may be that they stood *extra ordinem paginarum* (cf. 9 praef. 1–2) in the ancient editions, which would further complicate the layering of entries to the book.

5. On dedications in Martial, see Nauta 2002.120–32. As he points out (129), Martial's multiple dedications were a novelty.

6. *Si quis tam ambitiose tristis est ut apud illum in nulla pagina latine loqui fas sit, potest epistula vel potius titulo contentus esse.*

7. *Epigrammata illis scribuntur qui solent spectare Florales. non intret Cato theatrum meum, aut si intraverit, spectet.*

8. The story goes that Cato turned up at the theater during the celebration of the *Florales*. The festival included *ludi scaenici* at which it was customary for the audience to demand that the mimes strip naked for them; on this occasion the mere presence of Cato made them hesitate. Informed of this, Cato left the show, to great applause (Valerius Maximus 2.10.8). For an excellent account of the use of Cato as a foil by early imperial poets, see Connors 2000.210–14.

9. *Absit a iocorum nostrorum simplicitate malignus interpres nec epigrammata mea inscribat: improbe facit qui in alieno libro ingeniosus est.* Shackleton Bailey prints Heinsius's conjecture *inscribat* for the mss. *scribat*, which may not need emendation. For *inscribat* in the

sense I have given it, see *CIL* 6.24799, *quisquis hoc monumentum alio
. . . quo nomine inscripserit.* Tanner (1986.2665) has an intriguing interpretation of the mss. reading: "*Scribat* here will refer to writing out
abbreviations read from an inscription in their full form."

10. Elsewhere, Martial complains that others were circulating scurrilous
epigrams under his name (7.12, 7.72, 10.3).

11. See Gowing 2005.102–31 for the memory of the Republic under the Flavians, which Gowing sees as waning in this period.

12. *Spero me secutum in libellis meis tale temperamentum ut de illis queri
non possit quisquis de se bene senserit, cum salva infimarum quoque
personarum reverentia ludant; quae adeo antiquis auctoribus defuit ut
nominibus non tantum veris abusi sint sed et magnis. mihi fama vilius
constet et probetur in me novissimum ingenium.*

13. Freudenburg 2001; Galán Vioque 2002.105. See also Pliny 6.21.5–6.

14. *Mihi fama vilius constet et probetur in me novissimum ingenium,*
5–6. What does *vilius constet* mean? The preamble suggests that fame
bought at the price of the discomfiture of others is not worth having,
but it is also possible that offense to the great is too high a price for the
author to pay for fame. I suspect that Martial is covering the second,
more anxious, meaning under the first. When he follows this up with
*et probetur in me novissimum ingenium*, does he really mean, as the
*communis opinio* has it, that ingenuity is the last thing (*novissimum*)
he wants to make his claim to fame, or does he want us to approve his
"up to date *ingenium*"?

15. *Sic* scribit *Catullus, sic Marsus, sic Gaetulicus, sic quicumque*
perlegitur.

16. Citroni (1975.14–15) emphasizes the epitaphic connotations of the *hic*
with which the poem begins. But, as Howell (1979.102) reminds us, *hic
est ille* is also the conventional phrase used to point somebody out in a
public place (5.13.3, *sed toto legor orbe frequens et dicitur "hic est"*). He
cites Cicero *Tusc.* 5.36.103; Plautus *Capt.* 786–87; and, for *requiris* in
this context, Tacitus *Dial.* 7.4.

17. Compare 1.25, where Faustus is urged to publish his books and earn
fame in his lifetime. The poem ends *cineri gloria sera venit.*

18. There is a superb treatment of the relation between this poem (and 1.2)
and Horace *Ep.* 1.20 in Roman 2001.126–29.

19. Roman (2001.128) sees an ironic echo of the end of Horace c. 1.1:
*quodsi me lyricis vatibus insere / sublimi feriam vertice sidera*; Horace
c. 1.1.36. The book's ambition is marked by an allusion to the words
of Ennius's epitaph (*volito vivus per ora virum, Epigr.* 18, Vahlen), but

these aspirations are mocked by the picture of the slave/book tossed in a blanket "toward the stars," a prank of schoolboys and soldiers (see Howell 1980 ad loc.).

20. On *rhonchi* as "coarse tastes" and *nasum* as a literary term, see Connors 2000.220–24. The extra associations with the arena that I see here are paralleled in 4.86.7–8, where the same use of *rhonchus* is followed by a reference to the *tunica molesta*.

21. Larash (2004.92–171) discusses the model of spectacle and theater for the relation between author and *lector*.

22. In 1.24 Decianus is addressed in a poem mocking those who simulate virtue and in 1.39 he is again praised for his old-style virtue. With this ending, compare 4.75: Nigrina is greater than Euadne and Alcestis because she proved her love for her husband without having to die (*certo meruisti pignore vitae / ut tibi non esset morte probandus amor*, 7–8). Howell (1980.127) notes that by juxtaposing the swollen epicisms of line 3 with the bald simplicity of line 4, Martial translates the contrast between Cato and Decianus into the mode of literary style.

23. For more on Catullus's *passer*, see 7.14 and 11.6.16.

24. See Fitzgerald 1995.129. Also Selden 1992.464–67.

25. Martial's reception of Catullus will be dealt with at length in chapter 6; here it should be noted that Catullus's presence is quite prominent in Martial's first book. Other poems in which there is a significant dialog with Catullus in Book 1 are 66, 92, 109, 112.

26. The negative connotations of *bellus*, which is a favorite word of Catullus (3.14, 8.16, 24.7, 81.2, 78.3, 22.2), are also brought out in 3.63. Note that the previous poem (3.62) mocks a man who thinks himself *magnus* but is in fact *pusillus*. For *bellus*, see also Pliny 4.25.3.

27. A play on names links Catullus (7), Cato (8), and Cotta (9). Catullus himself juxtaposed his own name to Cato's, as though one were a diminutive of the other (c. 56.3).

28. In 6.32 a similar contrast is made between Cato's suicide and Otho's, to the advantage of the latter.

29. On *amicus Caesaris* see Nauta 2002.344, n. 69, with citations.

30. These epigrams recall those attributed to Seneca, on Cato (*Anthologia Latina* 397–99, 414, 432) and Pompey (400–404, 406, 413, 438, 454–56).

31. The story is recounted in Pliny 3.16 and Dio 60.16.5.

32. Howell (1980.137–38) has an interesting account of its fortunes.

33. Compare Statius *Silvae* 2.5.

34. Pig and boar are distinguished as dishes at 8.22 (*invitas ad aprum, ponis mihi, Gallice, porcum*). Notice also that the previous poem, 1.41, ends with a play on the name Tettius *Caballus*.

35. Martial castigates a *turba* in rather similar terms at the end of *Spec.* 26. A rhinoceros, much to the crowd's fury, failed to show a proper war-like spirit, but eventually it rallied to give the crowd what it came for. Martial concludes: *i nunc et lentas corripe, turba, moras* (26.12).

36. On the bad emperor as solitary diner, see Braund 1996.43–52. Braund focuses on Pliny's *Panegyricus*, where it is Domitian himself who provides the example of the bad emperor in this respect!

37. The piously traumatized enemy, Porsena (1.21.3, 1.21.5), finds his counterpart in the Domitian, before whom the Dacian boy needn't fear for his life (1.22.6).

38. The meaning of *maior . . . charta minorque* has not been settled and the problem has played an important role in the ongoing argument about prepublication texts in Martial. Is Martial referring to two different collections, both containing the same poems on the lion and the hares, rather than to the repetition of the theme within the book? Friedländer (1886) argued that Martial here refers to two collections of epigrams, which would later become part of this book, both of which contained epigrams on the lions and hares. He was followed by Citroni 1975 in his commentary. The theory that Martial presented selected patrons with private collections of epigrams before these same epigrams were integrated into published books was most influentially formulated by White (1974). He there argues that presentation poems from these *libelli* found their way into published books, where they do not make sense unless we assume that the *libellus* referred to is such a prepublication text. Fowler (1995.43–45) argued against White 1974, that we do not need to refer to prepublication texts in order to make sense of poems such as 1.44 and that *maior . . . charta minorque* should be taken either as "every scrap of paper" or as a reference to the dual roll/codex publication of Book 1. White (1996) replies to Fowler and argues that *charta* must mean "book roll" rather than "piece of paper" (404–5, n. 16). In my opinion Nauta (2002.108–20) has convincingly shown that presentation poems that refer to *libelli* are referring to the published book and not to prepublication texts. But Nauta, who makes a powerful argument against the existence of prepublication texts for nonimperial addressees, believes that *minor charta* here does refer to a collection of lion and hares poems which had been presented to the emperor and had subsequently come into general circulation (like the *Liber spectaculorum*). Be that as it may, the inclusion of this poem in a book that repeats the theme of the lion and the hares six times means that it cannot help raise the issue of repetition within the book.

39. Epigram 1.50 also travesties a formula from Homer: *Si tibi Mistyllos cocus, Aemiliane, vocatur, / dicatur quare non Taratalla mihi?*

40. There is considerable controversy about this epigram, and particularly the first line (surveyed in Nauta 2002.370). Is Martial saying that if he doesn't pad his books they will be too short, and his trouble go to waste; that if he doesn't publish the same poems in several collections they risk being forgotten; or that if he doesn't recycle material from shorter, more ephemeral collections in his published books, his efforts go to waste?

41. This "exchange" with Stella may remind us of an earlier complaint from a reader, the distich in which Domitian speaks of the unequal exchange between himself, who gives Martial a *naumachia*, and the poet, who gives the emperor a book (1.5). There, too, Martial plays with sameness and difference, as the enormous differential in the two "gifts" is muted by the equivalently Greek and polysyllabic words for the things exchanged (*naumachia, epigrammata*).

42. Epigram 10.59.3–4 (*dives et ex omni posita est instructa macello/ cena tibi, sed te mattea sola iuvat*).

43. A point that is also made at 10.100.

44. *Una est in nostris tua, Fidentine, libellis / pagina, sed certa domini signata figura, / quae tua traducit manifesto carmina furto,* 1.53.1–3.

45. Citroni 1975.181. The language used of the swan and the nightingales, conventional figures for poets, is, appropriately, poetic.

46. On the basis of his poetry? This looks like the request of a prospective client to be included by a patron, a relationship usually called *amicitia*; see Citroni 1975 ad loc. on the use of *inspice* (6) for examining wares.

47. See Starr 1987 for a succinct account of the circulation of books. It is striking that the subject of plagiarism is common in Martial's first two books, but not after that. The following poems in Book 1 deal with plagiarism: 38, 52, 53, 63, 66, and 72. Howell (1980.168), following Citroni (1975.96), attributes the prominence of this theme in Book 1 to the "greater risk of plagiarism run by unpublished poems. Once M. had got into his stride, and was publishing books at fairly regular intervals, the risk was lessened."

48. Compare 1.72: "Fidentinus is a poet with my poems as Aegle buys her teeth and Lycoris changes her complexion. By the same means as you are a poet you will have a head of hair when you are bald."

49. Martial urges the plagiarist to seek out poems known only to the *virginis pater chartae* (1.66.7), and to buy *pumicata fronte si quis [liber] est nondum / nec umbilicis cultus atque membrana* (10–11), a delicious

parody of Catullus c. 1, where the virgin Muse is asked to protect Catullus's poems for posterity.

50. At *De beneficiis* 7.4.1, Seneca points out that there are many things for which one man is the owner of the object (*dominus rei*) and the other of its use (*usus*): *Libros dicimus esse Ciceronis; eosdem Dorus librarius suos vocat, et utrumque verum est. Alter illos tamquam auctor sibi, alter tamquam emptor adserit; ac recte utriusque dicuntur esse, utriusque enim sunt, sed non eodem modo. sic potest Titus Livius a Doro accipere aut emere libros suos.* This is quoted by Salles (1992.167). Notice also Martial's distinction between *auctor* and *emptor* in 9.99.

51. See Valette-Cagnac 1997.153ff. on plagiarism and recitation.

52. Pliny *Ep.* 2.10.2–3, *enotuerunt quidam tui versus et invito te claustra sua refregerunt. Hos nisi retrahis in corpus, quandoque ut errones aliquem, cuius dicantur, invenient.*

53. See Howell 1980.230.

54. This surprise may well reflect the Catullan poem that Martial is here alluding to (c. 15). Commending himself and his loves/boy to Aurelius, Catullus asks him to protect them/him not from the man in the street, but from himself! I have argued elsewhere that Catullus's poem concerns the anxieties of publication, which is certainly what Martial makes of it. See Fitzgerald 1995.46–49.

55. On the role of the *adsertor* in Roman slave law, see Buckland 1908.652–3.

56. It occurs, for instance, three times in Book 2 (18, 32, and 68); cf. also 3.46. Martial refers to the patron as *dominus* and *rex* at 1.112.1, 4.83.5, 10.10.5, and 12.60.14.

57. In 5.18 Quintianus is an *amicus dives*. For *meus poeta*, cf. 9.84.8, with Nauta 2002.77 on the words for patron; also White 1993.278, n. 34, citing Horace *Ep.* 1.7.11; Ovid *Tr.* 5.7.22; *Pont* 4.15.38; Crinagoras *AP* 6.229.6.

58. Reading forward sequentially from 1.52 to 1.54 it appears that in 1.52 relations between authors and poems are intertwined with relations between people, but in 1.53 and 1.54 these two kinds of relations are separated out and feature in one poem each, as though to undo the knot.

59. It is worth quoting the words of Starr at length: "Since bookshops enjoyed no special status above that of any luxury shop, that very commonality of commercial status may hint that literature was becoming something that could be bought and sold like perfume or expensive fabric. Since literature had been and remained a symbol of social status, its reduction to marketable commodity may indicate a weakening

of the hold of the traditional aristocracy on the control of access to social status. In earlier Roman society, one had to be a member of an aristocratic group to acquire access to works that circulated primarily within that group. In this later period, bookstores made it at least theoretically possible for access to literature to precede and perhaps even facilitate access to refined circles" (Starr 1987.223).

60. As a noun, *venalis* means "newly imported slave," probably contrasting with the book/slave of 1.3, who is to be thought of as a *verna* (houseborn slave).

61. The Ovidian allusions, all from the exile poetry, are listed in Citroni 1975.226.

62. For the directions, compare Ovid *Tr.* 3.1 and *Pont.* 4.5.

63. In 3.46.1–2 Martial sends a freedman in his stead to Candidus's *salutatio*. That poem is an inversion of this one to the extent that the freedman is described in terms that conjure up the book. Explaining the advantages that the freedman has over himself, Martial points out that the freedman could perform servile tasks such as clearing a way for Candidus with his elbow (*cunctos umbone repellet*, 4; the book, of course, has an *umbilicus*); furthermore the book can engage in flattery and insults inappropriate to the free man (7–10), just like the book of epigrams itself. Martial ends by saying that as *amicus* he will perform any duty that a freedman can't (11–12). The foregoing description of what the freedman can do makes the difference between them one of relative directness.

64. *De primo dabit alterove nido / rasum pumice purpuraque cultum / denaris tibi quinque Martialem. / "tanti non es" ais? sapis, Luperce,* 1.117.15–18.

65. In this *penultimate* poem of the book, Martial echoes the directions to the bookstore of Secundus (freedman of Lucensis) in the *second* poem of the book. Secundus is selling the codex, Atrectus the book roll. From 1.113 we learn that we can acquire Martial's juvenilia at Q. Valerianus Pollio's.

66. Compare 1.113, in which Martial tells us that his juvenilia are for sale at the bookstore of Quintus Valerianus Pollio; if, that is, we want to waste an hour. This is another way of marking Book 1 as the beginning of a mature oeuvre.

67. On slaves in Martial, see Garrido-Hory 1981.

68. Compare 8.3.5ff. for a literary application of this topos. Howell (1980) has an excellent account of kepotaphs (293–94).

CHAPTER 4

1. Studies of the relation between poems in Martial's books have for the most part not been interpretive, as can be seen from the miscellaneous list of verbal connections between contiguous poems in Williams 2004.10 and Scherf 2001. Barwick (1958) identifies "cycles" of (not necessarily contiguous) poems related in subject matter; Merli (1993) looks at the ordering of epigrams in relation to courtly strategies. Garthwaite (1990, 1993, 1998a, and 1998b) and Holzberg (n.d.) are closer to the approach I will be taking. See also Lorenz 2004.

2. Barwick 1958. A cycle of consecutive poems dealing with the same person: 2.21–23, all about the invitation chaser Selius (interestingly, they are all addressed to Postumus). A scattered cycle, all on Domitian's edict on seating in the theater: 5.8, 14, 23, 25, 27, 35, 38, 41.

3. Lorenz (2004.265–67) suggests *fellatio*.

4. The point, then, would be comparable to 3.54: *cum dare non possim quod poscis, Galla rogantem / multo simplicius, Galla, negare potes.* For another sequence of epigrams playing on various senses of *dare*, see 2.21, 2.24 and 2.25 with Garthwaite 2001.52.

5. See Nauta 2002.122–24 on "giving" or "sending" as dedication.

6. On this book, see Johnson 2005.

7. Roller 2001.146–54.

8. Other examples are 1.4–5, 1.39–40, 2.91–92, 6.64–65.

9. Howell (1980) cites two apotropaic inscriptions that quote this epigram, an interesting reversal of the more familiar relation between inscription and literary epigram.

10. Catullus c. 12 is the ancestor of these poems that praise one person by blaming another.

11. We could compare 8.31 and 8.32 as comic and serious version of "exiles" petitioning the emperor, with 8.32 making an oblique appeal to the emperor and 8.31 assuring the addressee that his request is futile.

12. The two scholars who have done most to encourage a suspicious mode of reading Martial's praise are Ahl (1984a and 1984b) and Garthwaite (1990, 1993, 1998a, and 1998b). The case against is put by Roemer 1994, Henriksen 1998–1999.1, 18f.; Johnson 1997; Coleman 1998b; and others. For more theoretical or broader discussion of the issues involved, see Bartsch 1994, Kennedy 1992, and Dewar 1994. Lorenz (2002.45–50) summarizes the debate.

13. A similar phrase occurs in Seneca's *De beneficiis* 3.26–7, in a passage about accusations in the reign of Tiberius. An ex-praetor, Paulus, called

for his chamber pot to relieve himself during a dinner. Unfortunately, he happened to have a gem engraved with the emperor's image on his finger. The informer Maro called the other guests to witness that the emperor's image had been brought into proximity with what is indecent (*admotam esse imaginem obscenis*). Fortunately, Paulus's slave, equally eagle-eyed, had anticipated him and removed the ring, which he showed to the guests in his own hand, thus saving his master. Martial 9.66 provides a rare example of a poem that contains both obscenity and a reference to Domitian. On Martial's handling of obscenity in connection with Domitian, see Lorenz 2002.142–62.

14. Book 11 takes a novel approach to this issue, hailing the *libertas* afforded by the new emperor, Nerva, as, among other things, the freedom to speak plain Latin (i.e., obscenity). "This book is mine" (*iste liber meus est*, 11.2.8), which is to say that the books written under Domitian were not. There is nothing about purity and temples here, so clearly there is room for maneuver when it comes to putting obscenity and the emperor on the same page; Martial even quotes an obscene poem by Augustus to make the point (11.20). On Book 11, see Lorenz 2002.210–18.

15. Proximity: *coram*, 5.2.8; *tam prope*, 5.3.5; *ingenio . . . propiore*, 5.5.2; *intra limina sanctioris aulae*, 5.6.8. Garthwaite 1998b contains a good discussion of this opening sequence, which notes the theme of Domitian's distance. Garthwaite points out that "in toying with the theme of oracular and literary possession [Myrtale's chewing of laurel], the poem neatly and playfully reflects the motifs of the preceding panegyrics" (160). On the importance of proximity at court, see Wallace-Hadrill 1996.285–93.

16. Domitian's ruddy complexion was remarked on by both Suetonius (*Dom.* 18) and Tacitus (*Agricola* 45.2). The latter comments that it served to protect Domitian from shame (*rubor, quo se contra pudorem muniebat*). Is Martial making a sly joke here?

17. A nice example of the "one could truly say" topos is provided by 4.34, where Attalus's worn toga is allowed to be "snowy"—not so much "snow-white" as "chilly" (*Sordida cum tibi sit, verum tamen, Attale, dicit, / quisquis te niveam dicit habere togam*, 1–2). Here insult and praise share the same words.

18. Holzberg 2002.66–67 puts it neatly (a propos 1.6): "Panegyrisches Sprechen ist hier ganz einfach epigrammatischen und damit witzigen Sprechen untergeordnet, ohne dass der verherrlichte lächerlich gemacht wird."

19. A very interesting juxtaposition highlights the fact that in Martial what "can truly be said" replaces the truth. Epigram 8.75 is basically a labored pun prepared by an elaborate story about a Lingonian who twists his ankle returning home; since he is only attended by one small slave, he has to be carried on a passing litter borne by four public slaves, who are persuaded to jettison the corpse they are carrying to a pauper's grave. "This is one you could truly address as 'dead Gaul,'" Martial concludes (*merito dici . . . potest*, 16). The next poem is addressed to a *Gallicus* who is always importuning Martial to tell him the truth about his recitations and oratory. It begins by picking up the *merito dici . . . potest* with which previous poem ends: "Tell me the truth, Marcus, tell it please; there's nothing I hear more gladly" (*Dic verum mihi, Marce, dic amabo; / nil est quod magis audiam libenter*, 8.76.1–2). From the previous poem we know he's asking the wrong person. And, sure enough, Martial manages to tell Gallicus, not the truth, but what is "truer than true" (*vero verius*, 7), namely that he does not willingly hear the truth (*verum, Gallice, non libenter audis*, 8). In this particular encounter, Gallicus could truly (*merito*) be called "a dead Gaul"! Poems 7.28 and 5.63 are even more inscrutable, or double-edged, in their truth-telling, and together they imply that all parties are involved in a conspiracy not to tell, or hear, the truth.

20. For instance, Coleman (1998b.337), on panegyric: "The ideology pervading the Epigrams is so alien to our modern way of thinking that we have to be particularly careful about importing our own ethical standards into an interpretation of what Martial is doing." Also Dewar 1994.5: "The extravagance of the medium [panegyric] with the high value it placed on the sheer extravagance of idea and expression alike, will always be alien in some measure to the modern reader."

21. Meter requires either something more or something less in this line. For the problem and various solutions, see Grewing 1997 ad loc.

22. Compare the bee in amber of 4.32 (*credibile est ipsam sic voluisse mori*, 4), which is followed by a poem addressed to someone who wants to be mentioned in Martial's poetry but has a metrically intractable name.

23. As a thief, too, he is returned to servile status, thievishness being one of the stereotypical characteristics of the slave (cf. 11.54.6). On *barbarismus*, see Grewing 1997 ad loc. As Grewing points out, the juxtaposition of *Cinnam* and *Cinname* suggests that there is only a letter's difference between them.

24. Grewing 1997.164, citing *CIL* 3.2507.

25. Grewing 1997.134 cites 2.20, 1.29, and 1.38 for the play with *suus*. For a comparable poem on purchased hair, see *AP* 11.68 (Lucillius).

26. Compare the juxtapositions of gender domination and social subordination noted in note 53, below.

27. Compare 14.1.5: *divitis alternas et pauperis accipe sortes.*

28. Cf. 1.42 and 1.43; also 8.75 and 8.76. Maltby (N.d.) cites 5.43 and 5.44 (*dentes* and Dento), 5.45 and 5.46 (Bassa and *basia*), 5.47 and 5.48 (Philo and *amor*/Encolpos).

29. Kay (1985 ad loc.), who points out that a Stoic Chaeremon was tutor to Nero.

30. Poet and Stoic are not so far removed, for both are proverbially poor. The description of Chaeremon's poverty has been transferred from the next poem, where we might expect an account of the poet's poverty to accompany the invitation.

31. For more on this poem, see Fitzgerald 2000.48–50.

32. On this, see Fitzgerald 2000.51–68.

33. Compare 11.22 and 11.43 for the "when is an anus not an anus" theme. The words *utere parte tua* (12.96.12) recur at 11.22.10 (parodying *Aen.* 12.932, *utere sorte tua*).

34. Some interesting examples are 2.68, 2.18, 2.32, and 3.46.

35. On positionality in this poem, see Fitzgerald 1995.50–51. On oral sex in Martial, see Parker 1994.

36. On this epigram's relation to the traditions of the *Carmina latina epigraphica*, see Morelli 2005.155–58.

37. Notice that 11.93, a straightforward insult, alludes to this poem (*o scelus, o magnum facinus*, 3; cf. 11.91.3, *ah scelus, ah facinus*); as Kay (1985) points out, we expect 11.93 also to be a lament, but it turns out to be quite the opposite—it's a pity that the poet Theodorus wasn't burnt along with his house!

38. Compare the sequence 1.77 and 1.78, where the noble suicide of Festus is celebrated (1.78) after a poem in which the ever-pale Charinus is revealed to be a cunnilinctor (1.77). The final line of 1.77 is *cunnum Charinus lingit et tamen pallet*. Poem 1.78 begins with an extended description of the wasting disease from which Festus was suffering, a disease which attacked his face (perhaps the same as Canace's): *Indignas premeret pestis cum tabida fauces / inque ipsos vultus serperet atra lues*, 1–2. Building up to Festus's chosen instrument of death (sword), Martial describes an alternative as oral pollution: *nec tamen obscuro*

*pia polluit ora veneno*, 5. Here, too, we are required to make a definite effort to avoid contaminating the second poem with the first (and so duplicating the spread of Festus's disease).

39. Client service is figured as slavery, for instance, in the following epigrams from Book 2: 2.68.4, 2.18.7, 2.32.7, 2.53 passim.

40. Other examples of masters castigated for beating slaves are 2.66, 3.13, and 3.94. In all of these cases, though, it is Martial who castigates the cruel master, or mistress. With this epigram, compare Juvenal 6.490–96, which it may have inspired.

41. On this poem, see Fitzgerald 2000.32–33.

42. Epigram 8.24 features a favorite pun of Martial's, on *libellus* (1), both "petition" and "book" (almost "poetry"); compare 11.1.5. This particular *libellus* is a petition that will have wide currency, contributing to the deification of the emperor on two levels.

43. On slaves and mythology, see Fitzgerald 2000.5–6.

44. On this concept, see Oliensis 1995.

45. I prefer the reading of T, in which the slave flirts with the guest (*avertam vultus, tamquam mihi pocula Gorgon / porrigat atque oculos oraque nostra* petat, 9.25.6) to that of b, accepted by Shackleton Bailey (1993), who prints *tegam* for *petat*.

46. Compare 9.39, where the emperor's birthday coincides with that of Rufus's wife; Rufus has two causes for celebration.

47. But perhaps competition is not entirely absent from 9.24, for to worship is to make a claim on the being who is worshiped, and Martial claims the emperor from Carus by including Carus's statue in his epigram.

48. Hylas, another figure connected with Hercules, is brought into 9.25 at line 7. Henriksen (1998–1999 ad loc.) cites *AP* 6.126 (Dioscorides), on a Cretan warrior, Hyllus, who has the Gorgon on his shield. This may have suggested Martial's reference to the Gorgon (5).

49. Compare Valerius Maximus 1 praef.: *reliquos enim deos accepimus, Caesares dedimus*. Quoted by Gowing 2005.50.

50. Under the marriage laws of Augustus, legal privileges, including certain rights of inheritance, were granted to parents of three or more children. The emperor could confer the *ius trium liberorum* on any individual regardless of marital or parental status. Martial seems to have been granted the *ius* by Titus (3.95.5–6, 9.97.5–6), so it is puzzling that he attributes it here to Domitian. See Williams 2004.279. Martial makes specific requests to the emperor twice in the corpus: once for the right to use water from the Aqua Marcia for his house on the

Quirinal (9.18) and once for the *ius trium liberorum* here. For satirical poems on the *ius,* see 8.31 and 9.66.

51. For the book as Martial's child, cf. 10.104.15, perhaps inspired by Ovid's exile poetry (*Tristia* 1.1.115, 3.1.57).

52. Compare 5.1.8 (*sospite quo gratum credimus esse Iovem*) and 7.60.2 (*quem salvo duce credimus Tonantem*).

53. For juxtapositions in which social subordination is compensated by gender domination compare 11.23 and 11.24. Epigrams 2.30 and 2.31 provide another example: in the first poem, Martial is the poor client asking for a loan (and receiving advice instead), and in the second he is the swaggering Romeo boasting of how well Chrestina "gives." Notice also the trade-off between being the client of a patron and the man of a woman in 3.30.3–4: *unde tibi togula est et fuscae pensio cellae / unde datur quadrans? unde vir es Chiones?* (and compare 3.53 and 3.54 for a juxtaposition that works similarly).

54. Martial's marital status has been much disputed. Sometimes he poses as a married man (3.92, 4.24, 11.43, 11.104) and sometimes as unmarried (2.49, 10.8, 11.19, 11.23). The general consensus is that, whether or not Martial ever married, the wife of the epigrams is a literary construct. See Sullivan 1991.25–26; Watson and Watson 2003.3; Williams 2004.279–80. *Valebis* here may allude to the formal language of divorce (see Williams 2004 ad loc.).

55. I take Regulus's question to mean that he did not receive a copy of Book 1. For other explanations having to do with the publication history and titles of Martial's books, see Williams 2004.282–83.

## CHAPTER 5

1. Citroni (1995.44) cites the solitary precedent of Catullus, c. 14b. On Martial and the *lector,* see Larash 2004 (21–91 on the Ovidian connection).

2. See Kenney 1982 and Starr 1987.

3. Nauta 2002.120–31, with his bibliography.

4. See especially *Ep.* 1.20, with Oliensis 1995. Also on Horace, Habinek 1998.98–102.

5. However, Spisak (1997) argues that Martial's special relationship with his reader owes much to satire.

6. Citroni 1995.436–39.

7. Citroni (1995.465, n. 5) lists the relevant passages.

8. In *Tristia* 3.1, the *lector amice* (2) to whom the book addresses itself on its arrival in Rome, and into whose plebeian hands it consigns itself after being ejected from the public libraries (81–82), is contrasted with the *princeps* to whom it addresses its prayer for mercy. See Newlands 1997.74.

9. Citroni 1995.462–64. Compare Pliny 9.23 on his fame as an author among people who do not know him by sight; also 9.11 (his books selling in Vienne).

10. Martial numbers his books more frequently than any previous Latin poet (cf. 5.1, 5.15, 6.1, 6.85, 7.17, 8 praef., 8.3, 10.2, 12.4). Henderson (2002.79–82) has a good treatment of this. Again, Ovid is Martial's model (*Amores* 1. epigr.; *Fasti* 1.723–24; Citroni 1995.443–44).

11. Book 9 praef.: *quem non miraris sed, puto, lector, amas*; cf. 4.49.10: *laudant illa, sed ista legunt*.

12. This contract is nicely encapsulated in 1.1, where the reader eagerly devours Martial's epigrams and gives him fame in return. However, by succumbing to the reader's desire, and accepting the reward of fame, Martial has consigned himself to poverty, or so he says (5.16).

13. Compare Pliny 1.2.6 on what the *bibliopolae* tell him.

14. On booksellers, see Kenney 1982.15–22. Martial names booksellers who stock his books at 1.2, 1.117, 4.72, and 13.3.

15. Albeit a *primipilus* (Aulus Pudens: 1.31, 5.48, 6.58). See White 1975 and Roman 2001.141–43 on the diffusion of patronage in Domitian's Rome. Sullivan (1991.16) gives the figure of about 140 identifiable personages in Martial's poetry, few of whom overlap with those mentioned by Statius and Pliny the Younger. Nauta (2002.58–73) surveys Martial's patrons.

16. Nauta 2002.39–49. Damon 1997 argues plausibly that the positive version of patron-client relations in the poems addressed to named individuals is fleshed out by a more cynical picture in the poems addressed to the pseudonymous.

17. This differential access is dramatized in 7.26, for instance, where Martial instructs his scazon to greet Apollinaris and to let his ear be the first to hear it.

18. See Nauta 2002.46 on "isolated vocatives." Nauta shows that there is a remarkable consistency in the kind of material addressed to any given named individual. Saller (1983) argues, against White 1978, that Martial needed and received material support from his patrons. Nauta (2002.80) makes the interesting observation that Martial acknowledges

the receipt of gifts eight times, but never the receipt of money, although Pliny 3.21 is evidence that he received it.

19. Cavallo 1999.79.

20. One factor that makes the author's copy more valuable is that it is less likely to be marred by uncorrected copyist's errors (Henriksen 1998–1999 ad loc.).

21. Martial 4.82, 5.80, 7.26, 7.97, 11.106. For Martial's leisured *lector*, see 11.3.1–2.

22. White 1974 and 1996.

23. Fowler 1995, answered by White 1996. Nauta 2002.107–20 and 365–74 is a judicious survey of the evidence, coming down against White's contention that the published books contain dedication poems transferred from *libelli*, but arguing that Martial did produce unpublished *libelli* for the emperor.

24. *Transire* is the usual term (*tu qui transis et leges hunc titulum*, CIL 14.1873.3). Valette-Cagnac (1997.75–82) describes the convention by which epitaphs seek to attract the attention of busy passersby (cf. *occupatus*, 11.106.2).

25. On Martial's female readers, see Larash 2004.172–230.

26. Epigram and *mentula*: 1.35.5, 3.69.2.

27. Is the echo of 1.1 in 7.17 evidence that the codex edition to which it refers consists of these seven books? See Galán Vioque 2002 ad loc., for a survey of opinions.

28. A point made by Galán Vioque (2002.141). On the reciprocal bestowing of fame by poet and patron, see Puelma 1995.443.

29. The stimulating discussion of the circulation of *decus* in Bowditch 2001.47–50 is very relevant to this preface.

30. Or possibly for the book itself. Once again, Ovid's exile poetry would be the model (*Ex Ponto* 1.1.3: *hospitio peregrinos, Brute, libellos, excipe . . .*).

31. White (1972.56f.) cited Henriksen 1998–1999.52.

32. *Clarissimus* becomes a title signifying membership of the senatorial order by the time of Trajan; see Henriksen 1998–1999.52.

33. Notice the juxtaposition of *cinis* and *vivat*; for *vivat*, compare 1.88.8: *hic tibi perpetuo tempore vivet honor.*

34. On this letter and on Pliny and Martial, see Henderson 2002.44–58.

35. Contrast the beginning of 7.33, where Pliny writes to Tacitus *Auguror, nec me fallit augurium, historias tuas immortales futuras; quo magis illis (ingenue fatebor) inseri cupio.*

36. The comparison of Pliny to Cicero in 10.19 works rather like the busts that will surround Martial in Avitus's library.

37. Domitian became *censor perpetuus* in 85; see Jones 1992.106–7. Martial himself makes the point that obscenity is incompatible with the sanctity of the emperor (8 praef.) and in the case of Books 5 and 8 declares that they will be free of obscene material since they approach the emperor. In 5.2 he makes a clear distinction between those readers to whose taste for *nequitiae procaciores* (3) the previous four books have catered, and the emperor, together with *matronae puerique virginesque* (1), who are the target audience of this book. However, in Book 11, with the change of regime from Domitian to Nerva, Martial makes the return of obscenity synonymous with the return of *libertas*. On epigrams and the *pudicus princeps*, see Lorenz 2002.111–208.

38. On Ovid *Tristia* 3.1, see Newlands 1997.73–75 ("having been rejected by state institutions and by the emperor himself, the personified book turns to the private citizen").

39. Compare 7.72, where it is the *Saturnalia* that provide the *sic* guaranteeing Martial's innocence. In 7.12 the reader replaces not only Martial's *dominus*, but also Ovid's *domina* (*perque tuam faciem, magni mihi numinis instar, Amores* 3.11.47).

40. Significantly, the poem whose first line featured the emperor as *dominus* ends by characterizing the *lector* as *liber*.

41. Bowditch 2001.50.

42. In 7.80 Faustinus is again involved in the dissemination of Martial's poetry.

43. On Domitian's edict against defamatory texts, see Suet. *Dom.* 8.3.

44. Especially if the analogy with Ovid is felt. Compare Ovid's acknowledgment of the reader at the end of *Tristia* 4 and the boast that concludes the *Metamorphoses* (*Met.* 15.875–75; cf. Martial, *pigra per hunc fugies ingratae flumina Lethes / et meliore tui parte superstes eris*, 10.2.7–8). Martial's recourse to the reader in a situation where the favor of the emperor is at risk reminds us of Ovid's similar appeal to the reader in *Tristia* 3.1. Compare also *Tristia* 4.10.123–32, which moves from *Livor* (123) to the *candidus lector* in the final line of the poem (*sive favore tuli, sive hanc ego carmine famam, / iure tibi grates, candide lector, ago*, 131–32).

45. On Book 10 and Martial's attitude toward imperial ideology and the emperor, see Fearnley 2003.

46. If Ovid is alluding to the displeasure of Augustus when he claims that *Iovis ira* cannot touch the survival of his work (*Met.* 15.871), there is a

parallel to be drawn with Martial, whose poetry will outlast the monuments of Domitian.

47. Suetonius *Dom.* 23, with Jones 1996 ad loc.

48. Compare *Omnes . . . libelli mei, domine, quibus tu famam, id est vitam, dedisti, tibi supplicant; et, puto, propter hoc legentur,* 8 praef. 3–5. On the location of the Pliny poem in Book 10 (10.19), see Henderson 2002.44–58.

49. Poem 12.4 in Shackleton Bailey's numbering; for the problem of numbering, see Lorenz 2002.234.

50. Fortunately for Martial, earlier books had included poems addressed to Nerva. In both 8.70 and 9.26 Martial cites Nero's respect for the future emperor's poetry. Notice that 9.26 comes shortly after 9.24, on Domitian's portrait.

51. This is one of only two occasions in Martial's oeuvre where the emperor is made to speak. The other is 1.5, which also implies that an atmosphere of casual joking prevails between emperor and poet.

52. Compare 5.25.11–12: *o frustra locuples, o dissimulator amici, / haec legis et laudas? quae tibi fama perit.*

53. In fact, in 5.16 the example of Alexis, supposedly a slave given to Vergil by Maecenas, bring us back to the world of the court. It is a favorite example of Martial, but a particularly telling one in this context. Martial has just complained that his book is a *conviva* and *comissator,* a dinner companion whose company is enjoyed gratis (*et tantum gratis pagina nostra placet,* 9); it was at a dinner that Vergil reputedly admired Alexis, waiting at table, and received him as a gift from Maecenas. Compare 8.55, where Maecenas makes the gift of Alexis an afterthought to the offer of money. Immediately he sees the lovely attendant, Vergil conceives his *arma virumque* (for the double entendre on *arma,* see Adams 1982.21).

54. Martial's nearest equivalent to the alien might be the frozen centurion, thumbing the book among the Getic snows (11.3).

55. *Dissimulas? Facies me, puto,* caus*idicum* (5.15.14), recalls *tu causa es, lector amice, mihi* (5.15.2).

56. Nauta 2002.96–105.

57. Compare 1.2.2, where the codex is figured as the *comes* of a traveler.

58. The figure of the book as *conviva* to be enjoyed free may also allude to a recent development in the workings of patronage, namely the failed attempt of Domitian to restore the *cena* as return for the observances of the client in place of the *sportula* (money or small basket of comestibles) that had taken its place (Suetonius *Dom.* 7). Insofar as the dinner

replaced money, the *conviva* could be represented as free (cf. 3.30.1: *spor-tula nulla datur; gratis conviva recumbis*; 3.60.1: *cum vocer ad cenam non iam venalis ut ante*; 4.68.1: *invitas centum quadrantibus et bene cenas*). After Domitian revoked his attempt to reinstate the *cena*, it could retro-spectively be seen as a way of avoiding the payment that itself marks the degradation of patron-client relations to a financial formality.

59. Howell (1995 ad loc.) cites Quintilian's disapproval of this "piracy" (*Inst. Or.* 12.7.11–12).

CHAPTER 6

1. For an extended treatment of "the hermeneutics of reception" see Martindale (1993.35), who quotes Borges to the effect that "every writer creates his own precursors.".

2. Gaisser 1993, chap. 5.

3. Gaisser 1993.244–46.

4. For this argument, see Giangrande 1975.

5. Bloom 1973. On the relation between Catullus and Martial, see Offer-mann 1980; Newman 1990.75–103; Gaisser 1993.200–211; Swann 1994 (with the review of Batstone 1998); Grewing 1996.

6. In taking the line that Martial deliberately banalizes Catullus, I dis-agree with the view that Martial persistently misunderstood Catullus due to inadequacies of sensibility. Offermann 1980 is the best example of this attitude.

7. Kay 1985.165–66 is a good survey of *captatio* in Martial and beyond.

8. Compare 8.54, where the wish that a certain Catulla were either less beautiful or less chaste (with an allusion to Catullus 49) suggests a metapoetic agenda concerning Martial's relation to Catullus.

9. Offermann (1980.116–17) puts this poem in the category of Martial's "continuations" of Catullan poems (*fateor*, 1).

10. On Catullus c. 13, see Fitzgerald 1995.98–100.

11. As the Watsons (2003 ad loc.) point out, dead bodies were anointed not only prior to burial or cremation (*unguitur*), but also at the funeral feast at which the dead were present, but could not partake (*non cenat*).

12. On this topic, see Offermann 1980.121–24.

13. Offermann (1980.124) remarks that *pilosus* (4) and *hircoso* (5) are both Catullan words (cc. 16.10, 33.7, 71.7).

14. Unless we read Martial's cunnilinctor back into Catullus c. 9, so that the poet greets Veranius fresh from ministering to his Lesbia.

15. Though often Martial combines Catullus with other poets. Catullus with Marsus and Pedo: 1 praef., 5.5.6; Catullus with Marsus: 2.71.3 and 7.99.7; Pedo and Marsus only: 2.77.5. On the collocation, see Newman 1990.79–81. For Catullus alone, see 4.14.13, 10.78.16, 10.103.5.

16. On the Latin invitation poem, see Edmunds 1982. Dettmer (1989) deals with the relation between Catullus c. 13 and Philodemus's poem.

17. On 11.52, see Gowers (1993.264–67), who comments "with *belle*, Martial flaunts tastefulness, and disclaims it as a laughable value."

18. A motif that is found in Greek epigram; see Lucillius, *AP* 11.10.

19. The combination of deference and mockery that Martial manages is in no way incompatible with the encomiastic purpose of his poem. As Nauta has observed (2002.30–31), it is the relationship between poet and patron that is on display in poems like this.

20. The classic example of Martial turning down the emotional heat on one of Catullus's poems of inner torment is 1.32, a self-satisfied version of c. 85 (*Non amo te, Sabidi, nec possum dicere quare: / hoc tantum possum dicere, non amo te*). As Offermann (1980.125) remarks, the reader gets the distinct impression that Martial enjoys his aversion to Sabidius.

21. Both poems end with knowledge (*cum tantum sciat esse basiorum*, c. 5.13; *quisquam, vivere cum sciat, moratur*? 5.20). In Catullus, the knowledge of others is threatening to the lovers, but in Martial the knowledge of the friends is rendered useless by the demands that others make on them.

22. *OLD* has this use of *verna* under the meaning "vulgar, town-bred person." The most common meaning of *verna* is "home-born slave," which is relevant here since *vernae* were often encouraged to be cheeky, as Howell (1980 ad loc.) points out in a helpful note.

23. Compare the similar substitution of Rome for the Spain of Catullus's c. 9 in 12.54.

24. Fitzgerald 1995.93–98.

25. Or rather, their cheap slaves (*viles pueri salariorum*, 1.41.8), who may themselves be taking Catullus's slangy *leporum differtus puer* (12.8–9) to the level of real degradation (one step down from the *verna*).

26. Grewing (1996.346) suggests that Martial's reference to Cecrops (*Cecropio monte*, 6.34.4) parallels Catullus's naming of Battus (alluding to Callimachus) at c. 7.6. There would be a closer parallel if we were to see in Martial's *Oceani fluctus* (6.34.2) a sly allusion to the name of the bouncer (*dissignator*) in the theater (5.23, 5.27, 6.9). This allusion would anticipate the scene of the emperor's arrival in the theater and would be as emblematic of Martial's poetic world as Catullus's *Batti . . . sepulcrum* is of his.

27. On this simile, see Grewing 1996.345–47, who points out that Domitian's appearance is that of a god (347). Gaisser (1993.235) observes, "Here, characteristically, Martial has replaced the content of Catullus's imagery with a picture from his own crass world, but he has also achieved a *tour de force* of the flatterer's art: by the blandness of the preceding images he highlights the applause for Domitian."

28. Martial pretends to misunderstand Catullus's counting in order to produce his concluding epigrammatic point (*pauca cupit qui numerare potest*). See Grewing 1996.348–49. Typically, Offermann (1980.122) sees this as a plain misunderstanding.

29. Grewing (1996.349–51) has some good remarks on the social background to Martial's shift from free to slave and heterosexual to homosexual. As he points out, Catullus had done his own homosexual version of the kiss poems to Lesbia in his Iuventius poems (especially c. 48).

30. The phrase *passerem Catulli* could also allude to poems in the style of Catullus, written for the boy. See Kay 1985 ad loc. Catullus's book (in some form or other) was known as the *Passer* (Martial, 1.7.3, 4.14.4; Pliny 9.25).

31. Dindymus is probably to be thought of as a eunuch (cf. 11.81.1 and 6.39.21). The theme of castration has already been introduced by the allusion to Saturn's castration of Uranus (*falciferi senis*, 11.6.1).

32. *AP* 7.185, 7.371, 7.467, 7.632, 7.643 (Laurens 1965.319).

33. Epigrams 9.56 and 9.103 and the "Earinus cycle" (9.11–13, 16–17, 36) are good examples, all in a single book.

34. It is preceded by the genuine article, a poem on Stella's slave Argynnus (or possibly the statue of a boy; see Galán Vioque 2002 ad loc.).

35. His metrically awkward wife, Violentilla, receives the Greek pseudonym matching the previous line's "Lesbia."

36. Aulus Pudens receives poems of erotic content also in 6.54 and 8.63.

37. Connors 2000.227–28.

38. See Geyssen 1999.719, n. 2, for other forbears of this topographical poetry, including Terence *Ad.* 573–84; Horace *Sat.* 1.9; and *Aeneid* 8, reworked by Propertius in 4.1.

39. On Ovid and Martial, see Siedschlag 1972; Pitcher 1998; Williams 2002; Larash 2004.21–91 ; and, most important, Hinds n.d..

40. Roman 2001.124.

41. The opening of 1.70 (*Vade salutatum pro me, liber . . .*) recalls another exile poem of Ovid *Tristia* 3.7 (*Vade salutatum, subito perarata, Perillam*). On Martial 1.70 and Ovid, see Geyssen 1999.

42. One might add Geyssen's (1999.735) interpretation of Martial's disclaimer: poetry that is written for a number of patrons involves too

many salutations; Martial would prefer one Maecenas instead. This poem, then, is implicitly directed at Domitian, as the allusions to Ovid's itinerary (taking in places that are associated with Augustus) implies.

43. "In a manner which Ovid would recognize, Martial is acutely aware of the importance of being at the centre of affairs, and so is determined to remain there. By referring back to aspects of Ovid's exile poetry Martial is able to present himself as the superior of Ovid, and acceptable to the emperor. He uses these themes from the centre, not the periphery, and so transforms the experience of Ovid into something new and acceptable. Ovid's exile and death on the fringes of the empire did not mean that his influence was ended, or that Latin poetry could not develop. Martial repatriates it" (Pitcher 1998.71–72).

44. Pitcher 1998.68.

45. There are good remarks on Martial in Spain in Woolf 2003.218–20.

46. Pitcher 1998.61–62.

47. Labate 1987.103–12, who cites *Tristia* 5.1.39–45.

48. Labate 1987.105–6, citing *Ex Ponto* 3.4.17, 37–40, 51–60.

49. Labate 1987.107.

50. In the *serus spectator* who, having arrived late from far away, is instructed by Martial on what he has missed (*Spec.* 27 [24]) we may see the Ovidian book which is shown around Rome in *Tristia* 3.1.27–32.

51. Martial 4.82, 5.80, 7.26, 7.97, 11.106.

52. Compare *Tristia* 4.10.131–32 (*sive favore tuli, sive hanc ego carmine famam, / iure tibi grates, candide lector, ago*).

53. For instance, 1.107, 5.16.11–12, 8.55, and 11.3.7–11, discussed below. See Geyssen 1999 735–6 and, for a broader view, Roman 2001.138–45.

54. He had, after all, written in praise of Nerva before he became *princeps*. In 9.26 sending poems to Nerva is sending coals to Newcastle (cf. Ovid *Ex Pont.* 4.2.9–13).

55. Martial uses the expression *Quid mihi vobiscum est?* again, facetiously, at 2.22: Postumus used to kiss him with one lip, now he does with both, in spite of having being mocked (in 2.10 and 12). What use is Martial's poetry to him?

56. On Jonson, see Clark 2002, chap. 5.

57. Reinhardstöttner 1887. In Burmeister's *Amphitryo* Alcmena makes a convenient Virgin Mary.

58. Connections between the Old and New Testaments are made at every level. For instance, Martial's *Spec.* 7 begins with a simile comparing the criminal crucified in the arena to Prometheus. Burmeister's *qualiter* introduces a figure of the crucifixion from the Old Testament, the

bronze snake that Moses suspended on a pole which healed the Israel-ites who looked at it of snakebite (Numbers 21; John 3). Naturally, the criminal himself becomes Christ. In Burmeister's version of Martial's three poems on the dead sow (*Spec.* 14, 15, 16) a poem on Susanna's chastity introduces one of the death of Christ (life in death) and an-other on the virgin birth.

59. Sullivan 1991.282.


CONCLUSION

1. Henderson 2002.xi.
2. Henderson 2002.195, n. 5.
3. Terdiman 1985.125.
4. Terdiman 1985.127.

# WORKS CITED

Adams, J. 1982. *The Latin Sexual Vocabulary*. Baltimore.

Ahl, F. M. 1984a. "The Rider and the Horse: Politics and Power in Roman Poetry from Horace to Statius." *ANRW* 2.32.1:40–124.

———. 1984b. "The Art of Safe Criticism in Rome." *American Journal of Philology* 105:174–208.

Austin, C., and G. Bastianini. 2002. *Posidippi pellaei quae supersunt omnia*. Milan.

Barton, C. 1993. *The Sorrows of the Ancient Romans: the Gladiator and the Monster*. Princeton.

———. 1994. "Savage Miracles: the Redemption of Lost Honor in Roman Society and the Sacrament of the Gladiator and the Martyr." *Representations* 45:41–69.

Bartsch, S. 1994. *Actors in the Audience: Theatricality and Doublespeak from Nero to Hadrian*. Cambridge, Mass.

Barwick, K. 1958. "Zyklen bei Martial und in der Kleinen Gedichten des Catull." *Philologus* 102:284–318.

———. 1959. *Martial und die Zeitgenössische Rhetorik*. Berlin.

Batstone, W. 1998. Review of *Martial's Catullus: The Reception of an Epigrammatic Rival*, by Bruce Swann. *Classical Philology* 93:286–89.

Baudrillard, J. 1994. *Simulacra and Simulation*. Trans. Sheila Faria Glaser. Michigan.

Benjamin, W. 1970. *Illuminations*. Trans. Harry Zohn. London.

Bergmann, B. and C. Kondoleon. 1999. *The Art of Ancient Spectacle*. New Haven.

Bloom, H. 1973. *The Anxiety of Influence*. Oxford.

Bowditch, L. 2001. *Horace and the Gift Economy of Patronage*. Berkeley.

Boyle, A., and W. Dominik, eds. 2003. *Flavian Rome: Culture, Image, Text*. Leiden.

Bramble, J. 1982. "Martial and Juvenal." In *Cambridge History of Classical Literature: Latin Literature*, ed. E. Kenney and W. Clausen, 597–623. Cambridge.

Brantlinger, Patrick. 1983. *Bread and Circuses: Theories of Mass Culture as Social Decay*. Ithaca.

Braund, S. Morton. 1996. "The Solitary Feast: a Contradiction in Terms?" *Bulletin of the Institute of Classical Studies* 41:37–52.

Buckland, W. W. 1908. *The Roman Law of Slavery*. Cambridge.

Burmeister, J. 1612. *Martialis Renati: Parodiarum sacrarum partes tres quibus obposita M. Val. Martialis epigrammata*. Goslar.

Burnikel, W. 1980. *Untersuchungen zur Struktur des Witzepigramms bei Lukillios und Martial*. Wiesbaden.

Cameron, A. 1993. *The Greek Anthology from Meleager to Planudes*. Oxford.

Camille, Michael. 1996. "Simulacrum." In *Critical Terms for Art History*, ed. Robert Nelson and Richard Shiff, 31–44. Chicago.

Carratello, Ugo. 1965a. "Orfeo e l'orsa (nota a Marziale *spect.* 21–21b)." *Giornale italiano di filologia* 18:131–45.

———. 1965b. "Omnis Caesareo cedit labor amphitheatro! (Note a Mart. *spect. lib.*)." *Giornale italiano di filologia* 18:294–324.

———. 1980. *M. Valerii Martialis: Epigrammaton liber*. Perugia.

Cavallo, G. 1999. "Between Volumen and Codex: Reading in the Ancient World." In *A History of Reading in the West*, ed. G. Cavallo and R. Chartier, 64–89. Cambridge.

Citroni, M. 1975. *M. Valerii Martialis: Epigrammaton liber primus*. Florence.

———. 1988. "Pubblicazione e dediche dei libri in Marziale." *Maia* 40:3–39.

———. 1989. "Marziale e la letteratura per i Saturnali (poetica dell'intrattenimento e cronologia della pubblicazione dei libri)." *Illinois Classical Studies* 14:201–26.

———. 1995. *Poesia e lettori in Roma antica: Forme della communicazione letteraria*. Rome.

Clark, Michael. 2002. "In a Martial Hand: Studies in the Epigram in Early Modern Britain." D.Phil. diss., Oxford University.

Coleman. K. 1986. "The Emperor Domitian and Literature." *ANRW* 2.32.5, 3087–3115.

———. 1990. "Fatal Charades: Roman Executions Staged as Mythological Enactment." *Journal of Roman Studies*, 80:44–73.

———. 1993. "Launching into History: Aquatic Displays in the Early Empire." *Journal of Roman Studies* 83:48–75.

———. 1998a. "The *Liber spectaculorum*: Perpetuating the Ephemeral." In Grewing 1998.15–36.

———. 1998b. "Martial Book 8 and the Politics of AD 93." *Papers of the Leeds International Latin Seminar* 10:337–57.

———. 1999. "Informers on Parade." In Bergmann and Kondoleon 1999:231–46.

Colton, R. 1991. *Juvenal's Use of Martial's Epigrams: A Study of Literary Influence*. Las Palmas.

Connors, C. 2000. "Imperial Space and Time: The Literature of Leisure." In *Literature in the Roman World: A New Perspective*, ed. Oliver Taplin, 208–34. Oxford.

Coppola, A. 1999. "Fra Alessandro e gli Aeneadi, da Tiberio a Traiano." *Athenaeum* 87:447–56.

Courtney, E. 1993. *The Fragmentary Latin Poets*. Oxford.

Crary, Jonathan. 1988. "Spectacle, Attention, Counter-Memory." *October* 50:97–107.

Damon, C. 1997. *The Mask of the Parasite: A Pathology of Roman Patronage*. Ann Arbor.

Debord, Guy. 1983. *The Society of the Spectacle* (trans. of *La société du spectacle*). Detroit.

———. 1998. *Comments on the Society of the Spectacle*. London.

Dettmer, H. 1989. "Catullus 13: A Nose Is a Nose Is a Nose." *Syllecta Classica* 1:75–85.

Dewar, M. 1994. "Laying It on with a Trowel: The Proem to Lucan and Related Texts." *Classical Quarterly* 44:199–211.

Dickey, E. 2002. *Latin Forms of Address: From Plautus to Apuleius*. Oxford.

Dixon, S. 1993. "The Meaning of Gift and Debt in the Roman Elite." *Echos du Monde Classique* 12:451–64.

Dupont, F. 1985. *L'acteur-roi, ou le théâtre dans la Rome antique*. Paris.

Edmondson, J. C. 1996. "Dynamic Arenas: Gladiatorial Presentations in the City of Rome and the Construction of Roman Society during the Early Empire." In *Roman Theater and Society*, ed. William Slater, 69–112. Michigan.

Edmunds, L. 1982. "The Latin Invitation Poem: What Is It? Where Did It Come From?" *American Journal of Philology* 103:184–88.

Fearnley, H. 2003. "Reading the Imperial Revolution: Martial, *Epigrams 10*." In Boyle and Dominik 2003.613–35.

Feldherr, A. 1998. *Spectacle and Society in Livy's History*. Berkeley.

Fitzgerald, W. 1995. *Catullan Provocations: Lyric Poetry and the Drama of Position*. Berkeley.

———. 2000. *Slavery and the Roman Literary Imagination*. Cambridge.

Foucault, M. 1979. *Discipline and Punish*. Trans. Alan Sheridan. New York.

Fowler, D. 1995. "Martial and the Book." *Ramus* 24:31–58.

Freudenburg, K. 2001. *Satires of Rome: Threatening Poses from Lucilius to Juvenal.* Cambridge.

Friedländer, L. 1886. *M. Valerii Martialis Epigrammaton Libri.* Leipzig.

Gaisser, J. 1993. *Catullus and His Renaisance Readers.* Oxford.

Galán Vioque, G. 2002. *Martial, Book VII: A Commentary.* Leiden.

Gamberale, L. 1993. "Fra epigrafia e letteratura. Note a Marziale 10.71." *A&R* 38:42–54.

Garrido-Hory, M. 1981. *Martial et l'esclavage.* Paris.

Garthwaite, J. 1990. "Martial, Book 6, on Domitian's Moral Censorship." *Prudentia* 22:12–22.

———. 1993. "The Panegyrics of Domitian in Martial, Book 9." *Ramus* 22:78–102.

———. 1998a. "Patronage and Poetic Immortality in Martial, Book 9." *Mnemosyne* 51:161–75.

———. 1998b. "Putting a Price on Praise: Martial's Debate with Domitian in Book 5." In Grewing 1998.157–72.

———. 2001. "Reevaluating Epigrammatic Cycles in Martial, Book Two." *Ramus* 30:46–55.

Geyssen, J. 1999. "Sending a Book to the Palatine: Martial 1.70 and Ovid." *Mnemosyne* 52:718–36.

Giangrande, G. 1975. "Catullus' Lyrics on the *Passer*." *Museum Philologum Londoniense* 1:137–46.

Gowers, E. 1993. *The Loaded Table: Representations of Food in Roman Literature.* Oxford.

Gowing, A. 2005. *Empire and Memory: The Representation of the Roman Republic in Imperial Culture.* Cambridge.

Grewing, F. 1996. "Möglichkeiten und Grenzen des Vergleichs: Martials Diadumenos und Catulls Lesbia." *Hermes* 124:333–54.

———. 1997. Martial, *Buch VI: Ein Kommentar.* Goettingen.

———, ed. 1998. *Toto Notus in Orbe: Perspektiven der Martial-Interpretation.* Stuttgart.

Gunderson, E. 1996. "The Ideology of the Arena." *Classical Antiquity* 15:113–51.

———. 2003. "The Flavian Amphitheatre: All the World's a Stage." In Boyle and Dominik 2003.637–58.

Gunning, T. 1994. "An Aesthetics of Astonishment: Early Film and the (In)Credulous Spectator." In *Viewing Positions: Ways of Seeing Film,* ed. L. Williams, 114–33. New Brunswick.

Gutzwiller, K. 1998. *Poetic Garlands: Hellenistic Epigrams in Context.* Berkeley.

Habinek, T. 1998. *The Politics of Latin Literature: Writing, Identity, and Empire in Ancient Rome.* Princeton.

Hallett, J. 1977. "*Perusinae Glandes* and the Changing Image of Augustus." *American Journal of Ancient History* 2:151–71.

Hardie, A. 1983. *Statius and the Silvae: Poets, Patrons, and Epideixis in the Greco-Roman World.*

Hardie, P. 2002. *Ovid's Poetics of Illusion.* Cambridge.

Henderson, J. 1998. *Fighting for Rome: Poets and Caesars, History and Civil War.* Cambridge.

———. 2002. *Pliny's Statue: The Letters, Self-Portraiture, and Classical Art.* Exeter.

Hennig, J.-L. 2003. *Martial.* Paris.

Henriksen, C. 1998–1999. *Martial, Book IX: A Commentary.* Uppsala.

Hinds, S. 1998. *Allusion and Intertext: Dynamics of Appropriation in Roman Poetry.* Cambridge.

———. N.d. "Martial's Ovid/Ovid's Martial."

Hoffer, S. 1999. *The Anxieties of Pliny the Younger.* Atlanta.

Holzberg, N. 1988. *Martial.* Heidelberg.

———. 2002. *Martial und das antike Epigram.* Darmstadt.

———. N.d. "Onomato-Poetics: A Linear Reading of Martial 7.67–70."

Hopkins, K. and M. Beard. 2005. *The Colosseum.* London.

Housman, A. E. 1901. "Two Epigrams of Martial." *Classical Review* 15:154–55 = Housman, *Classical Papers*, vol. 2, *1897–1914*, ed. J. Diggle and F. Goodyear, 536–38. Cambridge.

Howell, Peter. 1980. *A Commentary on Book One of the Epigrams of Martial.* London.

———. 1995. *Martial: The Epigrams, Book 5.* Warminster.

Hutchinson, G. 2003. "The Catullan Corpus, Greek Epigram, and the Poetry of Objects." *Classical Quarterly* 53:206–21.

Jameson, Fredric. 1991. *Postmodernism; or, the Cultural Logic of Late Capitalism.* Durham.

Janson, T. 1964. *Latin Prose Prefaces.* Stockholm.

Johnson, M. 1997. "Martial and Domitian's Moral Reforms." *Prudentia* 29:24–70.

Johnson, W. R. 2005. "Small Wonders: The Poetics of Martial, Book Fourteen." In *Defining Genre and Gender in Latin Literature*, ed. W. Batstone and G. Tissol, 139–50. New York.

Jones, B. 1992. *The Emperor Domitian.* London.

———. 1996. *Suetonius: Domitian.* London.

Kay, N. 1985. *Martial, Book XI: A Commentary.* London.

Kellum, B. 1997. "Concealing/Revealing: Gender and the Play of Meaning in the Monuments of Augustan Rome." In *The Roman Cultural Revolution,* ed. Thomas Habinek and Alessandro Schiesaro, 158–81. Princeton.

———. 1999. "The Spectacle of the Street." In Bergmann and Kondoleon 1999.283–99.

Kennedy, D. 1992. "'Augustan' and 'Anti-Augustan': Reflections on Terms of Reference." In *Roman Poetry and Propaganda in the Age of Augustus,* ed. A. Powell, 26–58. London.

Kenney, E. 1982. "Books and Readers in the Roman World." In *Cambridge History of Classical Literature,* vol. 2, *Latin Literature,* 3–32.

Ker, W. 1919. *Martial: Epigrams.* 2 vols. Cambridge, Mass.

Labate, M. 1987. "Elegia triste ed elegia liete: Un caso di riconversione letteraria." *Materiali e discussioni per l'analisi dei testi classici* 19: 91–129.

Larash, P. 2004. "Martial's Lector, the Practice of Reading, and the Emergence of the General Reader in Flavian Rome." Ph.D. diss., University of California, Berkeley.

Laurens, P. 1965. "Martial et l'épigramme grecque du ler siècle ap. J.-C." *Revue des Études Latines* 43:315–41.

Laurens, P. 1989. *L'abeille dans l'ambre: Célébration de l'épigramme de l'époque alexandrine à la fin de la Renaissance.* Paris.

Lausberg, M. 1982. *Das Einzeldistichon: Studien zum antiken Epigramm.* Munich.

Lehan, R. 1998. *The City in Literature: An Intellectual and Cultural History.* Berkeley.

Leigh, M. 1997. *Lucan: Spectacle and Engagement.* Oxford.

Lindsay, W. M. 1903. *The Ancient Editions of Martial.* Oxford.

Lorenz. S. 2002. *Erotik und Panegyrik: Martials epigrammatischer Kaiser.* Tübingen.

———. 2004. "Waterscape with Black and White: Epigrams, Cycles, and Webs in Martial's *Epigrammaton Liber Quartus.*" *American Journal of Philology* 125:255–78.

Malnati, T. 1988. "Juvenal and Martial on Social Mobility." *Classical Journal* 83:133–41.

Maltby, R. N.d. "Names as a Linking Device in Martial." Manuscript.

Manley, L. 1985. "Proverbs, Epigrams, and Urbanity in Renaissance London." *English Literary Renaissance* 15:247–76.

Martindale, C. 1993. *Redeeming the Text: Latin Poetry and the Hermeneutics of Reception*. Cambridge.

Merli, E. 1993. "Ordinamento degli epigrammi e strategie cortegiane negli esordi dei libri I–XII di Marziale." *Maia* 45:229–56.

Morelli, A. 2005. "*Toto notus in orbe?* The Epigrams of Martial and the Tradition of the *Carmina latina epigraphica*." *Papers of the Langford Latin Seminar* 12:151–75.

Moretti, G. 1992. "L'arena, Cesare e il mito: Appunti sul De spectaculis di Marziale." *Maia*, n.s., 44:55–63.

Nauta, R. 2002. *Poetry for Patrons: Literary Communication in the Age of Domitian*. Leiden.

Newlands. C. 1997. "The Role of the Book in *Tristia* 3.1." *Ramus* 26:57–79.

———. 2001. *Statius' Silvae and the Poetics of Empire*. Cambridge.

Newman, J. 1990. *Roman Catullus and the Modification of the Roman Sensibility*. Hildesheim.

Nicolet, C. 1980. *The World of the Citizen in Republican Rome*. London.

Nisbet, G. 2003. *Greek Epigram in the Roman Empire: Martial's Forgotten Rivals*. Oxford.

Offermann, H. 1980. "Uno tibi sim minor Catullo." *Quaderni Urbinati di Cultura Classica* 34:107–39.

Ogilvie, R. M. 1965. *A Commentary on Livy, Books 1–5*. Oxford.

Oliensis, E. 1995. "Life after Publication: Epistles 1.20." *Arethusa* 28:209–24.

Pailler, J.-M. 1981. "Martial et l'espace urbain." *Pallas* 28:79–87.

———. 1990. "Le poète, le prince et l'arène: À propos du livre des spectacles de Martiale." In *Spectacula I: Gladiateurs et amphithéâtres*, ed. C. Domergue, C. Landes, and J.-M. Pailler, 179–83. Lattes.

Parker, H. 1994. "Innocent on the Face of It: An Overlooked Obscenity in Martial (6.6)." *Mnemosyne* 47:380–83.

Pitcher, R. 1998. "Martial's Debt to Ovid" in Grewing 1998.59–76.

Potter, David. 1996. "Performance, Power, and Justice in the High Empire." In *Roman Theater and Society*, ed. William J. Slater, 129–59. Ann Arbor.

Puelma, M. 1995. "Dichter und Gönner bei Martial." In *Labor et Lima: Kleine Schriften und Nachträge*, ed. M. Puelma, 415–66. Basle.

———. 1996. "*Epigramma–epigramma*: Aspekte einer Wortgeschichte." *Museum Helveticum* 53:123–39.

Reeve, M. 1983. "Martial." In *Text and Transmission: A Survey of the Latin Classics*, ed. L. D. Reynolds, 329–44. Oxford.

Reinhardstöttner, Karl von. 1887. "Johannes Burmeister's christlicher Martial." *Vierteljahrsschrift fur Kultur und Literatur der Renaissance* 2:283–95.

Reinhold, M. 1971. "Usurpation of Status and Status Symbols in the Roman Empire." *Historia* 20:275–302.

Richlin, A. 1992. *The Gardens of Priapus: Sexuality and Aggression in Roman Humor.* 2nd ed. Oxford.

Robert, L. 1968. "Dans l'amphithéâtre et dans les jardins de Neron. Un épigramme de Lucillius." In *Comptes Rendus/Académie des Inscriptions et Belles-Lettres*, 280–88.

Roberts, C. H., and T. C. Skeat. 1983. *The Birth of the Codex.* London.

Roller, M. 1998. "Pliny's Catullus: The Politics of Literary Appropriation." *Transactions of the American Philological Association* 128:265–304.

Roller, M. 2001. *Constructing Autocracy: Aristocrats and Emperors in Julio-Claudian Rome.* Princeton.

Roman, L. 2001. "The Representation of Literary Materiality in Martial's *Epigrams.*" *Journal of Roman Studies* 91:113–45.

Römer, F. 1994. "Mode und Methode in der Deutung panegyrischer Dichtung der nachaugusteischen Zeit." *Hermes* 122:95–113.

Ross, D. 1969. *Style and Tradition in Catullus.* Cambridge, Mass.

Saggesse, P. 1994. "Lo Scurra in Marziale." *Maia* 46:53–59.

Saller, R. 1983. "Martial on Patronage and Literature." *Classical Quarterly* 33:246–57.

———. 2000. "Status and Patronage." In *The Cambridge Ancient History*, 2nd ed., vol. 11, *The High Empire*, 817–54. Cambridge.

Salles, C. 1992. *Lire à Rome.* Paris.

Sauter, F. 1934. *Der Römische Kaiserkult bei Martial und Statius.* Stuttgart.

Scherf, J. 1998. "Zur Komposition von Martials Gedichtbüchern 1–12." In Grewing 1998:119–38.

———. 2001. *Untersuchungen zur Buchgestaltung Martials.* Munich.

Schwartz, V. 1998. *Spectacular Realities: Early Mass Culture in Fin-de-siècle France.* Berkeley.

Selden, D. 1992. "*Caveat lector*: Catullus and the Rhetoric of Performance." In *Innovations of Antiquity*, ed. R. Hexter and D. Selden, 461–512. New York.

Shackleton Bailey, D. 1990. *M. Valerii Martialis Epigrammata.* Stuttgart.

———. 1993. *Martial: Epigrams, Edited and Translated.* 3 vols. Cambridge, Mass.

Siedschlag, E. 1972. "Ovidisches bei Martial." *Rivista di filologia e di istruzione classica* 100:156–61.

Smith, B. H. 1968. *Poetic Closure: A Study of How Poems End.* Chicago.

Sobchak, V. 1990. "'Surge and Splendor': A Phenomenology of the Hollywood Historical Epic." *Representations* 29:224–49.

Sontag, S. 1977. *On Photography.* New York.

Spaeth, J. 1939. "Martial and the Pasquinade." *Transactions of the American Philological Association* 70:242–55.

Spisak. A. 1997. "Martial's Special Relationship with His Reader." In *Studies in Latin Literature and Roman History.* Vol. 8, ed. C. Deroux, 352–63. Brussels.

———. 1998. "Gift-Giving in Martial." In Grewing 1998.243–55.

Starr, R. J. 1987. "The Circulation of Literary Texts in the Roman World." *Classical Quarterly* 37:213–23.

Sullivan, J. 1991. *Martial: The Unexpected Classic.* Cambridge.

Swann, B. 1994. *Martial's Catullus: The Reception of an Epigrammatic Rival.* Hildesheim.

Szelest, H. 1960. "Die satirische Epigramme des Martials und das griechische Epigramm." *Meander* 15:518–30.

Tanner, R. 1986. "Levels of Intent in Martial," *ANRW* 32.4:2624–77.

Terdiman, R. 1985. *Discourse/Counter-Discourse: The Theory and Practice of Symbolic Resistance in Nineteenth-Century France.* Ithaca.

Valette-Cagnac, E. 1997. *La Lecture à Rome: Rites et Pratiques.* Paris.

Veyne, P. 1964. "Martial, Virgile et quelques épitaphes." *Revue des Études Antiques* 66:48–52.

———. 1976. *Le pain et le cirque.* Paris.

Wallace-Hadrill, A. 1996."The Imperial Court." In *The Cambridge Ancient History,* 2nd ed., vol.10, *The Augustan Empire: 43 BC–AD 69.* Cambridge.

Waters, K. H. 1963. "The Second Dynasty of Rome." *Phoenix* 17:198–218.

Watson, L., and P. Watson. 2003. *Martial: Select Epigrams.* Cambridge.

Weinreich, Otto. 1928. *Studien zu Martial.* Stuttgart.

White, P. 1972. "Aspects of Non-imperial Patronage in the Works of Statius and Martial." Ph.D. diss., Harvard University.

———. 1974. "The Presentation and Dedication of the *Silvae* and the *Epigrams.*" *Journal of Roman Studies,* 64:40–61.

———. 1975. "The Friends of Martial, Statius, and Pliny, and the Dispersal of Patronage." *Harvard Studies in Classical Philology* 79:265–300.

———. 1978. "*Amicitia* and the Profession of Poetry in Early Imperial Rome." *Journal of Roman Studies* 68:74–92.

————. 1993. *Promised Verse: Poets in Early Imperial Rome*. Cambridge, Mass.

————. 1996. "Martial and Pre-Publication Texts." *Echos du Monde Classique/ Classical Views*, 15:397–412.

Wiedemann, T. 1992. *Emperors and Gladiators*. London.

Williams, C. 2002. "Ovid, Martial, and Poetic Immortality: Traces of *Amores* 1.15 in the Epigrams." *Arethusa* 35:417–33.

————. 2004. *Martial: Epigrams, Book 2*. Oxford.

Williams, G. 1978. *Change and Decline: Roman Literature in the Early Empire*. Berkeley.

Wittmann, R. 1999. "Was There a Reading Revolution at the End of the Eighteenth Century?" in In *A History of Reading in the West*, ed. G. Cavallo and R. Chartier, 284–312. Cambridge.

Woolf, G. 2003. "The City of Letters." In *Rome the Cosmopolis*, ed. C. Edwards and G. Woolf, 203–21. Cambridge.

Wyke, M. 1997. *Projecting the Past: Ancient Rome, Cinema, and History*. London.

# INDEX·OF·EPIGRAMS

*Bold type indicates pages where the epigram itself appears.*

# INDEX

# DUPED

## *Why Innocent People Confess—and Why We Believe Their Confessions*

## Saul Kassin

Prometheus Books

Guilford, Connecticut

**Prometheus Books**

An imprint of The Rowman & Littlefield Publishing Group, Inc.
4501 Forbes Boulevard, Suite 200
Lanham, Maryland 20706
www.rowman.com

Distributed by NATIONAL BOOK NETWORK

British Library Cataloguing in Publication Information Available

**Library of Congress Cataloging-in-Publication Data**

Name: Kassin, Saul M., author.
Title: Duped : why innocent people confess and why we believe their confessions / Saul Kassin.
Description: Lanham, MD : Prometheus, [2022] | Includes bibliographical references and index. |
    Summary: "This conclusive and comprehensive book reveals the psychology behind why inno-
    cent men and women, intensely stressed and befuddled by the promises, threats, trickery, and
    deception of a police interrogation, are duped into confession, no matter how horrific the
    crime. Featuring riveting case studies, highly original research, work done in tandem with the
    Innocence Project, and quotes from individuals who confessed to crimes they did not commit,
    Duped tells the story of how this happens, how the system turns a blind eye, and how to make
    it stop"—Provided by publisher.
Identifiers: LCCN 2021038835 (print) | LCCN 2021038836 (ebook) | ISBN 9781633888081
    (cloth ; alk. paper) | ISBN 9781633888098 (epub)
Subjects: LCSH: Police questioning—Psychological aspects. | Confession (Law)—Psychological
    aspects. | Innocence (Psychology) | False arrest. | Judicial error. | Criminal psychology.
Classification: LCC HV8073.3 .K37 2022 (print) | LCC HV8073.3 (ebook) | DDC 363.25/4—dc23
LC record available at https://lccn.loc.gov/2021038835
LC ebook record available at https://lccn.loc.gov/2021038836

♾™ The paper used in this publication meets the minimum requirements of
American National Standard for Information Sciences Permanence of Paper
for Printed Library Materials, ANSI/NISO Z39.48-1992.